GrapeVine Studies

New Testament Overview

A Chronological Study of the Characters and Events of the New Testament from Matthew to Revelation.

Master Teacher

GrapeVine
Studies

Grapevine Studies
P.O. Box 2123
Glenrock, WY 82637
(307) 529-2019

Website: www.GrapevineStudies.com

Email: info@GrapevineStudies.com

New Testament Overview
Master
Teacher 2nd Edition

By Dianna Wiebe

Copyright 2019 by Grapevine Studies

ISBN: 978-1-59873-216-0

New Testament Overview

Inspiration

Deuteronomy 6:4-7 (NKJV)

Hear, O Israel: The Lord our God, the Lord is one! You shall love the Lord your God with all your heart, with all your soul, and with all your strength. And these words which I command you today shall be in your heart. You shall teach them diligently to your children, and shall talk of them when you sit in your house, when you walk by the way, when you lie down, and when you rise up.

Psalm 78:4b-7 (NKJV)

…Telling to the generation to come the praises of the Lord, and His strength and His wonderful works that He has done. For He established a testimony in Jacob, and appointed a law in Israel, which He commanded our fathers, that they should make them known to their children; that the generation to come might know them, the children who would be born, that they may arise and declare them to their children, that they may set their hope in God, and not forget the works of God, but keep His commandments.

Dedication

This lesson series is dedicated to my children Cody, Tabitha, Luke, and Zak.

I would also like to dedicate this book to all those parents and teachers who desire to diligently teach their children and their students the Word of God.

Acknowledgments

I thank the Lord God Almighty for His faithfulness through the years. The inspiration, creativity, and ideas for this study have all come from Him.

I would like to thank my husband, John, for all the prayers, support, and advice as I have written this book. Thank you to my wonderful children—Cody, Tabitha, Luke, and Zak—for your continuing love and support as I write books. I am blessed to be your mother!

Table of Contents

The Grapevine Mission

Our mission at Grapevine Studies is to provide believers with the tools they need to know God's Word and to disciple others. With our teaching method and Bible curriculums, parents and teachers can effectively disciple their children and students so that they are equipped to reach the world with the truth of the Gospel.

The Grapevine Teaching Method

Grapevine Studies teaches the Bible as if it were a puzzle, doing the frame first. Once the framework is in place (the timeline) then individual pieces (Bible passages, characters, and events) are much easier to place and understand in the context of the "whole puzzle" (the whole counsel of the Word of God).

This study will begin by teaching the timeline from birth of John to the final judgment. Students study each lesson by reading passages from the Bible and drawing (or taking notes on) each section of Scripture, using what we at Grapevine Studies call stick figuring. Stick figuring is using stick figures, symbols, colors, charts, and words to illustrate each Bible passage. This method allows students to interact with the Bible passage and be as creative as they desire. At the end of each lesson a set of review questions is given to ensure that students have grasped the essentials of the passage (the who, what, where, when, why, and how). Application of the lesson is for the teacher to determine based upon prayer, the class, the needs of individual students, and what that teacher feels the Lord has led him to emphasize. Each lesson ends with a Bible memory verse that is related to the lesson and the timeline.

Our prayer is that those who take this journey, both teachers and students, will expand in their knowledge of the Bible and grow in their love for the Lord and His Word. May God bless you richly as you study and teach His Word!

Teacher-Directed Doctrine

Grapevine Studies is pleased to be able to provide Bible curriculum to a variety of denominations. Our unique teacher-directed doctrinal approach provides a platform for each teacher/parent to explain specific doctrines as they arise within the lesson.

The Grapevine Studies
Statement of Faith

Bible: We believe that the Bible is the inspired, infallible, authoritative, complete Word of God and is accurate in all historical and scientific references.

God: We believe that there is one holy and perfect God, eternally existent in three persons—Father, Son, and Holy Spirit.

Jesus: We believe that Jesus Christ is true God and true man; in His virgin birth, sinless life, miracles, atoning death, bodily resurrection, ascension, and in His physical return.

Holy Spirit: We believe that the Holy Spirit is the divine third person of the triune God, sent to indwell, comfort, teach, and empower the believer, and to convict the unbeliever of sin.

Man: We believe man was originally created perfect, in the image and likeness of God, with an unbroken relationship with God. When the first man (Adam) disobeyed God, the perfect relationship between God and man was broken and the curse of sin and death entered all creation. All men are born with this sin nature and only the atoning work of the Lord Jesus Christ can remove man's sinful nature and restore the broken relationship with God.

Salvation: We believe that salvation (forgiveness of sin against God) is provided only through faith in the life, death, resurrection, and ascension of Jesus Christ for all who believe, repent, and receive the gift of eternal life. As a result of faith, works will follow.

Resurrection: We believe in the resurrection of both the believer (saved) and the unbeliever (unsaved); the believer to eternal life and the unbeliever to eternal damnation.

Grapevine Teacher Goals

Grapevine Studies assumes that all teachers of this curriculum will already have a personal and intimate relationship with the Lord, as well as a calling to teach the Word of God. At Grapevine Studies our goals for teachers are that you will:

- Learn more about the character of the God you serve and His Word.

- Be godly examples to your students.

- Effectively communicate the Word of God to this generation.

- Instruct only after having spent time in prayer, Bible reading, and study.

- Have sufficient preparation time for your own study without the need to gather, order, and put together multiple supplies for various activities.

- Learn along with your students.

Grapevine Student Goals

Grapevine Studies believes that students who are taught using reading, hearing, and drawing will have a higher retention rate than those who are just lectured. We also believe that teaching the Bible in a chronological and sequential format is best for long-term memory and life impact. At Grapevine Studies, our goals for students are that they will:

- Desire to serve the One that all history pointed toward: Jesus, the Christ, the Messiah. Once students become believers it is our goal that the use of our studies will help teach them to know God and live a holy life.

- See God's interaction and movement through history as He dealt with nations and individuals so that they will be able to recognize God's movement and interaction in their own lives.

- Have a Biblical framework in place that will encourage and inspire them to study further on their own, and to understand the context of the passages they read in the future.

- Learn from those who have lived before them.

Teacher and Student Supply List

Teacher supplies: Bible, Grapevine Studies Teacher Book, dry erase board & markers (8 colors), and Bible dictionary.

Student supplies: Bible, Grapevine Studies Student Book, and colored pencils. Middle School students will need a Bible Dictionary, Topical Bible, and Concordance.

Teaching Multi-Level Books

Daily Schedule

Day 1: Timeline Review Page
Day 2: Lesson page 1
Day 3: Lesson page 2
Day 4: Student Drawing Page

Weekly Schedule

Timeline Review Page (5 -10 minutes)
Lesson Pages 1 and 2 (30-35 minutes)
Student Drawing Page (5-15 minutes)

Before Class

Lesson Preparation: Nothing can replace the time a teacher spends in prayer with our Master Teacher, the Lord God Almighty. We also recommend you read the Scriptures and lesson notes before class.

Supplies needed for teaching:

- Bible
- Dry erase board or chalk board
- Dry erase markers or chalk
- Colored pencils
- Lesson pages for each student
- Bible Dictionary
- Atlas of the Bible Lands

Teaching the Lessons

Teacher Notes

Teacher Notes: The teacher notes are in green. They explain the important information that will need to be covered in the timeline and each section of the lessons. These notes will also be helpful for substitute teachers and can even be read to the students if desired.

Bible Dictionary: For each lesson, we have provided a few words that we recommend you look up in a Bible dictionary. These words will help when teaching the lesson and answering questions from your students. We recommend you checking definitions in more than on dictionary.

Maps: As part of the study you will periodically do some mapping. The maps for both teachers and Elementary and Middle School students are found in the back of their respective books.

Teaching the Timeline

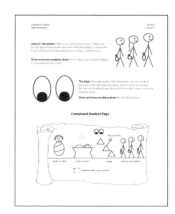

Teacher Narrative: The first lesson is the timeline. The teacher narrative in green explains the necessary information that will need to be taught at each point on the timeline. These notes are intended to be used as a guide, but they may be read aloud to the students if desired. Because the main goal of the timeline is to teach students the major events and the order in which they occur, I would caution against trying to give too much information during the timeline lesson. During subsequent lessons, students will learn more details about each of the characters and events on the timeline.

Stick Figuring: Students will begin this study by stick figuring the timeline. The timeline is a fun and interactive way to give students the big picture of what they will be learning in this study. This is also a great opportunity for you to discover what your students know about the characters and events in the study.

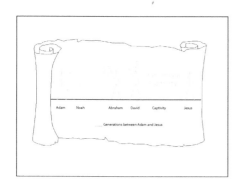

Simplifying or Trace the Stick Figures for Younger Students: Younger students may have a hard time drawing the entire stick figure in the space provided. If need, we recommend simplifying the drawings. For example, instead of a stick man, have students just draw the face. Another option for younger students is our Traceable version of the Early Elementary study. This options will allow younger students to keep up with older students and still draw the stick figures. Only Middle School students will note where the books of the Bible fit on the timeline.

Timeline Review Page

 Timeline Review: Students will begin each lesson, except Lesson 1, by reviewing the last three characters or events on the timeline. The timeline review is designed to set the context for the current lesson. The titles for each character/event will be given to the students, and they will need to draw the appropriate picture above the title. It is recommended that every two or three lessons you review the entire timeline, up to the point of your current lesson. Early Elementary students will only review the last three characters/events on the timeline while Elementary and Middle School students will review the last four characters/events.

Memory Verse Review: After students have reviewed the timeline, they will then review up to three previous memory verses. This review can be done verbally or by having the students write out the verses. Some students are encouraged to use a combination of speaking, writing, and stick figuring to memorize their verses.

Lesson Pages

Teacher Lesson Pages

Stick Figuring: After the Scripture is read, the teacher will stick figure that portion of Scripture onto the board. The amount of Scripture read can be reduced for younger students. While students are drawing, teachers can discuss that part of the lesson. Students can either draw what the teacher has drawn or draw their own interpretations of the Scripture. We encourage the use of colors and creativity. We have found that the more the students draw, the more they remember. For older Teacher students we have noted in the teacher books extra information they can add to their drawings. You will see Older, followed by a description of the extra information they can add. Some students may opt to take notes in this section.

Student Lesson Pages

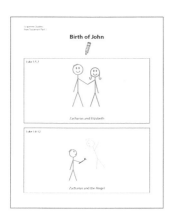

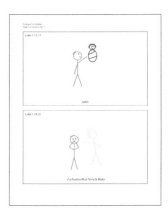

Early Elementary Pages: To ensure that little hands have plenty of room to draw, we have only two drawings per page for Early Elementary students. The Early Elementary students will use two pages to draw what is drawn on one page for Elementary and Middle School student pages.

Elementary and Middle School Pages: Students in these level will have four drawings per page. The teacher manual will show the Elementary and Middle School student page layout.

Lesson Pages Continued

Review Questions and Answers: This section gives teachers the questions and answers for the lesson review. These questions cover the who, what, when, where, why, and how of the lesson. We encourage teachers to add their own questions as time allows.

Application: At Grapevine Studies, we believe that teachers determine how to apply each lesson. We encourage our teachers to spend time in prayer to determine what to emphasize during that lesson. We have found this gives our teachers great freedom and is very effective. Notice that the last question is the application question for the lesson. The answer to this question will depend upon what the Lord has led you to emphasize in the lesson.

Early Elementary and Elementary for Early Elementary and Elementary

Character and Event Cards: Using blank index cards, the students will create their own Character and Event cards. On the front side, students will draw the main character or event from that lesson and label the character. On the back side, students will write the key facts you want them to remember related to the character or event. These cards can be used for games and review.

Drawing Review: This section is designed to allow students to review what they have learned through drawing. Encourage your students to be very creative and detailed on this page. This will help you and your students to see what they have learned.

Memory Verse: At the bottom of this page, we have left room to write out and/or stick figure the memory verse, however, it can also be done verbally.

Middle School for Middle School

Teachers: We have given page numbers for the answers that can be found in the Zondervan's Compact Bible Dictionary, Cruden's Compact Concordance and Nave's Compact Topical Bible (all published by Zondervan), but due to copyright restrictions we are unable to print the answers. Other Bible study tools can be used, but answers may differ.

Section Review

Questions and Timeline: The section review is given to review the previous lessons before moving on with the study. This review can be done verbally and within the context of games or challenges. Section reviews should be fun and should help students feel confident in what they are learning.

Timeline: The timeline will be reviewed up to the point of the section review. This will give students a chance to ensure that they can put the pieces of the timeline together before moving on.

Final Review

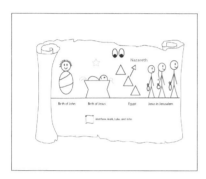

Questions: This review is designed to ensure that your students have mastered the information covered in each lesson. The questions should be familiar to them and will include their memory verses for the study. This is a unique way for you to show your students how much they have learned.

Timeline: The timeline review will give students a chance to put all the pieces of the timeline together one final time.

Page intentionally left blank

New Testament

~

Timeline

Adam: The Old Testament begins with the account of the creation week. On the sixth day God created the first man, Adam. Adam was created to have a perfect and complete relationship with God. When Adam sinned by disobeying God and ate the forbidden fruit, the relationship between God and man was broken. However, God promised Adam that one day the Messiah would come, would be born of a woman, and would restore the broken relationship between God and man.

Draw and have students draw: Adam.

Noah: Ten generations after Adam, Noah was born and lived. Noah built the ark and survived the Flood.

Draw and have students draw: Noah holding a hammer and plans for the ark.

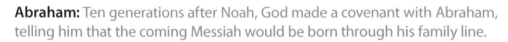

Abraham: Ten generations after Noah, God made a covenant with Abraham, telling him that the coming Messiah would be born through his family line.

Draw and have students draw: Abraham with a star of David, representing the covenant promise that God made with Abraham.

David: Fourteen generations after Abraham, a descendant of Abraham named David was born. David was the second king of Israel, and God promised him that through his family line the Messiah would come.

Draw and have students draw: King David.

Babylonian Captivity

Captivity in Babylon: Fourteen generations after David lived, the captivity of Judah took place.

Write and have students write: The Babylonian Captivity.

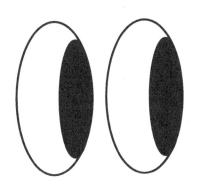

The Eyes: Throughout the Old Testament, our eyes looked forward to the Messiah, the One who would (1) be born of woman, (2) be born of the line of Abraham, and (3) be born of the line of David.

Draw and have students draw: Eyes looking forward.

Jesus: Fourteen generations after the captivity in Babylon, the Messiah was born just as Scripture had promised.

Draw and have students draw: .

Completed Student Page

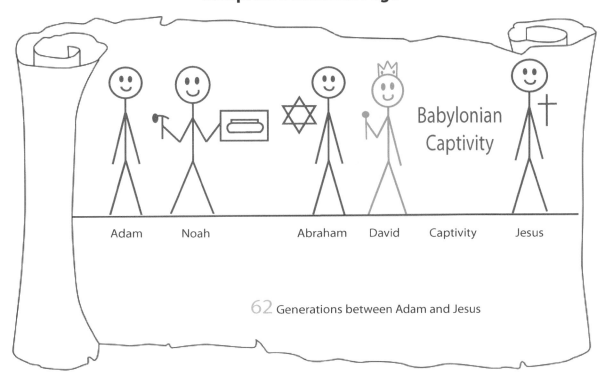

Adam   Noah   Abraham   David   Captivity   Jesus

Babylonian Captivity

62 Generations between Adam and Jesus

Birth of John: The first chronological event of the New Testament is the birth of John (commonly known as John the Baptist). An angel announced to Zacharias that he and his barren wife, Elizabeth, would have a son named John. Zacharias was told that John would be the man who would prepare the people for the coming Messiah.

Draw and have students draw: Baby John.

Birth of Jesus: The Old Testament had pointed to the coming Messiah, and the time had come for Him to be born (Galatians 4:4-5). The angel Gabriel appeared to a virgin named Mary to announce that she had been chosen by God to be the mother of the Messiah. Mary lived in Nazareth and was betrothed to man named Joseph. An angel appeared to Joseph, and a short time later Joseph and Mary married and traveled to Bethlehem, where Jesus was born. The angel announced Jesus' birth to the shepherds in the fields, and they traveled to Bethlehem to see the newborn baby. When Jesus was eight days old He was circumcised, and at forty days old He was presented in the temple, according to the Law. Our eyes at this time begin to look down, watching the Messiah who has come.

Draw and have students draw: Baby Jesus in the manger with a star above Him.

Egypt: Wise men from the East who had followed a star also came to worship Jesus. When the wise men arrived in Judea seeking to worship the newborn king of the Jews, the current king, Herod, was upset by their announcement and subsequent escape. Seeking to kill Jesus, Herod ordered the death of all male children age two and under living in and around Bethlehem. An angel told Joseph to take Mary and Jesus away, and the family escaped Herod's order by moving to Egypt, where they remained until the death of Herod. After Herod's death Joseph returned with his family, and they settled in a town called Nazareth.

Draw and have students draw: Three brown triangles, representing Egypt, and an arrow pointing to Nazareth.

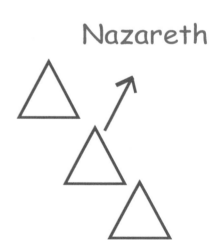

Jesus in Jerusalem: Little is recorded about Jesus' childhood except that at age twelve He went with His family to attend the Feast of Passover in Jerusalem in accordance with the Law.

Draw and have students draw: Jesus, Mary and Joseph walking to Jerusalem for Passover..

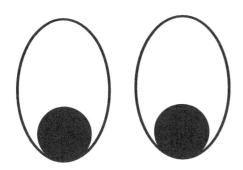

The Eyes: Throughout the Old Testament, our eyes looked forward to the Messiah, but when Jesus is born we change the eyes to looking down. Now that Jesus has come, we watch what He does.

Draw and have students draw: Eyes looking down.

Completed Student Page

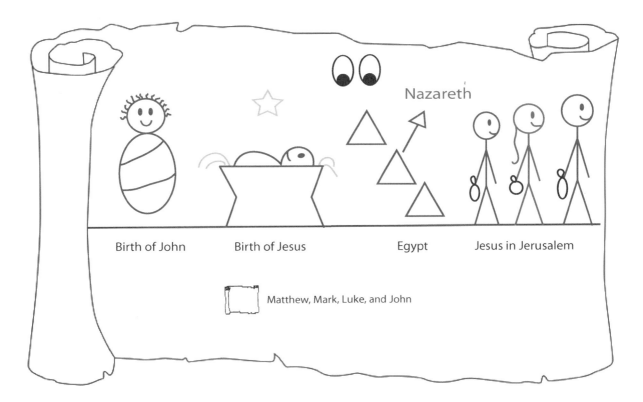

Birth of John   Birth of Jesus   Egypt   Jesus in Jerusalem

Matthew, Mark, Luke, and John

John Preached: As John became well known in the area, people asked if he was the Messiah. John clearly stated that he was not the Messiah but had only been sent to prepare the people for Him.

Draw and have students draw: John preaching.

John Baptized Jesus: Jesus went to the Jordan River, where John was baptizing, and asked John to baptize Him. As John baptized Jesus, God the Father spoke from heaven in an audible voice, and the Holy Spirit descended in the form of a dove. Jesus was about thirty years old at this time.

Draw and have students draw: John baptizing Jesus.

My Notes:

Jesus Was Tempted: Immediately after Jesus was baptized, the Holy Spirit led Jesus into the wilderness, where He fasted for forty days and nights. At the end of the fast, Satan came to tempt Jesus; Jesus responded to every temptation with the words, "It is written." Although Jesus was tempted throughout His lifetime, He never sinned. After Jesus was tempted, angels came and ministered to Him.

Draw and have students draw: Jesus resisting Satan.

My Notes:

Completed Student Page

John Preached   Jesus Baptized   Jesus Tempted

Matthew, Mark, Luke, and John

The Twelve Apostles: Once Jesus left the wilderness, He began to preach, and many disciples began to follow Him. After a night of prayer, Jesus chose twelve of His disciples and made them apostles.

Draw and have students draw: The twelve disciples.

Jesus Taught: Many times throughout the ministry of Jesus, we read that He was teaching. Jesus taught His apostles, His disciples, and many others.

Draw and have students draw: Jesus teaching.

My Notes:

Jesus Prayed: Many passages refer to Jesus praying. Some words used to describe Jesus at prayer are: alone, often, all night, and the Father's will.

Draw and have students draw: Jesus praying.

My Notes:

Completed Student Page

Twelve Apostles   Jesus Taught   Jesus Prayed

Matthew, Mark, Luke, and John

Lesson Goals and Key Points

BIRTH OF JOHN

The goal of this lesson is for the students to be introduced to John (the Baptist).

Key Points:
- Zacharias and Elizabeth were righteous people but had no children.
- The angel Gabriel appeared to Zacharias in the temple announcing that he and Elizabeth would have a son.
- Zacharias was struck mute for disbelief until John was named.
- Zacharias prophesied that John would prepare the way for the Messiah.
- John grew up strong in spirit and lived in the desert until it was time for him to prepare the children of Israel for their coming Messiah.

Memory Verse: Luke 1:80

BIRTH OF JESUS

The goal of this lesson is for the students to see that in the fullness of time God sent His Son into the world.

Key Points:
- The angel Gabriel announced to Mary, a virgin from Nazareth, that she would be the mother of the Messiah.
- After Gabriel spoke to Joseph, Joseph took Mary as his wife.
- Joseph and Mary traveled to Bethlehem to be registered.
- The Messiah, Jesus the Christ, was born in Bethlehem!
- Angels announced to shepherds the birth of Messiah.
- The shepherds worshiped Jesus.
- Joseph and Mary took Jesus to the temple, where both Simon and Anna prophesied over Him.

Memory Verse: Galatians 4:4-5

JESUS IN EGYPT

The goal of this lesson is for the students to learn some of the facts about events that surrounded the early years of Jesus' earthly life.

Key Points:
- The wise men had traveled from the East in order to worship the newborn king of the Jews.
- Herod sought to find Jesus.
- The wise men found Jesus, worshipped Him, and presented Him with gifts.

- Herod attempted to kill Jesus by killing all the male children two years old and younger living in and around Bethlehem.
- To escape from Herod, Joseph took Jesus and Mary to Egypt.
- Joseph returned with Mary and Jesus to Israel and settled in Nazareth, where Jesus grew up.

Memory Verse: Matthew 2:11

AT THE TEMPLE

The goal of this lesson is to look at the only event recorded regarding the childhood of Jesus.

Key Points:
- When Jesus was twelve years old, he accompanied His family to Jerusalem where they yearly celebrated the Passover feast.
- At the end of the feast, Jesus remained behind at the temple, listening and asking questions of the teachers.
- When Joseph and Mary could not locate Jesus among their traveling companions, they returned to Jerusalem.
- After finding Jesus at the temple being about His Father's business, the family returned to Nazareth, where Jesus was subject to them and continued to grow physically and spiritually.

Memory Verse: Luke 2:52

JOHN BAPTIZED JESUS

The goal of this lesson is for students to see the events marking the beginning of Jesus' three years of ministry.

Key Points:
- God sent John to prepare the people for Jesus.
- John preached repentance and baptism, and under John's preaching many repented and were baptized.
- Although many wondered if John was the Messiah/Christ, John always pointed to Jesus.
- Jesus came to John to be baptized.
- As Jesus was baptized, a voice spoke from heaven and the Holy Spirit descended in the form of a dove.

Memory Verse: Mark 1:9

NOTES

Page intentionally left blank

Middle School
Introduction to Study Tools

Today the Middle School lesson will just review the different Bible study tools. In the following lessons students will use each study tool at least once. I recommend looking through each additional study book to refresh your students on the function of each type of study tool.

Topical Bible

The topical Bible is used to do research on a specific topic or subject. In a topical Bible, subjects are listed with their definitions and/or references so that further research on that subject can be accomplished easily.

Bible Dictionary

In a Bible dictionary, subjects are listed with definitions and references so that students can have a clear understanding of the word(s) they are researching.

Concordance

In a concordance, words are listed with their Biblical references and a small portion of Scripture surrounding that word. This tool is designed to give students quick access to passages they are looking up.

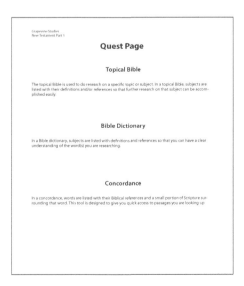

Birth of John

Memory Verse: Luke 1:80

Zacharias and Elizabeth

Read aloud: Luke 1:1-7

Discuss Zacharias and Elizabeth: In the days of Herod the Great, Zacharias was serving as a priest in the temple in Jerusalem. Zacharias and his wife, Elizabeth, were righteous, but they had no children and were advanced in years.

Draw and have students draw: Zacharias and Elizabeth.

Zacharias and the Angel

Read aloud: Luke 1:8-12

Discuss Zacharias and the Angel: While Zacharias was burning incense in the temple, an angel of the Lord appeared to him. (Review where the altar of incense was in the temple.)

Draw and have students draw: Zacharias and the angel of the Lord.

Look up the following words in a Bible Dictionary:

priest , righteous, walking, blameless

altar of incense

make ready

mute

prophesied

strong, manifestation

John

Read aloud: Luke 1:13-17

Discuss John: The angel told Zacharias that he and his wife would have a son, that they were to give him the name John, and that John would prepare the people for the coming of the Lord.

Draw and have students draw: The angel and Zacharias discussing John.

Zacharias Was Struck Mute

Read aloud: Luke 1:18-25

Discuss Zacharias Was Struck Mute: Zacharias questioned the news from the angel. The angel declared that he was Gabriel and was sent by God to give Zacharias the good news. Because of his unbelief, Zacharias was struck mute by Gabriel. After Zacharias completed his priestly duties he returned home, and shortly thereafter Elizabeth conceived.

Draw and have students draw: Zacharias struck mute by the angel.

Completed Student Page

Teacher Notes

John Was Born

Read aloud: Luke 1:57-58

Discuss John Was Born: Elizabeth gave birth to John, and her relatives and neighbors rejoiced with her.

Draw and have students draw: Zacharias and Elizabeth with baby John.

John Was Named

Read aloud: Luke 1:59-66

Discuss John Was Named: On the eighth day, when the time came to name the baby, Elizabeth told those present that he would be called John. When the people questioned Zacharias, he wrote to confirm the choice of the name John. At once Zacharias was no longer mute and immediately began praising the Lord.

Draw and have students draw: Zacharias showing a man the tablet with John's name on it.

Teacher Notes

Completed Student Page

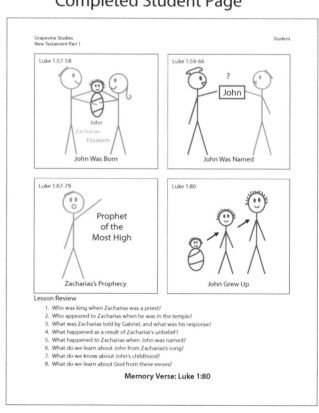

Zacharias's Prophecy

Prophet of the Most High

Read aloud: Luke 1:67-79

Discuss Zacharias's Prophecy: In Zacharias's prophecy, he recalled God's covenant with Abraham and David. Zacharias prophesied that John would be called "the prophet of the Most High" and would prepare the way of the Lord.

Draw and have students draw: Zacharias prophesying.

John Grew Up

Read aloud: Luke 1:80

Discuss John Grew Up: John grew up and was strong in spirit. He lived in the desert until the time when he was revealed to Israel.

Draw and have students draw: John growing up.

Lesson Review

1. Who was king when Zacharias was a priest? King Herod.

2. Who appeared to Zacharias when he was in the temple? The angel of the Lord, Gabriel.

3. What was Zacharias told by Gabriel, and what was his response? He and Elizabeth would have a son, but Zacharias did not believe Gabriel.

4. What happened as a result of Zacharias's unbelief? He was struck mute.

5. What happened to Zacharias when John was named? He could speak again and praised God.

6. What do we learn about John from Zacharias's song? John would be a prophet of the Most High and would prepare the way for the Lord.

7. What do we know about John's childhood? He grew up strong in the Lord and lived in the desert until his manifestation to Israel.

8. What do we learn about God from these verses? God calls and prepares people for service to Him.

Memory Verse: Luke 1:80

Early Elementary and Elementary

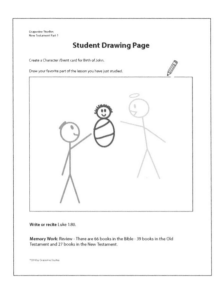

Information for the Birth of John card:

- Zacharias and his wife Elizabeth were righteous but had no children.
- The angel Gabriel appeared to Zacharias while he was serving as a priest in the temple and told him that he and Elizabeth would have a son.
- This son would prepare the people for the coming Messiah.
- Elizabeth and Zacharias named their son John.
- John grew strong in spirit and lived in the desert.

Memory Verse: Luke 1:80

Memory Work: Review - There are 66 books in the Bible - 39 books in the Old Testament and 27 books in the New Testament.

Middle School

Birth of Jesus

Topical Bible

Name the three people that Scripture records the angel *Gabriel* appearing to.

Daniel, Zacharias, and Mary (Nave's, page 167)

Bible Dictionary

What is a *manger*?

Zondervan's, page 342

Concordance

Give the passage that notes the first time the name *Jesus* is used in the Bible.

Matthew 1:21 (Cruden's, page 262)

Quest Question

Why do you think the authors of Matthew and Luke recorded Jesus' genealogy?

To confirm the New Testament prophecies that Jesus would be born of the lineage of Abraham and David.

Timeline Review

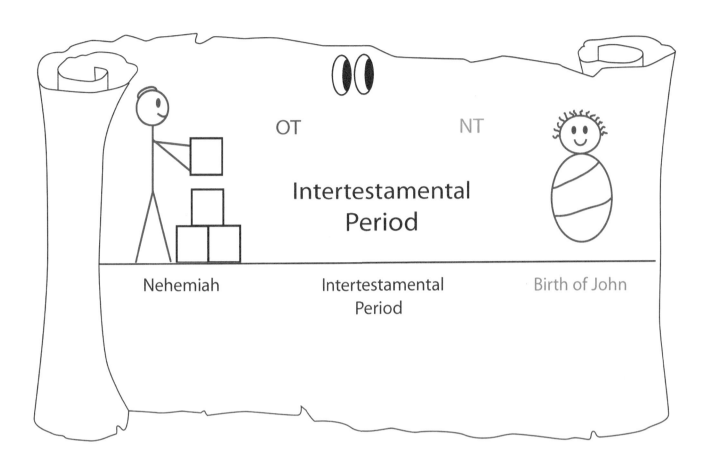

OT   NT

Intertestamental
Period

Nehemiah   Intertestamental   Birth of John
                        Period

Memory Verse Review

Luke 1:80

Memory Work: Review - There are 66 books in the Bible - 39 books in the Old Testament and 27 books in the New Testament.

Birth of Jesus

Memory Verse: Galatians 4:4-5

Mary and Gabriel

Read aloud: Luke 1:26-38

Discuss Mary and Gabriel: In the sixth month of Elizabeth's pregnancy, Gabriel was sent to Nazareth to Mary, a virgin, who was betrothed to Joseph. Gabriel told Mary that she would be the mother of the Son of God. Mary responded with wonder and obedience.

Map: Label the city of Nazareth.

Draw and have students draw: Mary at a table and Gabriel appearing to her.

Mary Went to See Elizabeth

Read aloud: Luke 1:39-45

Discuss Mary Went to See Elizabeth: Mary left Nazareth and went to see her relative Elizabeth. Elizabeth confirmed what the angel had told Mary, calling her "blessed among women."

Draw and have students draw: Mary reaching out to Elizabeth.

Look up the following words in a Bible Dictionary:

    betrothed

    Nazareth

    blessed

    just, Jesus

    swaddling cloths

    consolation of Israel, prophetess

Joseph and the Angel

Read aloud: Matthew 1:18-25

Discuss Joseph and the Angel: Before Joseph and Mary came together in marriage, Joseph discovered that Mary was pregnant. Joseph decided to divorce Mary quietly, but an angel of the Lord appeared to him assuring him that he was to take Mary as his wife. Joseph obeyed the angel and took Mary as his wife.

Draw and have students draw: The angel talking to Joseph.

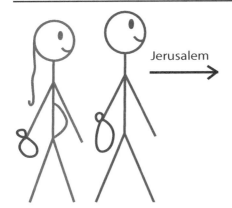

From Nazareth to Bethlehem

Read aloud: Luke 2:1-5

Discuss From Nazareth to Bethlehem: Caesar Augustus, emperor of Rome, decided that he wanted to take a census of all the earth. As a result, Joseph was required to register in Bethlehem. Joseph and Mary traveled to Bethlehem together.

Map: Label the city of Bethlehem.

Draw and have students draw: Mary and Joseph on their way from Nazareth to Bethlehem.

Completed Student Page

Teacher Notes:

Jesus Was Born

Read aloud: Luke 2:6-7, Galatians 4:4-5

Discuss Jesus Was Born: At God's appointed time and place, among God's chosen people, the Messiah was born of woman, of the line of Abraham, and of the line of David. Jesus was wrapped in swaddling cloth and laid in a manger because of the lack of room in the inn.

Draw and have students draw: Mary and Joseph looking at baby Jesus in the manger.

Teacher Notes

Completed Student Page

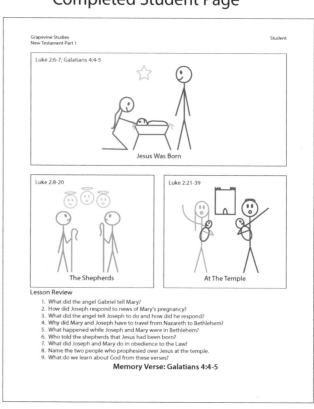

The Shepherds

Read aloud: Luke 2:8-20

Discuss The Shepherds: The first people to hear about the birth of Jesus were shepherds who were tending flocks near Bethlehem. The angel appeared to them telling them the wonderful news. Upon receiving this great announcement, the shepherds went to see Jesus. After seeing Jesus, the shepherds told all they met about the events they witnessed. When others heard, they marveled at the news.

Draw and have students draw: The shepherds and the angels.

At the Temple

Read aloud: Luke 2:22-39

Discuss At the Temple: Joseph and Mary took Jesus to the Temple in Jerusalem to fulfill the requirements of the law. While at the Temple, a priest named Simeon praised God that his eyes had seen Israel's salvation and blessed the family. Anna praised God and then spoke to those who were looking forward to the redemption of Jerusalem.

Draw and have students draw: Simeon and Anna praising God at the temple while holding baby Jesus.

Lesson Review

1. What did the angel Gabriel tell Mary? She would have a son, Jesus, the Son of God.

2. How did Joseph respond to news of Mary's pregnancy? He planned to divorce her.

3. What did the angel tell Joseph to do and how did he respond? The angel told Joseph to take Mary as his wife. Joseph obeyed the angel and took Mary as his wife.

4. Why did Mary and Joseph have to travel from Nazareth to Bethlehem? Because Caesar wanted all men to register, and Joseph was required to register in Bethlehem.

5. What happened while Joseph and Mary were in Bethlehem? Jesus was born.

6. Who told the shepherds that Jesus had been born? An angel of the Lord.

7. What did Joseph and Mary do in obedience to the Law? They went to the Temple and offered a sacrifice.

8. Name the two people who prophesied over Jesus at the temple. Simeon and Anna.

9. What do we learn about God from these verses? God keeps His promises and provides redemption for all men.

Memory Verse: Galatians 4:4-5

Early Elementary and Elementary

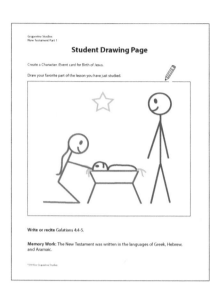

Information for the Birth of Jesus card:

- The angel Gabriel announced to Mary that she would be the mother of the Messiah, the Son of God.
- Joseph took Mary as his wife after an angel appeared to him.
- Joseph and Mary traveled from Nazareth to Bethlehem to register.
- In the fullness of time the Messiah was born of woman, of the line of Abraham, and of the line of David.

Memory Verse: Galatians 4:4-5

Memory Work: The New Testament was written in the languages of Greek, Hebrew, and Aramaic.

Middle School

Herod and the Wise Men

Topical Bible

What does the topical Bible tell us about *Herod the Great*?

Nave's, page 203

Bible Dictionary

Who were the *Magi*?

Zondervan's, page 337

Concordance

What two New Testament passages refer to *wise men*?

Genesis 41:8 and Exodus 7:11 (Cruden's page 547)

Quest Question

Compare how the shepherds, the wise men, and Herod responded to the birth of Jesus.

The shepherds and the wise men sought Jesus and worshipped Him. Herod sought to kill Jesus.

Timeline Review

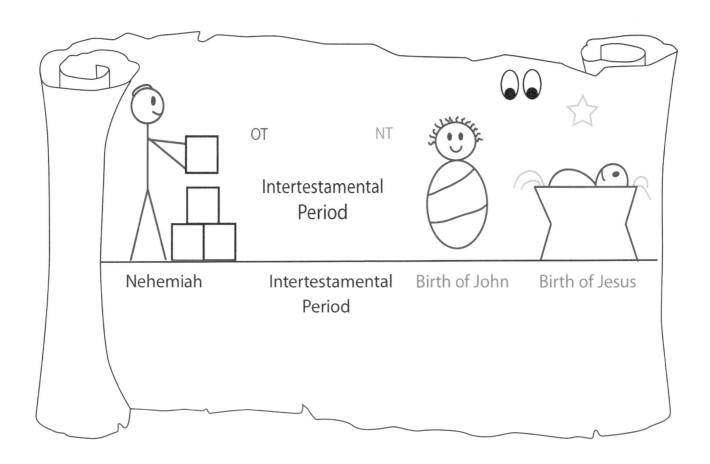

Nehemiah   Intertestamental Period   Birth of John   Birth of Jesus

Memory Verse Review

Galatians 4:4-5

Luke 1:80

Memory Work: The New Testament was written in the languages of Greek, Hebrew, and Aramaic.

Herod and The Wise Men

Memory Verse: Matthew 2:11

Herod and the Wise Men

Read aloud: Matthew 2:1-2

Discuss Herod and the Wise Men: After the birth of Jesus, wise men went to Jerusalem, having followed a star, seeking to worship the newborn king of the Jews.

Draw and have students draw: Herod and the wise men standing before him.

Herod's Quest

Read aloud: Matthew 2:3-8

Discuss Herod's Quest: When Herod heard that a king had been born among the Jews, he sought to find out where the Christ would be born. Herod consulted with the chief priests and scribes to determine where the Child would be born. He was told the prophecies indicated that the Messiah would be born in Bethlehem. Herod then directed the wise men to return to him and report the child's location.

Draw and have students draw: Herod questioning a scribe.

Look up the following words in a Bible Dictionary:

wise men

troubled

star, frankincense, myrrh

Egypt

Jesus and the Wise Men

Read aloud: Matthew 2:9-12

Discuss Jesus and the Wise Men: The Wise Men left Jerusalem and went to Bethlehem, where they found Jesus. They worshipped Him and presented Him with gifts. Before they left, they were warned in a dream not to go to back to Herod, so they took a different route to their home.

Draw and have students draw: The wise men before Jesus.

Completed Student Page   Teacher Notes

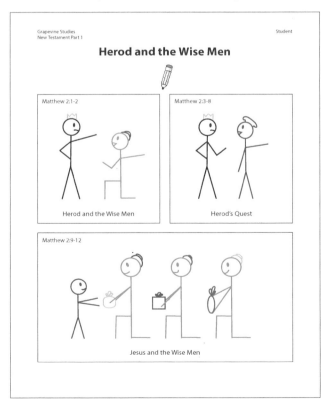

The Flight to Egypt

Read aloud: Matthew 2:13-15

Discuss the Flight to Egypt: The angel of the Lord told Joseph to take Mary and Jesus and flee to Egypt because Herod was seeking to kill Jesus.

Map: Label the country of Egypt.

Draw and have students draw: Joseph, Mary, and Jesus fleeing to Egypt.

Herod's Rage

Read aloud: Matthew 2:16-18

Discuss Herod's Rage: Herod was furious when he saw that the wise men had disobeyed his command by not returning to him to report the whereabouts of the child. As a result, Herod ordered the death of all male children two years old and younger living in and around Bethlehem.

Draw and have students draw: Herod ordering "death."

Teacher Notes

Completed Student Page

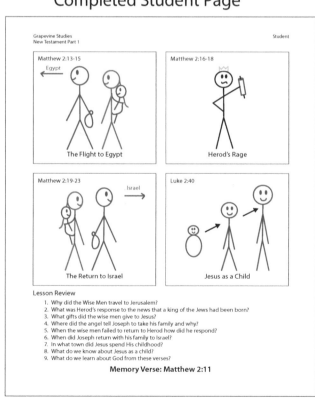

The Return to Israel

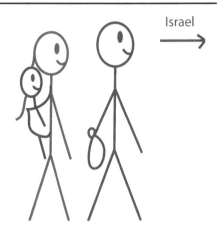

Israel

Read aloud: Matthew 2:19-23

Discuss The Return to Israel: Herod died, and Joseph had a dream in which the angel told him to return with his family to Israel. Joseph, Mary, and Jesus returned to Israel but settled in the land of Galilee, in a town called Nazareth, instead of Bethlehem.

Draw and have students draw: Joseph returning with Mary and Jesus to Nazareth.

Jesus as a Child

Read aloud: Luke 2:40

Discuss Jesus as a Child In Nazareth Jesus grew up physically and grew strong spiritually.

Draw and have students draw: Jesus growing up.

Lesson Review

1. Why did the wise men travel to Jerusalem? To worship the newborn king of the Jews.

2. What was Herod's response to the news that a king of the Jews had been born? He sought to locate the Child's birthplace from the chief priests, scribes, and wise men.

3. What gifts did the wise men give to Jesus? Gold, frankincense and myrrh.

4. Where did the angel tell Joseph to take his family and why? To Egypt because Herod was seeking to kill Jesus.

5. When the wise men failed to return to Herod, how did he respond? He ordered the death of all the children two years old and under living in and near Bethlehem.

6. When did Joseph return with his family to Israel? After the death of Herod.

7. In what town did Jesus spend His childhood? Nazareth.

8. What do we know about Jesus as a child? He grew up physically and became spiritually strong.

9. What do we learn about God from these verses? God desires and accepts the worship of all men, and like the wise men we should also seek to worship the Lord.

Memory Verse: Matthew 2:11

Early Elementary and Elementary

Information for the Herod and the Wise Men card:

- Wise men from the East followed a star that led them to find the newborn king of the Jews.
- Herod wanted to find and kill the newborn king.
- The wise men found Jesus, worshipped Him, and presented Him with gifts.
- Herod ordered the death of all the male children in the Bethlehem area age two and younger.
- Joseph fled with Mary and Jesus to Egypt, where they lived until Herod died.
- Jesus grew up in Nazareth, where He grew up physically and grew strong in spirit.

Memory Verse: Matthew 2:11
Memory Work: The Gospels: Matthew, Mark, Luke, and John.

Middle School

Jesus at the Temple

Topical Bible

Give three verses that deal with the institution of *Passover*.

Exodus 12:3-49, 23:15-18, 34:18; Leviticus 23:4-8; Numbers 9:2-5,13,14; 28:16-25; Deuteronomy 16:1-8,16; Psalm 81:3,5 (Nave's, page 354)

Bible Dictionary

What was the *temple*?

Zondervan's page 578

Concordance

Give the passage that notes the first time the word *Passover* is mentioned in the Bible.

Exodus 12:11 (Cruden's page 355)

Quest Question

During Jesus' childhood, did He live anywhere besides Nazareth, Israel?

Yes, Bethlehem and Egypt.

Timeline Review

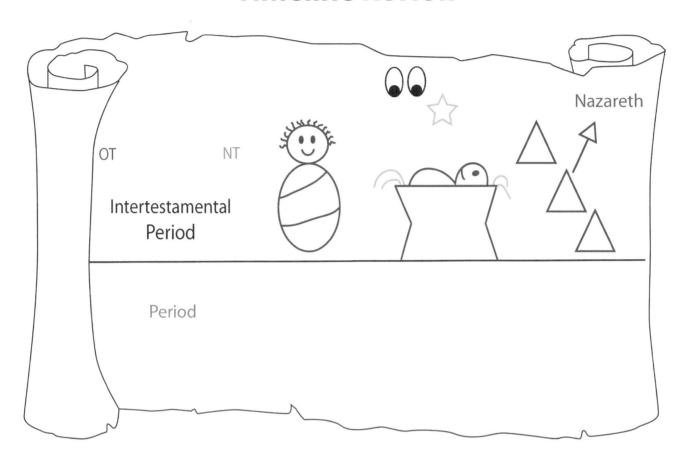

Memory Verse Review

Matthew 2:11

Galatians 4:4-5

Luke 1:80

Memory Work: The Gospels: Matthew, Mark, Luke, and John.

Jesus at the Temple

Memory Verse: Luke 2:52

Passover in Jerusalem

Read aloud: Luke 2:40-42, Exodus 23:14-17

Discuss Passover in Jerusalem: Following the return of Joseph, Mary, and Jesus from Egypt, Scripture records nothing more about Jesus' childhood except in Luke 2:40. As Jesus grew up, He grew strong in the Lord and was filled with wisdom and God's grace. In obedience to the Law (Ex. 23:14-17), Joseph took his family and went to Jerusalem for the celebration of the Feast of Passover.

Map: Label the city of Jerusalem.

Draw and have students draw: Joseph, Mary, and Jesus on their way to Jerusalem.

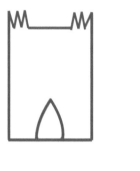

Jerusalem

Look up the following words in a Bible Dictionary:

Passover

wisdom

grace

teachers

stature

favor

Jesus Remained in Jerusalem

Read aloud: Luke 2:43

Discuss Jesus Remained in Jerusalem: After Passover Joseph and Mary left to go home but did not realize that Jesus had remained in Jerusalem and was not in their company.

Draw and have students draw: Jesus worshipping at the temple.

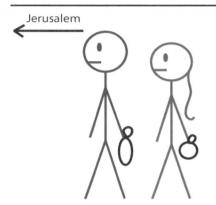

Joseph and Mary Returned to Jerusalem

Read aloud: Luke 2:44-45

Discuss Joseph and Mary Returned to Jerusalem: When Joseph and Mary could not locate Jesus among their traveling companions and family, they returned to Jerusalem in search of their son.

Draw and have students draw: Joseph and Mary returning to Jerusalem.

Completed Student Page

Teacher Notes:

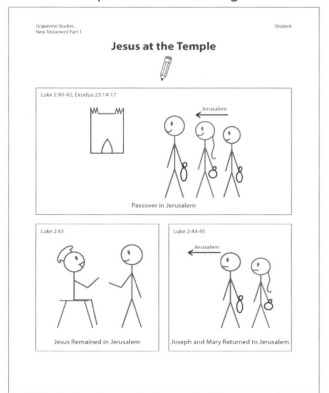

Jesus at the Temple

Read aloud: Luke 2:46-47

Discuss Jesus at the Temple: After three days, Joseph and Mary found Jesus in the temple listening to and asking questions of the teachers. The teachers were astonished at His understanding of the Law.

Draw and have students draw: Jesus talking to the teachers.

Teacher Notes

Completed Student Page

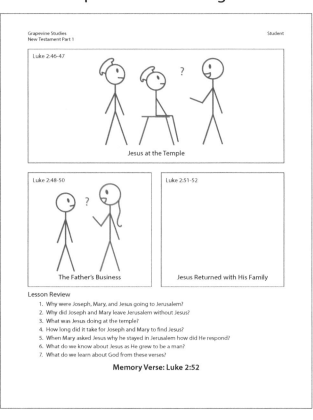

The Father's Business

Read aloud: Luke 2:48-50

Discuss The Father's Business: Upon finding Jesus, His mother questioned Him, and He responded that He had remained at the temple because He had to be about His "Father's business."

Draw and have students draw: Jesus talking to Mary.

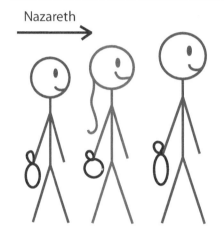

Nazareth

Jesus Returned with His Family

Read aloud: Luke 2:51-52

Discuss Jesus Returned with His Family: Jesus returned to Nazareth with Joseph and Mary and continued in subjection to them. He grew physically, gained wisdom, and found favor with men and in the sight of God.

Draw and have students draw: Jesus growing up.

Lesson Review:

1. Why were Joseph, Mary, and Jesus going to Jerusalem? To celebrate the Feast of Passover.

2. Why did Joseph and Mary leave Jerusalem without Jesus? They thought that Jesus was returning with them but traveling with some of their family or friends.

3. What was Jesus doing at the temple? He was listening and asking questions of the teachers.

4. How long did it take for Joseph and Mary to find Jesus? Three days.

5. When Mary asked Jesus why He stayed in Jerusalem, how did He respond? He was about His Father's business.

6. What do we know about Jesus as He grew to a be man? He was in subjection to His parents, grew up physically, gained wisdom, and found favor with men and in the sight of God.

7. What do we learn about God from these verses? God wants us to grow up, gain wisdom, and seek to find His favor.

Memory Verse: Luke 2:52

Early Elementary and Elementary

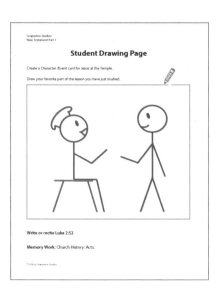

Information for the Jesus at the Temple card:

- When Jesus was twelve, He traveled with His family to Jerusalem to celebrate the Passover feast.

- Jesus remained at the temple listening to and asking questions of the teachers.

- It took Joseph and Mary three days to find Jesus in Jerusalem after they discovered He was not among their family and friends returning home to Nazareth.

- Jesus was found at the temple about His Father's business.

- Jesus grew up in obedience to His parents.

Memory Verse: Luke 2:52

Memory Work: Church History: Acts.

Middle School

John Baptized Jesus

Topical Bible

To whom is *baptism* administered in Scripture?

Nave's, page 49

Bible Dictionary

Define *repentance*.

Zondervan's, page 495

Concordance

Give the first reference to the *Holy Spirit* in the New Testament.

Luke 11:13 (Cruden's, page 244)

Quest Question

Why and how are people baptized today?

Answers will vary.

Timeline Review

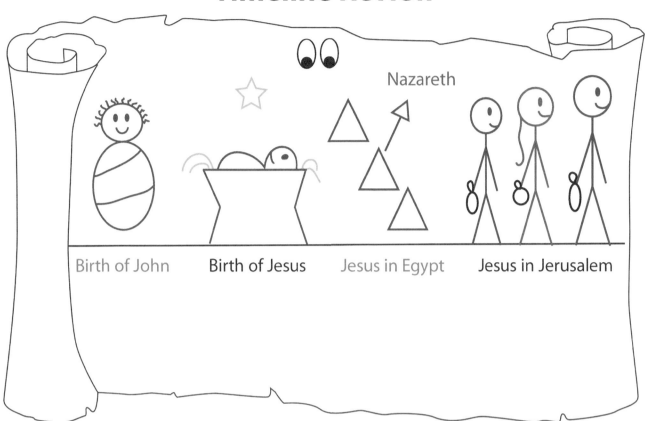

Birth of John   Birth of Jesus   Jesus in Egypt   Jesus in Jerusalem

Memory Verse Review

Luke 2:52

Matthew 2:11

Galatians 4:4-5

Luke 1:80

Memory Work: Church History: Acts.

John Baptized Jesus

Memory Verse: Mark 1:9

John

Read aloud: Luke 1:80, Matthew 3:4

Discuss John: John grew up strong in the Lord. He wore a camel-hair cloak with a leather belt and lived in the desert. His food was wild honey and locusts.

Map: Label the Jordan River.

Draw and have students draw: John.

John Preached Repentance

Read aloud: Matthew 3:1-6, Luke 3:1-6

Discuss John Preached Repentance: At the appointed time, John stepped forward and began to prepare the people for the coming of their Messiah. Being directed by God, John went into the region around the Jordan and preached repentance for the remission of sins. Many confessed their sins and were baptized.

Draw and have students draw: John preaching repentance.

Look up the following words in a Bible Dictionary:

strong

repentance

remission

confessed

Christ

baptize

fire

John Pointed to Jesus

Read aloud: Luke 3:15-16

Discuss John Pointed to Jesus: When people questioned whether John was the Messiah/Christ, John pointed out that he could only baptize with water but that the One coming was mightier than he and would baptize them with the Holy Spirit and with fire.

Draw and have students draw: John pointing to Jesus.

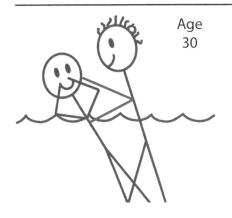

Age 30

John Baptized Jesus

Read aloud: Matthew 3:13-15, Luke 3:21

Discuss John Baptized Jesus: Jesus came to John to have John baptize him. John stated that he felt unworthy for such a task, but Jesus reminded him that it was part of God's plan. John then baptized Jesus in the Jordan River. Jesus was about thirty years old at this time, Luke 3:23.

Draw and have students draw: John baptizing Jesus.

Completed Student Page

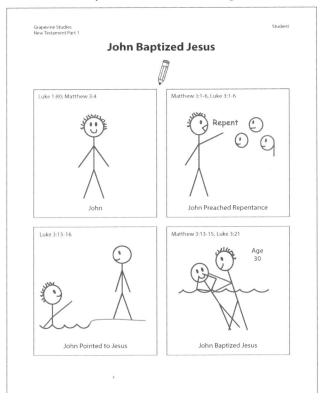

Teacher Notes:

Jesus and the Holy Spirit

Read aloud: Matthew 3:16-17, Luke 3:22

Discuss Jesus and the Holy Spirit: When Jesus came out of the water, the heavens opened and the Holy Spirit descended upon Him in the form of a dove. Then a voice spoke from heaven stating that Jesus was His beloved Son.

Draw and have students draw: A voice from heaven and a purple dove descending from heaven.

Teacher Notes

Completed Student Page

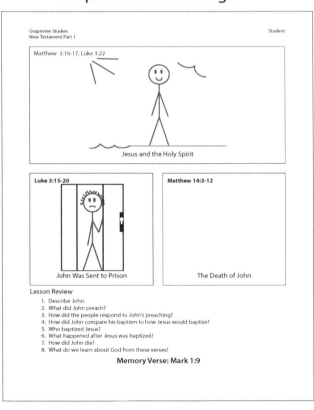

John Was Sent to Prison

Read aloud: Luke 3:15-20

Discuss John Was Sent to Prison: John preached to many people, including Herod the Tetrarch. John told Herod that his relationship with Herodias, his brother's wife, was sinful. For saying this John was put into prison.

Draw and have students draw: John in prison.

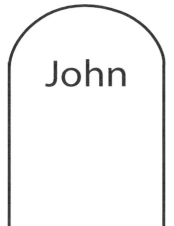

The Death of John

Read aloud: Matthew 14:3-12

Discuss The Death of John: Since we will not cover John later, it is important for your students to know what happened to him. Herod wanted to kill John, but he was afraid of the people. On Herod's birthday, the opportunity arose for John to be killed. Following John's death, his disciples buried him.

Draw and have students draw: John's grave.

Lesson Review:

1. Describe John. Strong in spirit, lived in desert, wore camel-hair clothing with leather belt, and ate wild locusts and honey.

2. What did John preach? Repentance.

3. How did the people respond to John's preaching? They confessed their sins and were baptized, and they wondered if John was the Messiah/Christ.

4. How did John compare his baptism to how Jesus would baptize? John baptized with water, but Jesus would baptize with the Holy Spirit and fire.

5. Who baptized Jesus? John.

6. What happened after Jesus was baptized? The Holy Spirit descended upon Jesus like a dove, and a voice spoke from heaven.

7. How did John die? Herod had him imprisoned and then beheaded.

8. What do we learn about God from these verses? God confirmed that Jesus is His Son as well as the promised Messiah.

Memory Verse: Mark 1:9

Early Elementary and Elementary

Student Drawing Page

Information for the John Baptized Jesus card:

- John prepared the people for the Messiah by preaching repentance and baptizing the people.

- John baptized Jesus in the Jordan River.
    1. After Jesus was baptized:
    2. The Holy Spirit descended upon Jesus in the form of a dove.

- John was put into prison and later beheaded.

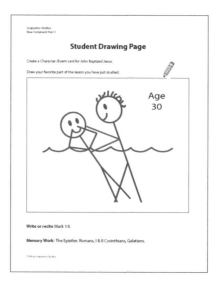

Memory Verse: Mark 1:9

Memory Work: The Epistles: Romans, I & II Corinthians, Galatians.

Section Review

1. Who was king when Zacharias was a priest? King Herod.

2. Who appeared to Zacharias when he was in the temple? The angel of the Lord, Gabriel.

3. What was Zacharias told by Gabriel, and what was his response? He and Elizabeth would have a son, but Zacharias did not believe Gabriel.

4. What happened as a result of Zacharias's unbelief? He was struck mute.

5. What happened to Zacharias when John was named? He could speak again and praised God.

6. What do we learn about John from Zacharias's song? John would be a prophet of the Most High and would prepare the way for the Lord.

7. What do we know about John's childhood? He grew up strong in the Lord and lived in the desert until his manifestation to Israel.

8. Recite Luke 1:80.

9. What did the angel Gabriel tell Mary? She would have a son, Jesus, the Son of God.

10. How did Joseph respond to news of Mary's pregnancy? He planned to divorce her.

11. What did the angel tell Joseph to do, and how did he respond? He obeyed the angel and took Mary as his wife.

12. Why did Mary and Joseph have to travel from Nazareth to Bethlehem? Because Caesar wanted all men to register, and Joseph was required to register in Bethlehem.

13. What happened while Joseph and Mary were in Bethlehem? Jesus was born.

14. Who told the shepherds that Jesus had been born? An angel of the Lord.

15. What did Joseph and Mary do in obedience to the Law? They went to the Temple and offered a sacrifice.

16. Name the two people who prophesied over Jesus at the temple. Simeon and Anna.

17. Recite Galatians 4:4-5.

18. Why did the wise men travel to Jerusalem? To worship the newborn king of the Jews.

19. What was Herod's response to the news that a king of the Jews had been born? He sought to locate the Child's birthplace from the chief priests, scribes, and wise men.

20. What gifts did the Wise Men give to Jesus? Gold, frankincense and myrrh.

21. Where did the angel tell Joseph to take his family and why? To Egypt because Herod was seeking to kill Jesus.

22. When the wise men failed to return to Herod, how did he respond? He ordered the death of all the children two years old and under living in and near Bethlehem.

23. When did Joseph return with his family to Israel? After the death of Herod.

24. In what town did Jesus spend His childhood? Nazareth.

25. What do we know about Jesus as a child? He grew up physically and became spiritually strong.

26. Recite Matthew 2:11.

27. Why were Joseph, Mary, and Jesus going to Jerusalem? To celebrate the Feast of Passover.

28. Why did Joseph and Mary leave Jerusalem without Jesus? They thought that Jesus was returning with them but traveling with some of their family or friends.

29. What was Jesus doing at the temple? He was listening and asking questions of the teachers.

30. How long did it take for Joseph and Mary to find Jesus? Three days.

31. When Mary asked Jesus why He stayed in Jerusalem, how did He respond? He was about His Father's business.

32. What do we know about Jesus as He grew to be a man? He was in subjection to His parents, He grew up physically, gained wisdom, and found favor with men and in the sight of God.

33. Recite Luke 2:52.

34. Describe John. Strong in spirit, lived in desert, wore camel-hair clothing with leather belt, ate wild locusts and honey.

35. What did John preach? Repentance.

36. How did the people respond to John's preaching? They confessed their sins and were baptized, and they wondered if John was the Messiah/Christ.

37. How did John compare his baptism to how Jesus would baptize? John baptized with water, but Jesus would baptize with the Holy Spirit and fire.

38. Who baptized Jesus? John.

39. What happened after Jesus was baptized? The Holy Spirit descended upon Jesus like a dove, and a voice spoke from heaven.

40. How did John die? Herod had him imprisoned and then beheaded.

41. Recite Mark 1:9.

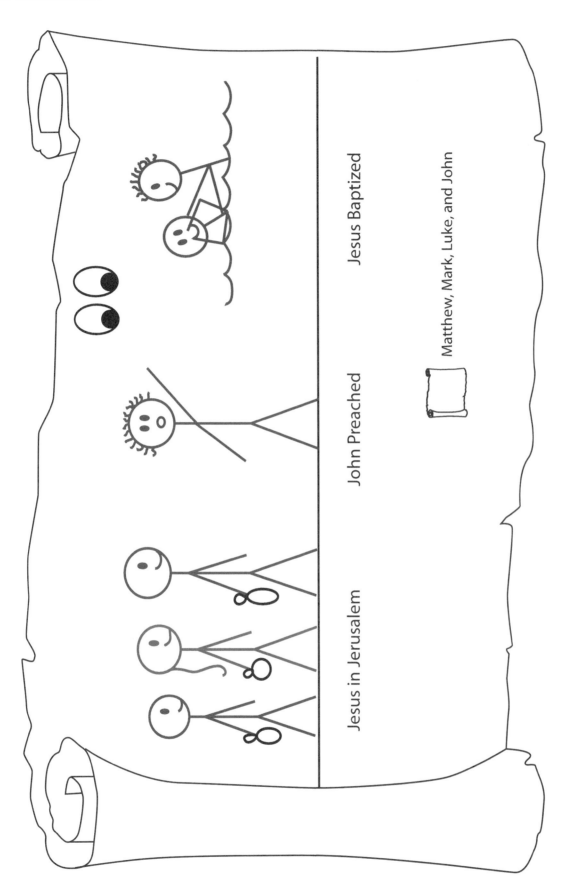

Jesus Baptized

Matthew, Mark, Luke, and John

John Preached

Jesus in Jerusalem

Lesson Goals and Key Points

JESUS WAS TEMPTED

The goal of this lesson is for the students to see that Jesus was tempted in all ways, yet remained without sin, so that He is now able to help us in our time of temptation.

Key Points:
- Jesus was led into the wilderness by the Holy Spirit and fasted there for forty days.
- Satan tempted Jesus, and each time Jesus responded with Scripture: "It is written."
- Jesus was tempted throughout His earthly life yet remained without sin.
- All men are tempted, but God will not allow us to be tempted beyond what we can bear and will always provide us with a way of escape.
- Jesus helps us in our time of temptation.

Memory Verse: Hebrews 4:15

SATAN

The goal of this lesson is to learn the different names and characteristics of Satan and then to study our defenses.

Key Points:
- Satan is known by many names which reveal his actions and character.
- The armor of God is given to us as a defense.
- Satan will spend eternity in the lake of fire.

Memory Verse: Revelation 20:10

THE TWELVE APOSTLES

The goal of this lesson is to learn about the twelve apostles.

Key Points:
- Jesus had many "disciples" but only twelve "apostles."
- The twelve apostles were commissioned and empowered by Jesus to preach the Gospel and heal those who were sick and demon-possessed.
- The life work of the apostles was to teach the word of God and pray.

Memory Verse: Matthew 28:19-20

JESUS TAUGHT

The goal of this lesson is to study some of the teachings of Jesus.

Key Points:
- Jesus taught that outward sins (actions) are a result of inward sins (thoughts and motives).
- When Jesus was asked what the greatest command was, He responded by saying to love God completely and also to love your neighbor as yourself.

Memory Verse: Matthew 22:37-39

JESUS PRAYED

The goal of this lesson is to observe how, when, and where Jesus prayed.

Key Points:
- Jesus often prayed alone.
- Jesus prayed at different times: in the morning, after ministering all day, and before His crucifixion.
- Jesus prayed in many places: in the wilderness, on a mountain, at Gethsemane.
- Jesus taught His disciples to pray.

Memory Verse: Mark 1:35

NOTES

Middle School

The Temptation of Jesus

Topical Bible Exercise

What are the two meanings of *temptation*?

Nave's, page 477

Bible Dictionary Exercise

Define *fasting*.

Zondervan's, pages 173

Define *sin*.

Zondervan's, page 557

Concordance Exercise
In what verse would I find the reference to "Jesus was in all points *tempted…*"?

Hebrews 4:15 (Cruden's, page 494)

Quest Question
Is being tempted the same as sinning? Explain your answer.

No, Jesus was tempted in all ways and yet without sin (Hebrews 4:15).

Timeline Review

Nazareth

Egypt Jesus in Jerusalem John Preached Jesus Baptized

Memory Verse Review

Mark 1:9

Luke 2:52

Matthew 2:11

Galatians 4:4-5

Memory Work: The Epistles: Romans, I & II Corinthians, Galatians.

The Temptation of Jesus

Memory Verse: Hebrews 4:15

Jesus Fasted

Read aloud: Matthew 4:1-2; Luke 4:1-2

Discuss Jesus Fasted: After being baptized and filled with the Holy Spirit, Jesus was led into the wilderness to be tempted/tested by Satan. While in the wilderness He fasted forty days and nights.

Draw and have students draw: Jesus being led into the wilderness/Jesus fasting and praying.

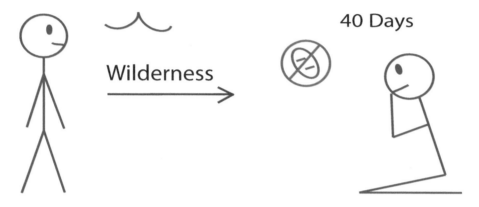

Stones to Bread

Read aloud: Matthew 4:3-4

Discuss Stones to Bread: Satan tempted Jesus to prove that He was the Son of God by turning stones to bread. Jesus responded by quoting Deuteronomy 8:3.

Jump Off the Temple

Read aloud: Matthew 4:5-7

Discuss Jump Off the Temple: Satan quoted Scripture to tempt Jesus to jump off the temple to prove that He was the Son of God. (It is interesting to note that when Satan quoted Scripture, he failed to quote all of Psalm 91:11-12.) Jesus responded by quoting Scripture.

Look up the following words in a Bible Dictionary:

tempted

fasted

weakness

Worship Satan

Read aloud: Matthew 4:8-10

Discuss Worship Satan: Satan showed Jesus all the kingdoms of the earth and their glory and said he would give Jesus all of them if Jesus would worship him. Jesus responded by quoting Scripture and then commanded Satan to leave.

Draw and have students draw: Write Jesus' responses and scripture that he used for each of Satan's temptations.

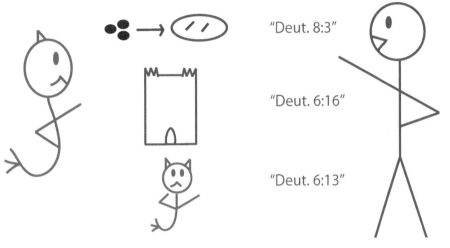

Completed Student Page

Teacher Notes:

Jesus After the Temptation

Read aloud: Matthew 4:11

Discuss Jesus After the Temptation: After Satan left, angels ministered to Jesus

Draw and have students draw: Jesus with an angel over Him.

Tempted but Without Sin

Read aloud: Hebrews 4:15

Discuss Tempted but Without Sin: Scripture tells us that Jesus was tempted in all ways, like we are, but did not sin.

Draw and have students draw: Jesus with temptation and no sin.

Teacher Notes

Completed Student Page

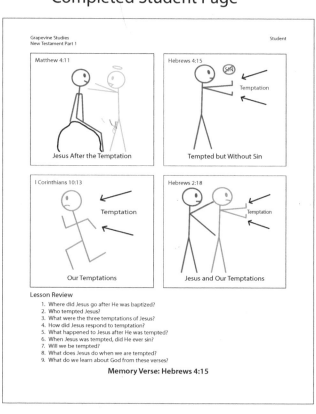

Our Temptations

Temptation

Read aloud: I Corinthians 10:13

Discuss Our Temptations: The Bible assures us that the temptations we face are common to all men. No temptation will be beyond what we can handle, and with every temptation God will provide us with a means of escape.

Draw and have students draw: Temptation coming to man and the man fleeing.

Temptation

Jesus and Our Temptations

Read aloud: Hebrews 2:18

Jesus and Our Temptations: Jesus was tempted so that He could help us in our temptations.

Draw and have students draw: Jesus helping us in our temptations.

Lesson Review:

1. Where did Jesus go after He was baptized? He was led into the wilderness to be tempted.

2. Who tempted Jesus? Satan.

3. What were the three temptations of Jesus? (1) stones to bread, (2) throw Himself off the temple, (3) worship Satan.

4. How did Jesus respond to temptation? "It is written" or with Scripture.

5. What happened to Jesus after He was tempted? The angels came and ministered to Him.

6. When Jesus was tempted, did He ever sin? NO!

7. Will we be tempted? Yes, but not beyond what we can bear.

8. What does Jesus do when we are tempted? He aids us and provides us with an escape.

9. What do we learn about God from these verses? God will not allow us to be tempted beyond what we can bear and will aid us when we are tempted and provide a way of escape.

Memory Verse: Hebrews 4:15

Early Elementary and Elementary

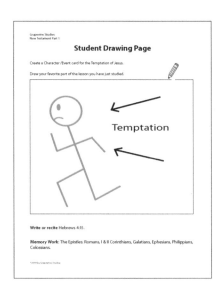

Information for the Temptation of Jesus:

- After Jesus was baptized, the Spirit led Him into the desert where He fasted for 40 days and was tempted by Satan.

- Jesus responded to Satan's temptations by quoting scripture.

- After Jesus was tempted, angels ministered to Him.

Memory Verse: Hebrews 4:15

Memory Work: The Epistles: Romans, I & II Corinthians, Galatians, Ephesians, Philippians, Colossians.

Middle School

Satan

Topical Bible

What do you learn about *Satan*?

Nave's, page 426

Bible Dictionary

Define *devil*.

Zondervan's, page 132

Concordance

How many verses refer to "fire and *brimstone*…"?

One: Revelation 21:8 (Cruden's, page 47)

Quest Question

What power does Satan have over unbelievers and believers? Explain your answer.

Answers will vary.

Timeline Review

Jesus in Jerusalem   John Preached   Jesus Baptized   Jesus Tempted

Memory Verse Review

Hebrews 4:15

Mark 1:9

Luke 2:52

Matthew 2:11

Memory Work: The Epistles: Romans, I & II Corinthians, Galatians, Ephesians, Philippians, Colossians.

Satan

Memory Verse: Revelation 20:10

Serpent of Old/Deceiver

Read aloud: Revelation 12:9

Discuss Serpent of Old/Deceiver: Satan is often referred to as the Serpent of Old because of his long history of deceiving man, starting in Genesis and ending in Revelation.

Draw and have students draw: A snake in a tree.

Devil or Satan

Read aloud: Revelation 12:9

Discuss Devil or Satan: Two formal names of our enemy.

Draw and have students draw: Satan.

Accuser of the Brethren

Read aloud: Revelation 12:9-10

Discuss Accuser of the Brethren: One of the strategies of Satan is to accuse the brethren, or true believers, before God..

Draw and have students draw: Satan before God, accusing a man.

Look up the following words in a Bible Dictionary:

    accuse, brethren

    light

    lies, truth

    dragon, angels

    strong, stand, wiles

    quench, fiery

    brimstone

Angel of Light

Read aloud: II Corinthians 11:14

Discuss Angel of Light: Another strategy of Satan is to appear as an angel of light for the purpose of deceiving men.

Draw and have students draw: Satan appearing as an angel of light.

Father of Lies

Read aloud: John 8:44

Discuss Father of Lies: Satan is not only a liar but the father of lies, with no truth in him.

Draw and have students draw: Satan with lies coming out of his mouth.

The Dragon

Read aloud: Revelation 12:7

Discuss The Dragon: Satan is also referred to as a dragon and the leader of angels (demons).

Draw and have students draw: Satan as a dragon.

Completed Student Page

Teacher Notes:

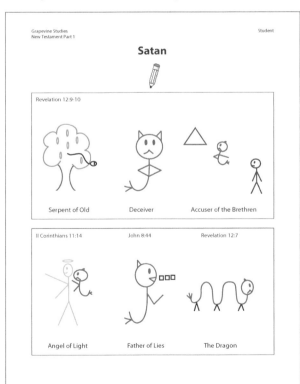

Our Defense

Read aloud: Ephesians 6:10-13
Discuss Our Defense: Before we look at our armor, we are reminded to rely upon the Lord's strength and not our own. Have students draw themselves and each part of the armor as they study.

Belt of Truth

Read aloud: Ephesians 6:14a
Discuss Belt of Truth: The first piece of armor is the belt of truth. Our faith and salvation are based upon the truth of who God is and His Word.
Draw and have students draw: A belt on your stick figure.

Breastplate of Righteousness

Read aloud: Ephesians 6:14b
Discuss Breastplate of Righteousness: Next is righteousness.
Draw and have students draw: The breastplate.

The Gospel

Read aloud: Ephesians 6:15
Discuss The Gospel: We are then ready to share the Gospel.
Draw and have students draw: The shoes.

Teacher Notes

Completed Student Page

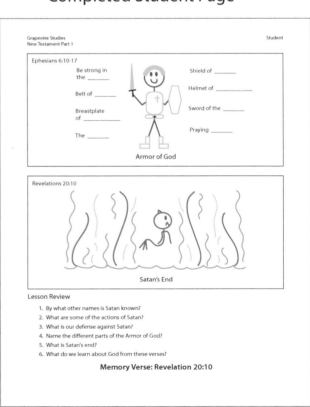

Shield of Faith

Read aloud: Ephesians 6:16
Discuss Shield of Faith: The shield is for extinguishing the darts thrown at us by Satan, the evil one.
Draw and have students draw: The shield.

Helmet of Salvation

Read aloud: Ephesians 6:17a
Discuss Helmet of Salvation: The helmet is given to us to protect our minds, for the Lord has given us a "sound mind."
Draw and have students draw: The helmet.

Sword of the Spirit

Read aloud: Ephesians 6:17b
Discuss Sword of the Spirit: The two-edged sword is given to us as weapon, and like Jesus we should use it to defeat Satan: "it is written." The sword is also an instrument that God uses to judge our thoughts and intentions.
Draw and have students draw: The sword.

Satan's End

Read aloud: Revelation 20:10

Discuss Satan's End: Satan's end will be in the lake of fire, forever and ever.

Draw and have students draw: Satan in the lake of fire.

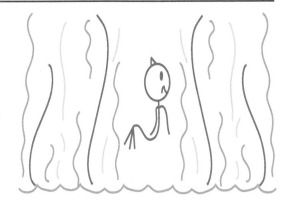

Lesson Review:

1. By what other names is Satan known? Serpent of Old, Deceiver, Devil, Satan, Accuser of the Brethren, Angel of Light, Father of Lies, and the Dragon.

2. What are some of the actions of Satan? Deceive, lie, accuse, etc.

3. What is our defense against Satan? Trust in the Lord, the Armor of God, and prayer.

4. Name the different parts of the Armor of God. Belt of Truth, Breastplate of Righteousness, Shoes to carry the Gospel, Shield of Faith, Helmet of Salvation, and the Sword of the Spirit.

5. What is Satan's end? The lake of fire, forever and ever.

6. What do we learn about God from these verses? God will judge Satan in the end, but until then God has given us what we need to stand against the evil one.

Memory Verse: Revelation 20:10

Early Elementary and Elementary

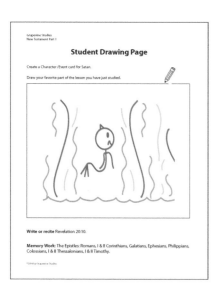

Information for the Satan card:

- Satan is known by many names:
  1. Serpent of Old
  2. Deceiver
  3. Devil
  4. Satan
  5. Accuser of the Brethren
  6. Angel of Light
  7. Father of Lies
  8. Dragon
- Our defense against Satan is the Word of God and the armor of God.
- Satan's end will be in the lake of fire.

Memory Verse: Revelation 20:10

Memory Work: The Epistles: Romans, I & II Corinthians, Galatians, Ephesians, Philippians, Colossians, I & II Thessalonians, I & II Timothy.

Middle School

The Twelve Apostles

Topical Bible

What is an *apostle*?

Nave's, page 29

Bible Dictionary

Define *disciple*.

Zondervan's, page 133

Concordance

Give one verse in which you find the names of the twelve *apostles*.

Matthew 10:2 (Cruden's, page 15)

Quest Question

Compare and contrast the religious leaders of Jesus' day with the apostles.

Answers will vary.

Timeline Review

Jesus in Jerusalem   John Preached   Jesus Baptized   Jesus Tempted

Teacher Note: The timeline review is the same as the last lesson because we added a lesson on Satan.

Memory Verse Review

Revelation 20:10

Hebrews 4:15

Mark 1:9

Luke 2:52

Memory Work: The Epistles: Romans, I & II Corinthians, Galatians, Ephesians, Philippians, Colossians, I & II Thessalonians, I & II Timothy.

The Twelve Apostles

Memory Verse: Matthew 28:19-20

Disciples and Apostles

Read aloud: Luke 6:12-13

Discuss Disciples and Apostles: A **disciple** is one who goes, learns from the teacher, and then imitates what he has learned. (Later this term is used to describe followers of Jesus.) An **apostle** was an eyewitness to Jesus' life who was empowered and commissioned to be sent forth to preach the Gospel. (Later this term was used to describe believers who were prominent leaders.)

Draw and have students draw: For **Disciple** draw a believer going, a teacher teaching with a disciple listening, and the disciple leaving and imitating his teacher. For **Apostle** draw a an apostle who has been commissioned (use a purple star to represent Jesus commissioning).

Disciples   Apostles

Look up the following words in a Bible Dictionary:

Disciple

Apostle

tax collector

power

baptize

Andrew and Simon Peter

Read aloud: John 1:35-36, 40-42

Discuss Andrew and Simon Peter: Andrew, a disciple of John the Baptist. Realizing that Jesus was the Messiah, Andrew began following Jesus. Andrew sought his brother, Simon Peter, told him of Jesus and then brought him to Jesus.

Draw and have students draw: Andrew and Simon Peter.

Andrew   Simon
(Peter)

Philip

Philip

Read aloud: John 1:43-44

Discuss Philip: Jesus called Phillip, who was from Bethsaida, to follow Him.

Draw and have students draw: Phillip.

Matthew

Read aloud: Matthew 9:9-13

Discuss Matthew: Jesus called Matthew (Levi), the tax collector to follow Him, and he did.

Draw and have students draw: Matthew.

Matthew

Completed Student Page

Teacher Notes:

James and John

Read aloud: Matthew 10:2-4

Discuss James and John: Sons of Zebedee who were fishermen and friends of Andrew and Simon.

Draw and have students draw: James and John.

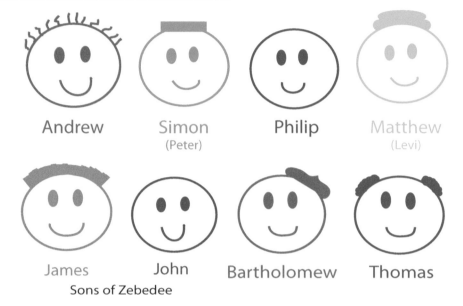

Andrew   Simon (Peter)   Philip   Matthew (Levi)

James   John   Bartholomew   Thomas

Sons of Zebedee

Teacher Notes

Completed Student Page

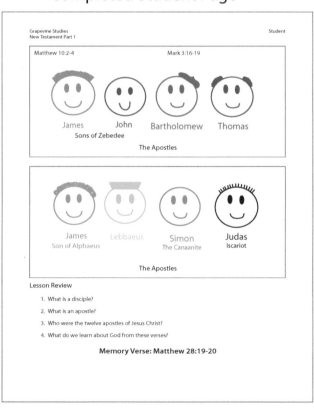

Bartholomew (Nathaniel), Thomas, James, Lebbaeus (Thaddaeus), Simon (the Canaanite) and Judas Iscariot

Read aloud: Mark 3:16-19

Discuss Bartholomew (Nathaniel), Thomas, James, Lebbaeus (Thaddaeus), Simon (the Canaanite) and Judas Iscariot: Jesus called a total of twelve disciples and made them apostles.

Draw and have students draw: The remaining apostles.

James
Son of Alphaeus

Lebbaeus

Simon
The Canaanite

Judas
Iscariot

Lesson Review:

1. What is a disciple? One who listens and learns and then acts upon what he has learned.

2. What is an apostle? One who is called, commissioned, and empowered to go forth.

3. Who were the twelve apostles of Jesus Christ? Andrew, Simon Peter, Philip, Matthew, James, John, Bartholomew, Thomas, James, Lebbaeus, Simon, Judas Iscariot.

4. What do we learn about God from these verses? God desires first that we become His disciple and then go and make other disciples.

Memory Verse: Matthew 28:19-20

Early Elementary and Elementary

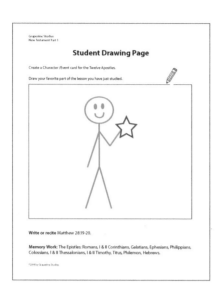

Add to The Twelve Apostles card:

- A disciple is one who listens, learns and then acts upon what he has learned.
- An apostle was an eye witness to Jesus' life who was empowered, commissioned, and sent forth to preach the gospel.
- Jesus had Twelve Apostles: Andrew, Simon Peter, Philip, Matthew, James, John, Bartholomew, Thomas, James, Lebbaeus, Simon, Judas Iscariot.

Memory Verse: Matthew 28:19-20

Memory Work: The Epistles: Romans, I & II Corinthians, Galatians, Ephesians, Philippians, Colossians, I & II Thessalonians, I & II Timothy, Titus, Philemon, Hebrews.

Middle School

Jesus Taught

Topical Bible

What do we read about *anger*?

Nave's, page 24

Bible Dictionary

What is *mammon*?

Zondervan's, page 339

Concordance

In what verse do we find the command *"Love* the Lord thy God with all your heart…"? (Love as a verb)

Deuteronomy 6:5 (Cruden's, page 302)

Quest Question

Now that Jesus has come, do we no longer need the Old Testament? Defend your answer.

Yes or No. Defenses will vary.

Timeline Review

| John Preached | Jesus Baptized | Jesus Tempted | Twelve Apostles |

Memory Verse Review

Matthew 28:19-20

Revelation 20:10

Hebrews 4:15

Mark 1:9

Memory Work: The Epistles: Romans, I & II Corinthians, Galatians, Ephesians, Philippians, Colossians, I & II Thessalonians, I & II Timothy, Titus, Philemon, Hebrews.

Jesus Taught

Memory Verse: Matthew 22:37-39

Murder and Anger

Read aloud: Matthew 5:21-24

Discuss Murder and Anger: As Jesus instructed His disciples, He often referred to what they had been taught in the Law (New Testament). The disciples knew what the Law taught about murder, but Jesus elaborated by addressing the inward issue of anger and expressions of anger.

Draw and have students draw: A man angry at another man.

Yes and No

Read aloud: Matthew 5:33-37

Discuss Yes and No: Jesus taught His disciples not to swear an oath by anything on earth or in heaven but instead let their "yes" be yes and their "no" be no.

Draw and have students draw: A woman saying "Yes" and another woman saying "No."

Look up the following words in a Bible Dictionary:

anger

swear

enemy

neighbor

charitable

mammon

Love Your Enemies

Read aloud: Matthew 5:43-45

Discuss Love Your Enemies: In place of hate and the actions associated with someone being our "enemy," Jesus taught that His disciples were to love, bless, do good to, and pray for their enemies.

Draw and have students draw: A man praying and blessing his enemy.

Charitable Deeds

Read aloud: Matthew 6:1-4

Discuss Charitable Deeds: When we do charitable deeds it should be for the Lord, and the only reward we should seek should be from Him.

Draw and have students draw: A man giving another man a drink with God/another man watching.

Completed Student Page

Teacher Notes:

Two Masters

Read aloud: Matthew 6:24

Discuss Two Masters: We all must choose who we will serve in our life: God or money.

Draw and have students draw: The symbols for God and money.

Do Not Worry

Read aloud: Matthew 6:25-34

Discuss Do Not Worry: God reminds us not to worry because He is able to provide for our every need. God demonstrates His provision throughout Creation.

Write and have students write: A man looking at flowers with birds above.

Teacher Notes

Completed Student Page

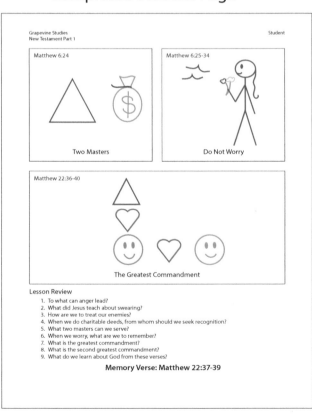

The Greatest Commandment

Read aloud: Matthew 22:36-40

Discuss The Greatest Commandment: When Jesus was asked "What is the greatest commandment?" He responded by saying that it is to love God completely and also love your neighbor as yourself.

Draw and have students draw: A man loving God and a man loving others.

Lesson Review:

1. To what can anger lead? Speaking evil against others, hate, and murder.

2. What did Jesus teach about swearing? We are not to swear but should let our "yes" mean yes and our "no" mean no.

3. How are we to treat our enemies? We are to love, bless, do good to, and pray for our enemies.

4. When we do charitable deeds, from whom should we seek recognition? God alone.

5. What two masters can we serve? God or mammon.

6. When we worry, what are we to remember? Creation and that God will take care of our needs.

7. What is the greatest commandment? Love God totally.

8. What is the second greatest commandment? Love our neighbor like we love ourselves.

9. What do we learn about God from these verses? God is concerned not only with our outward actions but also with our inward thoughts and attitudes.

Memory Verse: Matthew 22:37-39

Early Elementary and Elementary

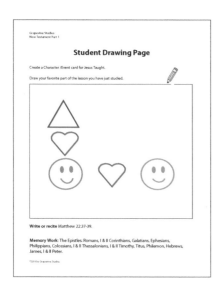

Information for the Jesus Taught card:

- Jesus taught
  1. The greatest commandment is to love God first and then love others.
  2. Our thoughts and attitudes will show in our actions.
  3. Do not swear.
  4. Love your enemies.
  5. Charitable deeds should be done for God to see and not for reward.
  6. No man can serve God and money.
  7. Do not worry.

Memory Verse: Matthew 22:37-39

Memory Work: The Epistles: Romans, I & II Corinthians, Galatians, Ephesians, Philippians, Colossians, I & II Thessalonians, I & II Timothy, Titus, Philemon, Hebrews, James, I & II Peter.

Middle School

Jesus Prayed

Topical Bible

What does *hallow* mean?

Nave's, page 192

Bible Dictionary

What is a *debt*?

Zondervan's, page 130

Concordance

What is the first verse of the Bible in which we find the word *pray*?

Genesis 20:7 (Cruden's, page 375)

Quest Question

To whom should we pray?

To God alone.

Timeline Review

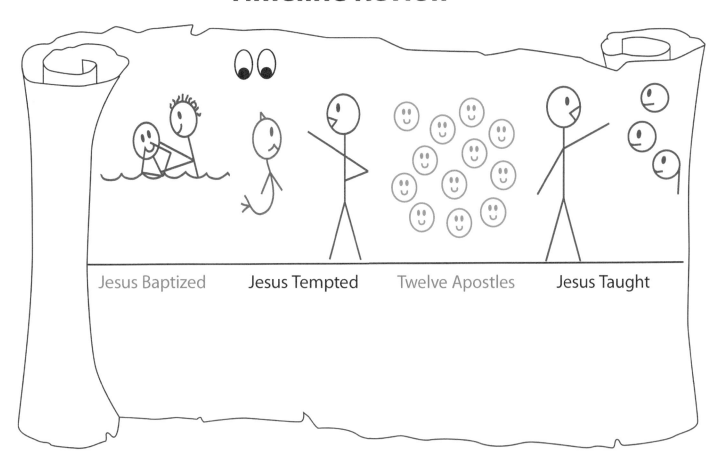

Jesus Baptized   Jesus Tempted   Twelve Apostles   Jesus Taught

Memory Verse Review

Matthew 22:37-39

Matthew 28:19-20

Revelation 20:10

Hebrews 4:15

Memory Work: The Epistles: Romans, I & II Corinthians, Galatians, Ephesians, Philippians, Colossians, I & II Thessalonians, I & II Timothy, Titus, Philemon, Hebrews, James, I & II Peter.

Jesus Prayed

Memory Verse: Mark 1:35

Alone

Read aloud: Matthew 14:23

Discuss Alone: Jesus often prayed alone. After He ministered to the crowds, He sent them away and then went alone to a mountain to pray.

Draw and have students draw: Jesus praying on a mountain alone, with the crowds leaving.

Early in the Morning

Read aloud: Mark 1:35

Discuss Early in the Morning: Jesus also prayed alone, early in the morning, in a solitary place.

Draw and have students draw: Jesus praying as the sun comes up over the horizon.

Look up the following words in a Bible Dictionary:

solitary

hypocrites

vain repetitions

heathen

hallowed

kingdom

After Teaching and Healing

Read aloud: Luke 5:15-16

Discuss After Teaching and Healing: After teaching and healing, Jesus went to pray in the wilderness.

Draw and have students draw: Jesus praying among trees.

All Night

Read aloud: Luke 6:12

Discuss All Night: Jesus also prayed on the mountain all night before choosing His disciples.

Draw and have students draw: Jesus praying on a mountain with a moon above.

Completed Student Page

Teacher Notes:

Before His Crucifixion

Read aloud: Mark 14:32-36

Discuss Before His Crucifixion: The night before Jesus was crucified, He went with His disciple to the Garden of Gethsemane to pray.

Draw and have students draw: Jesus praying over a rock.

When You Pray

Read aloud: Matthew 6:5-8

Discuss When You Pray: Jesus gave instructions for us to pray to Him, in secret and honestly, not in public for show.

Draw and have students draw: Themselves praying.

Teacher Notes

Completed Student Page

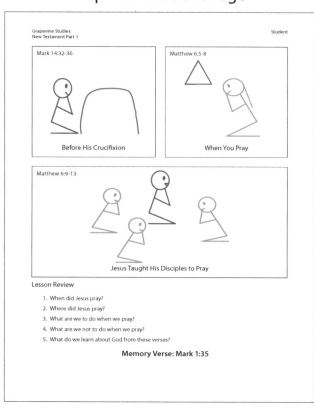

Jesus Taught His Disciples to Pray

Read aloud: Matthew 6:9-13

Discuss Jesus Taught His Disciples to Pray: When Jesus' disciples asked Him to teach them to pray, this is the prayer He taught them. I recommend your own personal study of the words used in this prayer, cross-referencing it with Luke 11:2-4.

Draw and have students draw: Jesus praying with His disciples.

Lesson Review:

1. When did Jesus pray? In the morning, at night, and after He had taught and healed.

2. Where did Jesus pray? On mountains and in solitary places.

3. What are we to do when we pray? Pray in secret, remembering God knows our needs.

4. What are we not to do when we pray? Pray to be seen by others and use vain repetitions and many words.

5. What do we learn about God from these verses? God wants us to pray using Jesus as an example.

Memory Verse: Mark 1:35

Early Elementary and Elementary

Student Drawing Page

Information for the Jesus Prayed card:

- Jesus gave us an example in prayer.
    1. He prayed in the morning, evening, and all night.
    2. After He had taught and healed.
    3. He prayed on mountains and in solitary places.
    4. He prayed often.
- Jesus taught His disciples to pray.

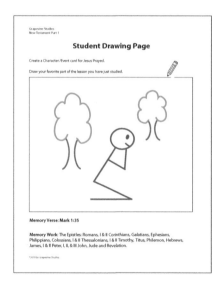

Memory Verse: Mark 1:35

Memory Work: The Epistles: Romans, I & II Corinthians, Galatians, Ephesians, Philippians, Colossians, I & II Thessalonians, I & II Timothy, Titus, Philemon, Hebrews, James, I & II Peter, I, II, & III John, Jude and Revelation.

Final Review

1. Who was king when Zacharias was a priest? King Herod.

2. Who appeared to Zacharias when he was in the temple? The angel of the Lord, Gabriel.

3. What was Zacharias told by Gabriel, and what was his response? He and Elizabeth would have a son, but Zacharias did not believe Gabriel.

4. What happened as a result of Zacharias's unbelief? He was struck mute.

5. What happened to Zacharias when John was named? He could speak again and praised God.

6. What do we learn about John from Zacharias's song? John would be a prophet of the Most High and would prepare the way for the Lord.

7. What do we know about John's childhood? He grew up strong in the Lord and lived in the desert until his manifestation to Israel.

8. Recite Luke 1:80.

9. What did the angel Gabriel tell Mary? She would have a son, Jesus, the Son of God.

10. How did Joseph respond to news of Mary's pregnancy? He planned to divorce her.

11. What did the angel tell Joseph to do, and how did he respond? He obeyed the angel and took Mary as his wife.

12. Why did Mary and Joseph have to travel from Nazareth to Bethlehem? Because Caesar wanted all men to register, and Joseph was required to register in Bethlehem.

13. What happened while Joseph and Mary were in Bethlehem? Jesus was born.

14. Who told the shepherds that Jesus had been born? An angel of the Lord.

15. What did Joseph and Mary do in obedience to the Law? They went to the Temple and offered a sacrifice.

16. Name the two people who prophesied over Jesus at the temple. Simeon and Anna.

17. Recite Galatians 4:4-5.

18. Why did the wise men travel to Jerusalem? To worship the newborn king of the Jews.

19. What was Herod's response to the news that a king of the Jews had been born? He sought to locate the Child's birthplace from the chief priests, scribes, and wise men.

20. What gifts did the Wise Men give to Jesus? Gold, frankincense and myrrh.

21. Where did the angel tell Joseph to take his family and why? To Egypt because Herod was seeking to kill Jesus.

22. When the wise men failed to return to Herod, how did he respond? He ordered the death of all the children two years old and under living in and near Bethlehem.

23. When did Joseph return with his family to Israel? After the death of Herod.

24. In what town did Jesus spend His childhood? Nazareth.

25. What do we know about Jesus as a child? He grew up physically and became spiritually strong.

26. Recite Matthew 2:11.

27. Why were Joseph, Mary, and Jesus going to Jerusalem? To celebrate the Feast of Passover.

28. Why did Joseph and Mary leave Jerusalem, without Jesus? They thought that Jesus was returning with them but traveling with some of their family or friends.

29. What was Jesus doing at the temple? He was listening and asking questions of the teachers.

30. How long did it take for Joseph and Mary to find Jesus? Three days.

31. When Mary asked Jesus why He stayed in Jerusalem, how did He respond? He was about His Father's business.

32. What do we know about Jesus as He grew to be a man? He was in subjection to His parents, He grew up physically, gained wisdom, and found favor with men and in the sight of God.

33. Recite Luke 2:52.

34. Describe John. Strong in spirit, lived in desert, wore camel-hair clothing with leather belt, ate wild locusts and honey.

35. What did John preach? Repentance.

36. How did the people respond to John's preaching? They confessed their sins and were baptized but they wondered if John was the Messiah/Christ.

37. How did John compare his baptism to how Jesus would baptize? John baptized with water but Jesus would baptize with the Holy Spirit and fire.

38. Who baptized Jesus? John.

39. What happened after Jesus was baptized? The Holy Spirit descended upon Jesus like a dove and a voice spoke from heaven.

40. How did John die? Herod had him imprisoned and then beheaded.

41. Recite Mark 1:9.

42. Where did Jesus go after He was baptized? He was lead into the wilderness to be tempted.

43. Who tempted Jesus? Satan.

44. What were the three temptations of Jesus? 1) stone to bread 2) throw Himself off the temple 3) worship Satan.

45. How did Jesus respond to temptation? "It is written" or with scripture.

46. What happened to Jesus after He was tempted? The angels came and ministered to Him.

47. When Jesus was tempted, did He ever sin? NO!

48. Will we be tempted? Yes, but not beyond what we can bear.

49. What does Jesus do when we are tempted? He aids us and provides us with an escape.

50. Recite Hebrews 4:15.

51. By what other names is Satan known? Serpent of Old, Deceiver, Devil, Satan, Accuser of the Brethren, Angel of Light, Father of Lies, and the Dragon.

52. What are some of the actions of Satan? Deceive, lie, accuse, etc.

53. What is our defense against Satan? Trust in the Lord, the Armor of God, prayer.

54. Name the different parts of the Armor of God. Belt of Truth, Breastplate of Righteousness, Shoes to carry the Gospel, Shield of Faith, Helmet of Salvation, and the Sword of the Spirit.

55. What is Satan's end? The Lake of Fire, forever and ever.

56. Recite Revelation 20:10.

57. What is a disciple? One who listens and learns and then acts upon what he has learned.

58. What is an apostle? One who is called, commissioned and empowered to go forth.

59. Who were the Twelve Apostles of Jesus Christ? Andrew, Simon Peter, Philip, Matthew, James, John, Bartholomew, Thomas, James, Lebbaeus, Simon, Judas Iscariot.

60. Recite Matthew 28:19-20.

61. To what can anger lead? Speaking evil against others, hate, and murder.

62. What did Jesus teach about swearing? We are not to swear but let our "yes" mean yes and our "no' mean no.

63. How are we to treat our enemies? We are to love, bless, do good to and pray for our enemies.

64. When we do charitable deeds, from whom should we seek recognition? God alone.

65. What two masters can we serve? God or mammon.

66. When we worry, what are we to remember? Creation and that God will take care of our needs.

67. What is the greatest commandment? Love God totally.

68. What is the second greatest commandment? Love our neighbor like we love ourselves.

69. Recite Matthew 22:37-39.

70. When did Jesus pray? In the morning, at night and after He had taught and healed.

71.   Where did Jesus pray? On mountains and in solitary places.

72.   What are we to do when we pray? Pray in secret remembering God knows our needs.

73.   What are we not to do when we pray? Pray to be seen by others and use vain repetitions and many words.

74.   Recite Mark 1:35.

For Early Elementary and Elementary Levels:

75.   How many books are in the Bible? 66.

76.   In what language was the New Testament written? Greek, Hebrew, and Aramaic.

77.   Name the Gospels. Matthew, Mark, Luke, and John.

78.   Name the Book of Church History. Acts.

79.   Name the Epistles? Romans, I & II Corinthians, Galatians, Ephesians, Philippians,   Colossians, I & II Thessalonians, I & II Timothy, Titus, Philemon, Hebrews, James, I & II Peter, I, II, & III John, Jude and Revelation.

Nazareth

Birth of John

Birth of Jesus

Egypt

Jesus in Jerusalem

Matthew, Mark, Luke, and John

Jesus Tempted

Jesus Baptized

John Preached

Matthew, Mark, Luke, and John

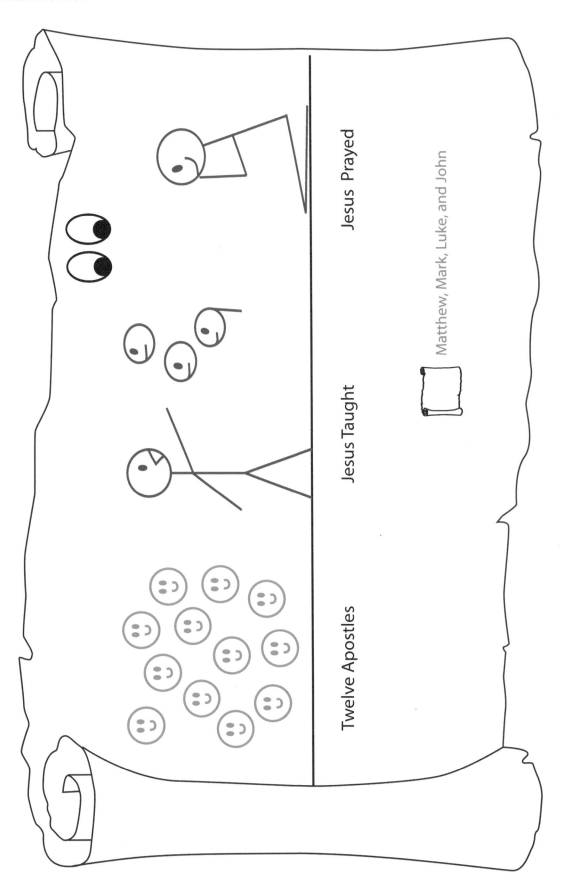

Jesus Prayed

Jesus Taught

Twelve Apostles

Matthew, Mark, Luke, and John

Map

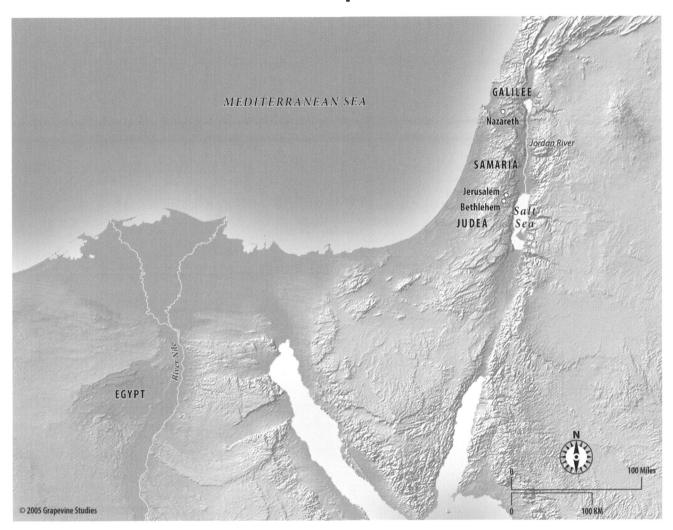

Label:

1. The city of Nazareth.

2. The city of Bethlehem.

3. The country of Egypt.

4. The Jordan River.

Page intentionally left blank

New Testament Overview
~
Part 2

Jesus and the Sea: One of the many miracles that Jesus performed was the calming of the sea in the midst of a storm. When Jesus spoke, Creation responded. After Jesus calmed the storm, His disciples marveled at what He had done and questioned among themselves who He was. At another point in Jesus' ministry, He also walked on water.

Draw and have students draw: Jesus in a boat speaking to the storm.

Jesus Fed the People: Jesus showed that He was concerned not only with the spiritual lives of those who sought to learn from Him but also their physical lives. Scripture records two separate accounts where Jesus fed multitudes, one time feeding 5,000 men (not including women and children) and another time feeding 7,000 men.

Draw and have students draw: Jesus holding bread and a fish.

My Notes:

Jesus Healed the Sick/Lame: Many times throughout Jesus' ministry, He healed people of various physical ailments. Jesus healed the deaf, the dumb, the blind, the mute, the lepers, and the lame.

Draw and have students draw: Jesus praying over a sick woman.

The Eyes: Throughout the Old Testament, our eyes looked forward to the Messiah, but when Jesus is born we change the eyes to looking down. Now that Jesus has come, we watch what He does.

Draw and have students draw: Eyes looking down.

Completed Student Page

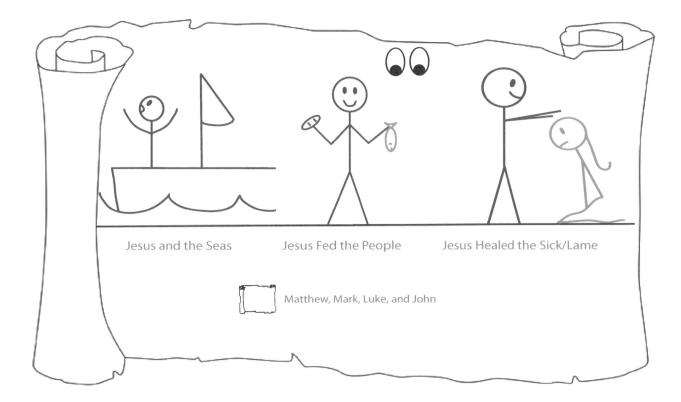

Jesus and the Seas   Jesus Fed the People   Jesus Healed the Sick/Lame

Matthew, Mark, Luke, and John

Jesus Healed the Demon-Possessed: In addition to the physical healings, Jesus also healed those who were demon-possessed. Many times Jesus cast out demons that had possessed and tormented men, women, and children. It is interesting to note that the demons knew that Jesus was the Messiah and that Jesus often commanded them to keep silent.

Draw and have students draw: Jesus casting a demon out of a man.

Jesus Raised the Dead: Although Jesus performed many miracles during His ministry, few compared with the people that Jesus raised from the dead. At the end of Jesus' time of ministry, He raised Lazarus from the dead after he had been in the tomb for four days. Word of Lazarus's resurrection by Jesus caused many Jews to believe that He was indeed the Messiah. Lazarus's resurrection also caused the unbelieving Jewish leaders to begin plotting to kill both Lazarus and Jesus.

Draw and have students draw: Jesus raising a man from the dead.

My Notes:

Jesus Entered Jerusalem: Jesus entered Jerusalem with His disciples to celebrate the Feast of Passover and to begin the last week of His earthly life. Jesus rode into Jerusalem on a donkey, and the people waved leafy branches and shouted "Hosanna!" This event is celebrated by Christians today on Palm Sunday. During this week Jesus went to the temple, removed the money changers, healed the sick, and taught. Also during this week, Judas began to plot with the chief priest, who sought to arrest and kill Jesus.

Draw and have students draw: Jesus riding on a colt.

My Notes:

Completed Student Page

Jesus Healed the Demon-Possessed   Jesus Raised the Dead   Jesus Entered Jerusalem

Matthew, Mark, Luke, and John

The Last Supper: At the Last Supper Jesus washed His apostles' feet and warned them of His coming death, telling them that they would all betray Him. After the meal Judas left, and Jesus instructed the eleven regarding the bread and the wine of the New Covenant. Jesus and the eleven then sang and departed to the Garden of Gethsemane.

Draw and have students draw: Jesus holding a cup and bread.

Draw The Garden of Gethsemane: Arriving at the garden, Jesus asked Peter, James, and John to go a little further into the garden with Him to pray. The apostles repeatedly fell asleep while Jesus prayed with such intensity that His sweat was as blood. Jesus' prayer during this time in the garden was that the Father's will would be done.

Draw and have students draw: Jesus praying near a tree.

Jesus Arrested: The chief priest, Pharisees, and Roman troops found Jesus in the garden, and there Judas betrayed Him. When Jesus was arrested, the eleven Apostles fled.

Draw and have students draw: Jesus in chains.

Jesus Put on Trial: After Jesus was arrested He was put on trial. Throughout the night and into the morning Jesus endured six individual trials, three religious and three civil. After Jesus was beaten and scourged, Pilate condemned Him to death by crucifixion

Draw and have students draw: Jesus on trial.

My Notes:

Completed Student Page

The Last Supper   The Garden of Gethsemane   Jesus Arrested   The Trials

Matthew, Mark, Luke, and John

Lesson Goals and Key Points

JESUS AND THE SEA

The goal of this lesson is to explore how Jesus demonstrated His power over the sea.

Key Points:
- Scripture records two instances where Jesus displayed His control over the wind and the sea.
- Jesus had the power to calm the wind and the sea when a tempest rose on the Sea of Galilee, threatening to capsize the boat He was riding in.
- Jesus also walked on the sea and called Peter out of the boat to do the same.

Memory Verse: Matthew 8:27

JESUS FED THE MULTITUDES

The goal of this lesson is to understand how Jesus cared for the spiritual condition and physical needs of people.

Key Points:
- On two separate occasions Jesus multiplied little to feed many.
- 1. With five loaves and two fish, Jesus fed 5,000.
- 2. With seven loaves and a few small fish, Jesus fed 7,000.
- Each time Jesus fed the multitudes, there were baskets of leftovers.

Memory Verse: Luke 9:16

JESUS HEALED THE SICK

The goal of this lesson is to see to how Jesus cared for those who were sick and lame.

Key Points:
- Throughout Jesus' ministry He healed the sick, deaf, mute, blind, lame, and diseased.
- Often the sick and lame were brought by others to Jesus to be healed.
- Many of those who were healed praised God and gave thanks to Jesus.
- People who saw the healings were amazed and praised God.

Memory Verse: Matthew 4:23

JESUS HEALED THE DEMON-POSSESSED

The goal of this lesson is to show how Jesus cared for those who were demon-possessed.

Key Points:
- Demons or unclean spirits possessed many people in Jesus' day.
- Often those who were demon-possessed came to Jesus, and He delivered and healed them.
- Jesus gave His disciples authority to cast out demons.
- Scripture warns that only believers have the authority to cast out demons in Jesus' name.

Memory Verse: Luke 9:1

JESUS RAISED THE DEAD

The goal of this lesson is to establish the fact that Jesus raised people from the dead.

Key Points:
- Scripture records that Jesus raised people from the dead, including the widow's son and Jairus' daughter.
- Jesus also raised Lazarus from the dead after he had been in the tomb four days.
- When Jesus raised Lazarus from the dead, many Jews believed.

Memory Verse: Luke 7:15

NOTES

Page intentionally left blank

Middle School

Quest Page

Topical Bible

How many times is the word *faith* used in the Old Testament and the New Testament?

Old Testament 2, New Testament nearly 500 (Nave's, page 149)

Bible Dictionary

Define the *watches of the night*.

Zondervan's, page 602

Concordance

In what other New Testament passages do we find a *tempest*?

Matthew 8:24, Acts 27: 18, 20, Hebrews 12:18, II Peter 2:17 (Cruden's, page 493)

Quest Question

What should be our response when the events of life seem to overtake us like a storm?

Matthew 8:25: We should respond like the disciples who, when they were caught in a storm, cried out to Jesus to save them.

Jesus and the Sea

Memory Verse: Matthew 8:27

Jesus and His Disciples

Read aloud: Matthew 8:23

Discuss Jesus and His Disciples: In the following passages, we will see that Jesus had power over Creation. When He spoke, Creation responded. One evening, after a day of ministry, Jesus and His disciples got into a boat and set out on the Sea of Galilee.

Map: Label the Sea of Galilee.

Draw and have students draw: Jesus in a boat with a disciple.

A Great Tempest Arose

Read aloud: Matthew 8:24

Discuss A Great Tempest Arose: After they set out on the sea, a great tempest suddenly came upon them. The waves threatened to overtake them, but Jesus slept in spite of the storm.

Draw and have students draw: The boat on stormy seas.

Look up the following words in a Bible Dictionary:

tempest

marveled

watch

worshipped

The Disciples Cried Out

Read aloud: Matthew 8:25

Discuss The Disciples Cried Out: The disciples, fearing that the boat would capsize, woke Jesus and cried out for Him to save them.

Draw and have students draw: The disciples and Jesus in the boat.

Jesus Calmed the Storm

Read aloud: Matthew 8:26-27

Discuss Jesus Calmed the Storm: Jesus arose and spoke to the wind and the sea. Immediately the winds stopped and the sea became calm. The disciples marveled that the winds and the sea obeyed Him.

Draw and have students draw: Jesus in the boat, speaking "peace" to the sea.

Completed Student Page

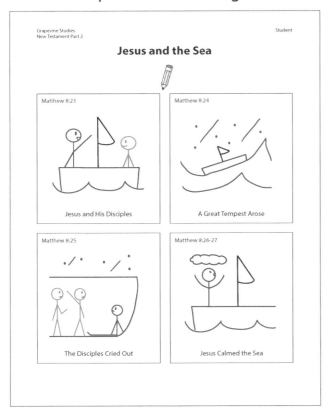

Teacher Notes

Jesus Prayed

Read aloud: Matthew 14:22-23

Discuss Jesus Prayed: Jesus often went alone upon a mountain to pray, even after a long day of ministry.

Draw and have students draw: Jesus on a mountain praying and a boat on the sea in the back ground.

Jesus Walked on Water

Read aloud: Matthew 14:24-25

Discuss Jesus Walked on Water: On one occasion, Jesus sent the disciples out across the Sea of Galilee in their boat. Jesus came to them walking on the water, which caused great fear among the disciples.

Draw and have students draw: Jesus walking on water.

Teacher Notes

Completed Student Page

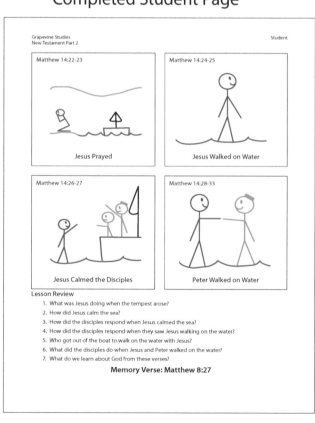

Jesus Calmed the Disciples

Read aloud: Matthew 14:26-27

Discuss Jesus Calmed the Disciples: Jesus spoke to the disciples to let them know that it was Him and not a ghost.

Draw and have students draw: Jesus walking on water and talking to the disciples who were in the boat.

Peter Walked on Water

Read aloud: Matthew 14:28-33

Discuss Peter Walked on Water: Peter asked Jesus to command him to come to Him on the water. When Peter got out of the boat, he looked at the waves, became afraid, and began to sink. Jesus seized Peter by the hand and asked him why he doubted. When the disciples saw these things happen, they proclaimed Jesus to be the Son of God.

Map: Label the Dead Sea, Jordan River and Mediterranean Sea.

Draw and have students draw: Peter walking on water with Jesus holding his hand.

Lesson Review

1. What was Jesus doing when the tempest arose? He was sleeping.

2. How did Jesus calm the sea? He spoke to the wind and the waves, and it was so.

3. How did the disciples respond when Jesus calmed the sea? They marveled.

4. How did the disciples respond when they saw Jesus walking on the water? They thought He was a ghost.

5. Who got out of the boat to walk on the water with Jesus? Peter.

6. What did the disciples do when Jesus and Peter walked on the water? They worshipped Jesus and proclaimed Him to be the Son of God.

7. What do we learn about God from these verses? God has control over all of Creation, and nothing that happens to us is out of His control.

Memory Verse: Matthew 8:27

Early Elementary and Elementary

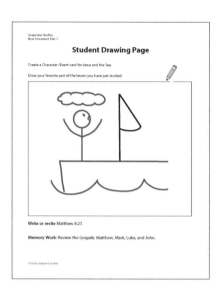

Information for the Jesus and the Sea card:

- On two separate occasions, Jesus interacted with the sea.
- Jesus showed that He had power over the wind and sea by commanding them to be at peace, and they were.
- Jesus demonstrated His power over the sea by walking on water and having Peter do the same.
- As a result of Jesus showing His power over the sea, the Disciples marveled and worshipped Him.

Memory Verse: Matthew 8:27

Memory Work: Review the Gospels: Matthew, Mark, Luke, and John.

Middle School

Jesus Fed the Multitudes

Topical Bible

How was *bread* prepared in biblical times?

Nave's, page 65

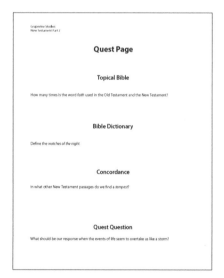

Bible Dictionary

Name some biblical *foods*.

Zondervan's, page 178-179

Concordance

Where in the Bible is *bread* first mentioned?

Genesis 14:18 (Cruden's, page 43)

Quest Question

Does Jesus meet the physical needs of men today? Give an example, preferably from your own life experience.

Yes; examples will vary.

Timeline Review

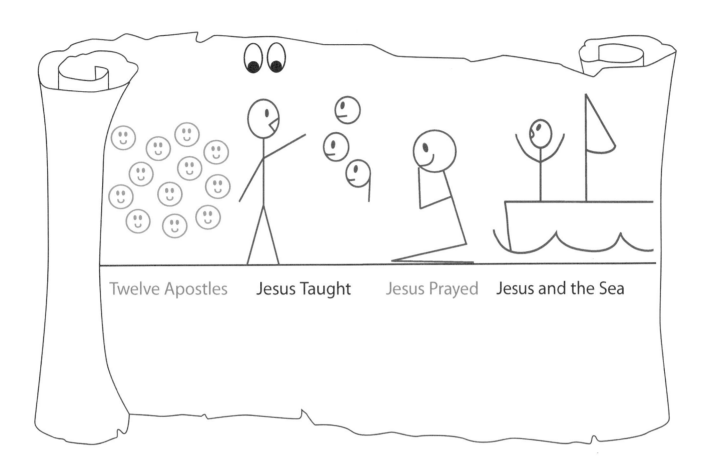

Twelve Apostles   Jesus Taught   Jesus Prayed   Jesus and the Sea

Memory Verse Review

Matthew 8:27

Mark 1:35

Matthew 22:37-39

Memory Work: Review the Gospels: Matthew, Mark, Luke, and John.

Jesus Fed the Multitudes

Memory Verse: Luke 9:16

Jesus and the Crowd

Read aloud: Luke 9:10-11

Discuss Jesus and the Crowd: Jesus and His disciples departed to a private place near Bethsaida, but when news spread of their whereabouts, a crowd gathered to hear Him. Jesus taught the people about the kingdom of God and healed many.

Draw and have students draw: Jesus talking to the crowd.

Fives Loaves and Two Fish

Read aloud: Luke 9:12-13

Discuss Fives Loaves and Two Fish: As evening approached, the twelve disciples spoke to Jesus about sending the people away for the night. Jesus desired to feed the people before sending them away, but the only food available was two fish and five loaves.

Draw and have students draw: Jesus with five loaves and two fish.

Look up the following words in a Bible Dictionary:

kingdom of God

Jesus Fed 5,000

Bethsaida

Read aloud: Luke 9:14-16

Discuss Jesus Fed 5,000: Jesus took the loaves and fish, blessed them, and gave them to the disciples to distribute among the 5,000 men (plus women and children).

Draw and have students draw: People eating the bread. Older students can note the location, Bethsaida.

Leftovers

Twelve Baskets of Leftovers

Read aloud: Luke 9:17

Discuss Twelve Baskets of Leftovers: When the people had eaten their fill, the disciples picked up twelve baskets full of leftovers.

Draw and have students draw: Two disciples with twelve baskets of leftovers.

Completed Student Page

Teacher Notes:

Jesus and the Crowd

Read aloud: Mark 8:1-4

Discuss Jesus and the Crowd: Word of Jesus had spread throughout the area. A crowd had been gathered for three days listening to Him. When Jesus looked upon them, He had compassion on them and desired to feed them. Being in the wilderness, the disciples asked how they could feed the crowd.

Draw and have students draw: Jesus teaching the crowd.

Seven Loaves

Read aloud: Mark 8:5

Discuss Seven Loaves: Jesus asked His disciples what food they had, and they told Him they had seven loaves of bread and a few small fish.

Draw and have students draw: Jesus with seven loaves and a few small fish.

Teacher Notes

Completed Student Page

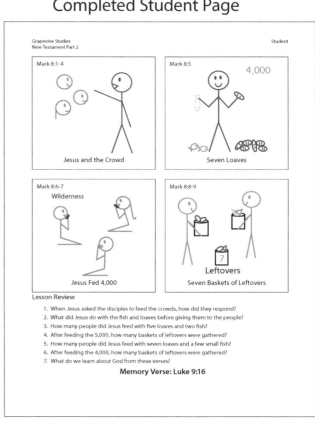

Jesus Fed 4,000

Wilderness

Read aloud: Mark 8:6-7

Discuss Jesus Fed 4,000: Jesus took the loaves and fish, and after giving thanks, He gave them to His Disciples to distribute to the crowd.

Draw and have students draw: People eating the bread. Older students can note the location, the wilderness.

Leftovers

Seven Baskets of Leftovers

Read aloud: Mark 8:8-9

Discuss Seven Baskets of Leftovers: When the people had eaten their fill, the disciples picked up seven large baskets full of leftovers. After the crowd had eaten, Jesus sent them home.

Draw and have students draw: Two disciples with seven baskets of leftovers.

Lesson Review

1. When Jesus asked the disciples to feed the crowds, how did they respond? By telling Jesus that they didn't have enough food to feed the crowds.

2. What did Jesus do with the fish and loaves before giving them to the people? He gave thanks and blessed the loaves and fish.

3. How many people did Jesus feed with five loaves and two fish? 5,000 men.

4. After feeding the 5,000, how many baskets of leftovers were gathered? 12.

5. How many people did Jesus feed with seven loaves and a few small fish? 4,000 men.

6. After feeding the 4,000, how many baskets of leftovers were gathered? 7.

7. What do we learn about God from these verses? God is not only concerned about our spiritual well-being but also about our physical needs. God is able to provide for our physical needs.

Memory Verse: Luke 9:16

Early Elementary and Elementary

Information for Jesus Fed the Multitudes card:

- On two separate occasions, Jesus fed multitudes of people.

- Jesus fed 5,000 men with five loaves of bread and two fish. Twelve baskets of leftovers were picked up.

- Jesus fed 4,000 men with seven loaves and a few small fish. Seven baskets of leftovers were picked up.

- Jesus cared not only for the spiritual needs of people but also their physical needs.

Memory Verse: Luke 9:16

Memory Work: Review the Book of Church History: Acts.

Middle School

Jesus Healed the Sick

Topical Bible

Name five *diseases* mentioned in the Bible that we still see in our day.

Nave's, page 122-123

Bible Dictionary

What was the *hem* of Jesus' garment?

Zondervan's, page 224

Concordance

In what New Testament books would we learn what the law has to say regarding *leprosy*?

Leviticus (Cruden's, page 287)

Quest Question

Does Jesus heal all those who ask Him to heal them? Defend your answers with at least one verse.

Timeline Review

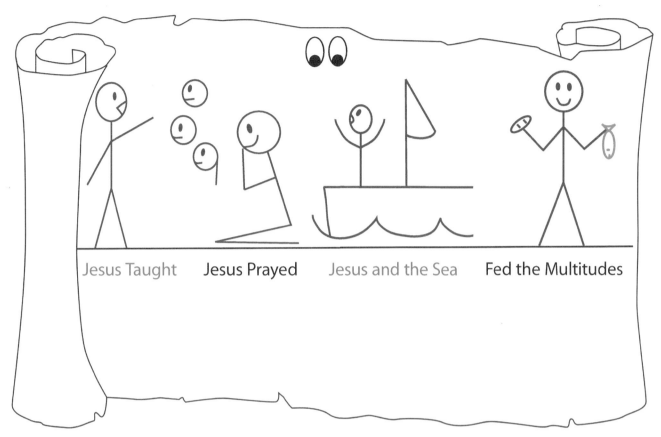

Jesus Taught   Jesus Prayed   Jesus and the Sea   Fed the Multitudes

Memory Verse Review

Luke 9:16

Matthew 8:27

Mark 1:35

Matthew 22:37-39

Memory Work: Review the Book of Church History: Acts.

Jesus Healed the Sick

Memory Verse: Matthew 4:23

Jesus in Galilee

Read aloud: Matthew 4:23-25

Discuss Jesus in Galilee: While Jesus was proclaiming the gospel in Galilee, people from the surrounding area came to hear Him and to be healed of various sicknesses and diseases.

Map: Label the region of Galilee.

Draw and have students draw: Jesus healing a woman and then the woman jumping for joy after being healed.

The Sick in Gennesaret

Read aloud: Mark 6:53-56

Discuss The Sick in Gennesaret: When the people of the area of Gennesaret heard that Jesus had come to their area, they ran and brought the sick to Him and He healed them.

Map: Label the city of Gennesaret.

Draw and have students draw: Jesus healing a man with spots and a woman waiting to be healed.

Look up the following words in a Bible Dictionary:

disease

hem of His garment

paralytic

impediment

leper

mute

The Paralytic and the Roof

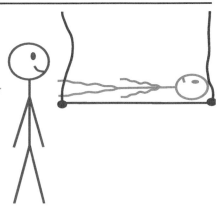

Read aloud: Mark 2:1-5

Discuss The Paralytic and the Roof: While Jesus was teaching, four men carried their friend, a paralytic, to Jesus. Because of the crowd, the men could not get him to Jesus, so they made a hole in the roof and lowered the paralytic man through the roof to Jesus.

Map: Label the City of Capernaum.

Draw and have students draw: The paralytic and Jesus.

The Paralytic Healed

Read aloud: Mark 2:6-12

Discuss The Paralytic Healed: Jesus forgave the paralytic of his sins and then healed him. Jesus wanted the scribes to understand that He had authority to heal and to forgive sins. The people were amazed. The paralytic arose from his mat and glorified God.

Draw and have students draw: Jesus and the healed paralytic with his mat.

Completed Student Page

Teacher Notes

The Deaf and Mute

Read aloud: Mark 7:31-35

Discuss The Deaf and Mute: A deaf and mute man was brought to Jesus, and Jesus took him aside and healed him.

Map: Label the cities of Tyre and Sidon; the region of the Decapolis.

Draw and have students draw: Jesus and a deaf and mute man, then the man speaking and hearing after being healed.

The Blind Beggar

Read aloud: Mark 10:46-52

Discuss The Blind Beggar: As Jesus and his disciples traveled out of Jericho, they passed Bartimaeus, a blind beggar. As Jesus neared, Bartimaeus called out to Jesus from among the crowd. Jesus called Bartimaeus to Himself and then healed him of his blindness.

Map: Label the city of Jericho.

Draw and have students draw: Bartimaeus being healed.

Teacher Notes

Completed Student Page

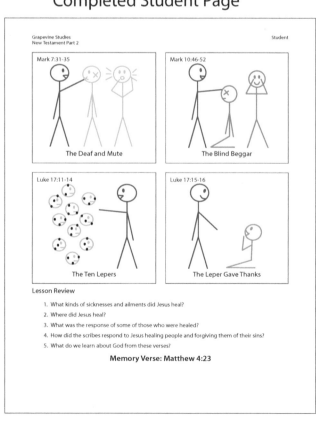

The Ten Lepers

Read aloud: Luke 17:11-14

Discuss The Ten Lepers: As Jesus traveled to Jerusalem, He passed through a village which had ten lepers living nearby. The lepers cried out to Jesus, and Jesus told them to go and show themselves to the priest (Leviticus 13-14). As the lepers were on their way to see the priest, they were healed.

Map: Label the region of Samaria.

Draw and have students draw: The lepers and Jesus speaking.

The Leper Gave Thanks

Read aloud: Luke 17:15-16

Discuss The Leper Gave Thanks: Only one of the ten lepers, a Samaritan, returned to give thanks and worship Jesus.

Draw and have students draw: One leper bowing down at Jesus' feet.

Lesson Review

1. What kinds of sicknesses and ailments did Jesus heal? The deaf, mute, blind, lepers and paralytics.

2. Where did Jesus heal? In various cities, on the roadways, and in homes.

3. What was the response of some of those who were healed? They thanked Jesus and worshipped and praised God.

4. How did the scribes respond to Jesus healing people and forgiving them of their sins? They questioned Jesus' authority to forgive sins.

5. What do we learn about God from these verses? God can heal those who are sick with any sickness, disease, or ailment.

Memory Verse: Matthew 4:23

Early Elementary and Elementary

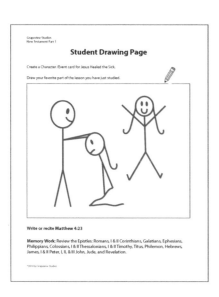

Information for the Jesus Heals the Sick card:

- Jesus healed many kinds of sicknesses and diseases. He healed those who were:
  1. Deaf
  2. Blind
  3. Mute
  4. Palsy
  5. Lepers
- Many of those who were healed worshipped and thanked Jesus for healing them.
- Jesus also forgave the sick of their sins.

Memory Verse: Matthew 4:23

Memory Work: Review the Epistles: Romans, I & II Corinthians, Galatians, Ephesians, Philippians, Colossians, I & II Thessalonians, I & II Timothy, Titus, Philemon, Hebrews, James, I & II Peter, I, II, & III John, Jude, and Revelation.

Middle School

Jesus Healed the Demon-Possessed

Topical Bible

Give a reference to the worship of *demons*.

Nave's, page 118

Bible Dictionary

Give some characteristics of *demons*

Zondervan's, page 131

Concordance

How many times are *unclean spirits* referred to in the Bible?

Nine (Cruden's, page 518)

Quest Question

Is demon possession real?

Yes!

Timeline Review

Jesus Prayed   Jesus and the Sea   Fed the Multitudes   Healed the Sick

Memory Verse Review

Matthew 4:23

Luke 9:16

Matthew 8:27

Mark 1:35

Memory Work: Review the Epistles: Romans, I & II Corinthians, Galatians, Ephesians, Philippians, Colossians, I & II Thessalonians, I & II Timothy, Titus, Philemon, Hebrews, James, I & II Peter, I, II, & III John, Jude, and Revelation.

Jesus Healed the Demon-Possessed

Memory Verse: Luke 9:1

Demon

Read aloud: None

Discuss Demon: An evil spirit who seeks the worship of men and tries to draw men away from the worship of the one true God.

Draw and have students draw: A man bowing down to an idol with a demon behind it.

Unclean Spirit

Read aloud: None

Discuss Unclean Spirit: An evil spirit who entices men to do evil and opposes God.

Draw and have students draw: A demon behind a man enticing him towards "evil."

Look up the following words in a Bible Dictionary:

demon

unclean spirit

demon possessed

synagogue

right mind

power

exorcise

Jesus Healed the Sick and Demon-Possessed

Read aloud: Mark 1:32-34; Luke 4:40-41

Discuss Jesus Healed the Sick and Demon-Possessed: There are many passages that speak of Jesus casting out demons. Jesus often healed people who came to Him whether they had a sickness/disease or were demon-possessed. Jesus demonstrated His authority over demons throughout His earthly ministry.

Draw and have students draw: Jesus casting a demon out of a man.

Completed Student Page

Teacher Notes:

Man in the Synagogue

Read aloud: Mark 1:21-27

Discuss Man in the Synagogue: When Jesus came to Capernaum, He taught in the synagogue. A man at the synagogue had an unclean spirit. Jesus rebuked the evil spirit and then cast it out of the man.

Draw and have students draw: The demon talking through a man to Jesus.

Man in the Tombs

Read aloud: Mark 5:1-20

Discuss Man in the Tombs: Upon arriving in the country of the Gadarenes, Jesus was confronted by a man who was demon-possessed. After Jesus cast out the demon, the people were amazed to find the man dressed and in his right mind. Jesus instructed him to tell others what the Lord had done for him.

Draw and have students draw: Jesus casting a demon out of a man with broken chains on.

Teacher Notes

Completed Student Page

Disciples and Demons

Read aloud: Luke 9:1-2; 10:17-20

Discuss Disciples and Demons: When Jesus sent out the seventy disciples, He commanded them to preach the kingdom of God and to heal the sick and demon-possessed. When they returned, they reported to Jesus all they had done. Jesus warned them not to focus on the fact that they had authority over demons but rather that their names were recorded in heaven.

Draw and have students draw: A demon fleeing and a book.

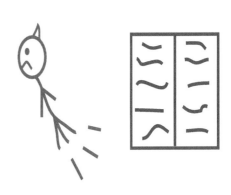

Warning

Read aloud: Acts 19:11-20

Discuss Warning: Paul cast out demons in the name of Jesus. Seven sons of a Jewish high priest tried to exorcise a demon by imitating Paul's method of using Jesus' name. The demon told these men that it knew Jesus and Paul but it did not know them. The demon then attacked the men and publicly humiliated them. This caused fear in the city of Ephesus, where God's Word was proclaimed and obeyed.

Draw and have students draw: A demon and men running away.

Lesson Review:

1. What is a demon? A spirit who seeks men who will worship it instead of the one true God.

2. What is an unclean spirit? An evil spirit who entices men to do evil and is opposed to God.

3. What did Jesus do when He encountered people who were possessed with an evil spirit? He rebuked and then cast out the demon/evil spirit.

4. What did the demons/unclean spirits say about Jesus? They called Him the Holy One of God and the Son of the Most High God.

5. To whom did Jesus give authority to cast out demons? His apostles and disciples.

6. What happened when men who were not believers tried to cast out demons? They were attacked and publicly humiliated.

7. What do we learn about God from these verses? God gives believers power to cast out demons in the name of Jesus.

Memory Verse: Luke 9:1

Early Elementary and Elementary

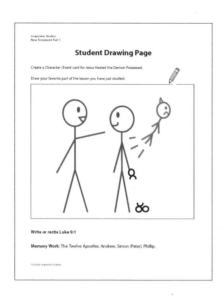

Information for Jesus Healed -Demon-Possessed:

- A demon is a spirit who seeks men who will worship it instead of the one true God.

- An unclean spirit is an evil spirit that entices men to do evil and is opposed to God.

- Jesus rebuked and cast demons out of many people.

- Jesus gave His disciples authority over demons.

Memory Verse: Luke 9:1

Memory Work: The Twelve Apostles: Andrew, Simon (Peter), Phillip.

Middle School

Jesus Raised the Dead

Topical Bible

How many different instances are there in the Bible of the *dead* being raised?

Nave's, page 113-114

Bible Dictionary

What did you learn about *widows*?

Zondervan's, page 605

Concordance

Give the Bible reference for "Mary whose brother *Lazarus*."

John 11:2 (Cruden's, page 285)

Quest Question

When Jesus and the early Church raised people from the dead, what did it prove?

Answers will vary.

Timeline Review

Jesus and the Sea   Fed the Multitudes   Healed-Sick   Healed - Demon Possessed

Memory Verse Review

Luke 9:1

Matthew 4:23

Luke 9:16

Matthew 8:27

Memory Work: The Twelve Apostles: Andrew, Simon (Peter), Phillip.

Jesus Raised the Dead

Memory Verse: Luke 7:15

Jesus and the Widow

Read aloud: Luke 7:11-13

Discuss Jesus and the Widow: As Jesus entered the town of Nain, he saw a dead man being taken out to be buried. He was the only son of his widowed mother. Jesus had compassion on the widow and told her not to weep.

Draw and have students draw: A widow and her dead son.

Jesus Raised the Dead Man

Read aloud: Luke 7:14-17

Discuss Jesus Raised the Dead Man: Jesus went to the coffin and told the young man to arise. The dead man arose and was returned to his mother. As news spread about this event, the people glorified God.

Draw and have students draw: The widow with her son and Jesus.

Look up the following words in a Bible Dictionary:

widow

compassion

prophet

afraid

groaning

glory of God

grave clothes

Jesus and Jairus

Read aloud: Luke 8:40-42, 49

Discuss Jesus and Jairus: Jairus came to Jesus to ask Him to come to his home because his only daughter was very sick. Before Jesus could respond, a man came to Jairus and told him that his daughter had died.

Draw and have students draw: Jesus and Jairus.

Jesus Raised the Girl

Read aloud: Luke 8:50-56

Discuss Jesus Raised the Girl: Jesus heard what the man said to Jairus, and he told Jairus not to fear. Jesus, along with Peter, James, and John, went with Jairus to his home. Jesus then raised the little girl from the dead.

Draw and have students draw: Jesus raising the girl from the dead.

Completed Student Page

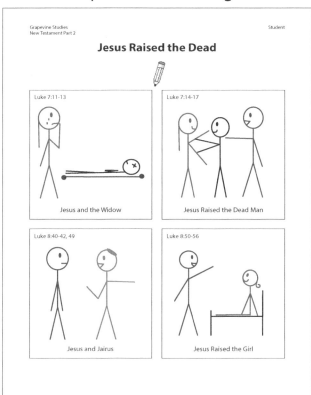

Teacher Notes:

Word Was Sent to Jesus

Read aloud: John 11:1-16

Discuss Word Was Sent to Jesus: Jesus loved Lazarus and his two sisters, Mary and Martha. When Lazarus became sick, his sisters sent word to Jesus. Lazarus died from the sickness before Jesus arrived.

Draw and have students draw: A woman sending a man away.

Lazarus Died

Read aloud: John 11:17-23

Discuss Lazarus Died: By the time Jesus arrived, Lazarus had been in a tomb four days. Jesus talked with Martha, assuring her that Lazarus would indeed be resurrected.

Draw and have students draw: Jesus talking to Martha.

Teacher Notes

Completed Student Page

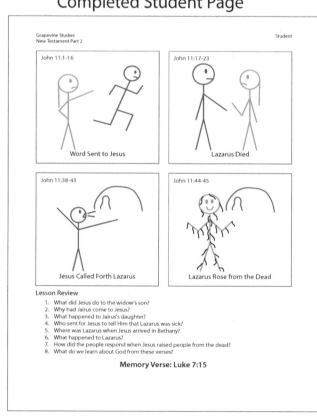

Grapevine Studies
New Testament Part 2

Student

John 11:1-16

Word Sent to Jesus

John 11:17-23

Lazarus Died

John 11:38-43

Jesus Called Forth Lazarus

John 11:44-45

Lazarus Rose from the Dead

Lesson Review
1. What did Jesus do to the widow's son?
2. Why had Jairus come to Jesus?
3. What happened to Jairus's daughter?
4. Who sent for Jesus to tell Him that Lazarus was sick?
5. Where was Lazarus when Jesus arrived in Bethany?
6. What happened to Lazarus?
7. How did the people respond when Jesus raised people from the dead?
8. What do we learn about God from these verses?

Memory Verse: Luke 7:15

Jesus Called Lazarus Forth

Read aloud: John 11:38-43

Discuss Jesus Called Lazarus Forth: When Jesus arrived at the tomb, He requested that the stone be removed from across the front. Jesus gave thanks and then called Lazarus forth.

Draw and have students draw: Jesus calling forth Lazarus at the tomb.

Lazarus Rose from the Dead

Read aloud: John 11:44-45

Discuss Lazarus Rose from the Dead: When Jesus called Lazarus out of the tomb, Lazarus came out of the tomb still wrapped in burial clothes. The Jews who were present with Mary saw that Jesus could raise the dead, and they believed.

Draw and have students draw: Lazarus coming out of the tomb covered in his burial clothes.

Lesson Review:

1. What did Jesus do to the widow's son? He raised him from the dead.

2. Why had Jairus come to Jesus? To request healing for his daughter.

3. What happened to Jairus's daughter? She died, and Jesus raised her from the dead.

4. Who sent for Jesus to tell Him that Lazarus was sick? His sisters, Mary and Martha.

5. Where was Lazarus when Jesus arrived in Bethany? In the tomb.

6. What happened to Lazarus? Jesus raised him from the dead.

7. How did the people respond when Jesus raised people from the dead? They glorified God, they questioned who Jesus was, and some believed.

8. What do we learn about God from these verses? God can raise people from the dead.

Memory Verse: Luke 7:15

Early Elementary and Elementary

Student Drawing Page

Information for Jesus Raised the Dead card:

- Scripture records that Jesus raised people from the dead including: the widow's son and Jairus' daughter.

- Jesus raised Lazarus from the dead after he had been in the tomb four days.

- After Lazarus was raised from the dead, many Jews believed.

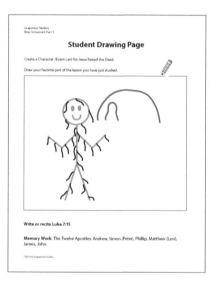

Memory Verse: Luke 7:15

Memory Work: The Twelve Apostles: Andrew, Simon (Peter), Phillip, Matthew (Levi), James, John.

New Testament Overview
~
Section Review

Section Review

1. What was Jesus doing when the tempest arose? He was sleeping.

2. How did Jesus calm the sea? By speaking to the wind and the waves, and it was so.

3. How did the disciples respond when Jesus calmed the sea? They marveled.

4. How did the disciples respond when they saw Jesus walking on the water? They thought He was a ghost.

5. Who got out of the boat to walk on the water with Jesus? Peter.

6. What did the disciples do when Jesus and Peter walked on the water? They worshipped Jesus and proclaimed Him to be the Son of God.

7. Recite Matthew 8:27.

8. When Jesus asked the disciple to feed the crowds, how did they respond? By telling Jesus that they didn't have enough food to feed the crowds.

9. What did Jesus do with the fish and loaves? He gave thanks and blessed the loaves and fish.

10. How many people did Jesus feed with five loaves and two fish? 5,000 men.

11. After feeding the 5,000, how many baskets of leftovers were gathered? 12.

12. How many people did Jesus feed with seven loaves and a few small fish? 4,000 men.

13. After feeding the 4,000, how many baskets of leftovers were gathered? 7.

14. Recite Luke 9:16.

15. What kinds of sicknesses and ailments did Jesus heal? The deaf, mute, blind, lepers, and those with palsy.

16. Where did Jesus heal? In various cities, on the roadways, and in homes.

17. What was the response of some of those who were healed? They thanked Jesus and worshipped and praised God.

18. How did the scribes respond to Jesus healing people and forgiving them of their sins? They questioned Jesus' authority to forgive sins.

19.   Recite Matthew 4:23.

20.   What is a demon? A spirit who seeks men who will worship it instead of the one true God.

21.   What is an unclean spirit? Evil spirit who entices men to do evil and is opposed to God.

22.   What did Jesus do when He encountered people who were possessed with an evil spirit? He rebuked and then cast out the demon/evil spirit.

23.   What did the demons/unclean spirits say about Jesus? They called Him the Holy One of God and the Son of the Most High God.

24.   To whom did Jesus give authority to cast out demons? His apostles and disciples.

25.   What happened to the men who were not believers when they tried to cast out demons? They were attacked and publicly humiliated.

26.   Recite Luke 9:1.

27.   What did Jesus do to the widow's son? He raised him from the dead.

28.   Why had Jairus come to Jesus? To request healing for his daughter.

29.   What happened to Jairus's daughter? She died, and Jesus came and raised her from the dead.

30.   Who sent for Jesus to tell Him that Lazarus was sick? His sisters, Mary and Martha.

31.   Where was Lazarus when Jesus arrived in Bethany? In the tomb.

32.   What happened to Lazarus? Jesus raised him from the dead.

33.   How did the people respond when Jesus raised people from the dead? They glorified God, they questioned who Jesus was, and some believed in Jesus.

34.   Recite Luke 7:15.

Jesus Healed the Sick/Lame

Jesus Fed the People

Jesus and the Seas

Matthew, Mark, Luke, and John

Jesus Raised the Dead

Jesus Healed the Demon-Possessed

Matthew, Mark, Luke, and John

Lesson Goals and Key Points

JESUS ENTERED JERUSALEM

The goal of this lesson is to examine the events surrounding the last few days of Jesus' earthly life, beginning with His triumphal entry into Jerusalem.

Key Points:
- After Jesus raised Lazarus from the dead, the chief priests began plotting how to kill both Jesus and Lazarus, because the people believed in Jesus.
- Jesus entered Jerusalem riding on a colt while the people greeted Him by spreading their cloaks on the road, singing, and waving leafy branches before Him.
- After entering Jerusalem, Jesus went to the temple area and chased out the money changers.
- Jesus also taught and healed people while in Jerusalem in the days preceding the Feast of Passover.

Memory Verse: Matthew 21:9

THE LAST SUPPER

The goal of this lesson is to understand the events that occurred as Jesus and the disciples celebrated the Passover meal.

Key Points:
- Jesus told His disciples about His coming death.
- Jesus celebrated the Passover meal with His disciples.
- Judas betrayed Jesus to the chief priest.
- Jesus warned His disciples that they would all stumble.

Memory Verse: John 13:1

THE GARDEN OF GETHSEMANE

The goal of this lesson is to see what took place in the Garden of Gethsemane.

Key Points:
- After the Passover meal, Jesus and the eleven apostles went to the Garden to pray.
- Jesus prayed that not His will but the Father's will would be done.
- While Jesus prayed the apostles slept.
- Judas betrayed Jesus in the garden.
- Jesus healed the servant's ear that was cut off by Peter.
- When Jesus was arrested the apostles fled.

Memory Verse: Mark 14:36

THE TRIALS OF JESUS

The goal of this lesson is to trace the three religious trials that Jesus went through on the last night of His life.

Key Points:
- Jesus was taken to Annas for His first trial.
- Jesus was taken to Caiaphas for His second trial.
- Peter denied Jesus three times.
- Jesus was beaten and mocked.
- Jesus was taken before Caiaphas and the Council, where He was condemned on the charge of blasphemy.

Memory Verse: Matthew 26:57

JESUS WAS CONDEMNED TO DEATH

The goal of this lesson is to trace the three civil trials that Jesus went through on the last night of His life.

Key Points:
- After Jesus was condemned by the Council, He was taken to Pilate to be questioned.
- Pilate sent Jesus to Herod Antipas after he found no fault in Him.
- Herod returned Jesus to Pilate.
- Pilate released Barabbas at the request of the crowd.
- Pilate washed his hands before the crowd to indicate that he did not believe that Jesus had done anything worthy of death.
- Jesus was then scourged and beaten.

Memory Verse: Matthew 27:26

NOTES

Middle School

Jesus Entered Jerusalem

Topical Bible

What does *hosanna* mean?

Nave's, page 210

Bible Dictionary

What do we learn about *money changers*?

Zondervan's, page 374

Concordance

How many times are *money changers* referred to in Scripture?

3 (Cruden's, page 323)

Quest Question

What are some of the reasons people go to Church? Why should we go to Church?

Answers will vary.

Timeline Review

Fed the Multitudes   Healed-Sick   Healed - Demon Possessed   Raised the Dead

Memory Verse Review

Luke 9:1

Matthew 4:23

Luke 9:16

Matthew 8:27

Memory Work: The Twelve Apostles: Andrew, Simon (Peter), Phillip, Matthew (Levi), James, John.

Jesus Entered Jerusalem

Memory Verse: Matthew 21:9

The Chief Priests Plotted

Read aloud: John 12:9-11

Discuss The Chief Priests Plotted: Word spread that Jesus had raised Lazarus from the dead, and many Jews came to see Jesus and Lazarus. Lazarus's resurrection caused many of the Jews to believe. This led the chief priests to plot to kill both Jesus and Lazarus.

Map: Review the location of the city of Jerusalem.

Draw and have students draw: Two chief priests with frowning faces.

Jesus Entered Jerusalem

Read aloud: Matthew 21:1-11

Discuss Jesus Entered Jerusalem: When Jesus reached the outlying area of Jerusalem, He told two of His disciples to go and bring him back a colt. Jesus rode the colt into Jerusalem, where the people laid leafy branches and their clothes on the road. The people also began to sing and praise Jesus with a song. Jesus was entering Jerusalem to celebrate the Feast of Passover.

Draw and have students draw: Two people waving palm branches and a coat on the ground.

Look up the following words in a Bible Dictionary:

chief priest

hosanna

Pharisee

money changers

scribes

wept

The Pharisees Responded

Read aloud: Luke 19:37-40

Discuss The Pharisees Responded: When the Pharisees heard the people singing worship songs to Jesus, they demanded that He tell the people to stop. Jesus responded by telling them that if the people were silent, the stones would cry out.

Draw and have students draw: Jesus, the people singing, and an angry Pharisee.

Jesus Wept over Jerusalem

Read aloud: Luke 19:41-44

Discuss Jesus Wept over Jerusalem: As Jesus came into Jerusalem, He wept over the city. Throughout Jewish history, the people had been waiting and praying for the coming of the Messiah. When He came, though, most did not recognize Him

Draw and have students draw: Jesus weeping over Jerusalem.

Completed Student Page

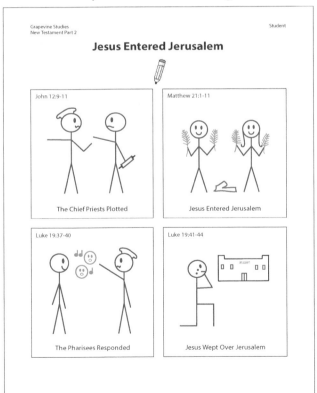

Teacher Notes:

Jesus Cleansed the Temple

Read aloud: Matthew 21:12-13

Discuss Jesus Cleansed the Temple: When Jesus entered the temple, He saw people buying and selling instead of praying. Jesus drove out the merchants and money changers and reminded the people that the temple was to be a place of prayer.

Draw and have students draw: Jesus turning over a table.

Jesus Healed and Children Sang

Read aloud: Matthew 21:14-16

Discuss Jesus Healed and Children Sang: After cleansing the temple, Jesus healed the blind and the lame there. The chief priests and scribes heard the children praising Jesus and became indignant.

Draw and have students draw: Jesus healing a man and children singing.

Teacher Notes

Completed Student Page

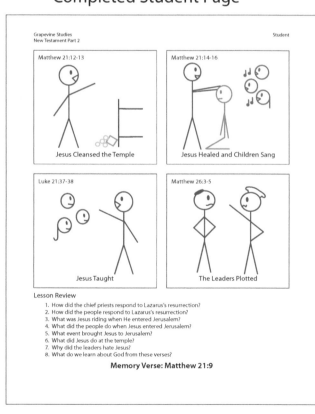

Jesus Taught

Read aloud: Luke 21:37-38

Discuss Jesus Taught: The week preceding the Passover feast, Jesus was in the temple teaching the people and preaching the Gospel (Luke 20:1).

Draw and have students draw: Jesus teaching a crowd.

The Leaders Plotted

Read aloud: Matthew 26:3-5

Discuss The Leaders Plotted: Although the chief priests, scribes, and leaders of the people wanted to kill Jesus, they were afraid to do so because of the people.

Draw and have students draw: A priest and a scribe plotting.

Lesson Review:

1. How did the chief priests respond to Lazarus's resurrection? They wanted to kill both Jesus and Lazarus.

2. How did the people respond to Lazarus's resurrection? Many of the people believed in Jesus.

3. What was Jesus riding when He entered Jerusalem? A colt that had not been ridden before.

4. What did the people do when Jesus entered Jerusalem? They threw leafy branches and coats on the road and sang to Him.

5. What event brought Jesus to Jerusalem? The Feast of Passover.

6. What did Jesus do at the temple? He drove out the money changers and merchants and then He taught and healed.

7. Why did the leaders hate Jesus? Because the people believed in Him and followed Him.

8. What do we learn about God from these verses? Jesus is God, and He is worthy of both our praise and our prayers.

Memory Verse: Matthew 21:9

Early Elementary and Elementary

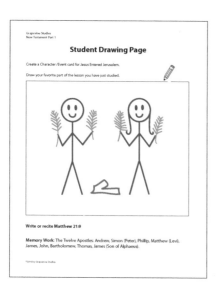

Information for Jesus Entered Jerusalem card:

- After Jesus raised Lazarus from the dead the chief priest began plotting how to kill both Jesus and Lazarus.

- When Jesus entered Jerusalem riding on a colt, the people sang and laid their cloaks and leafy branches on the road before Him.

- While in Jerusalem, Jesus went to the Temple where He removed the money changers and reminded the people that the Temple was a place of prayer.

- During the days before the Feast of Passover, Jesus healed and taught.

Memory Verse: Matthew 21:9

Memory Work: The Twelve Apostles: Andrew, Simon (Peter), Phillip, Matthew (Levi), James, John, Bartholomew, Thomas, James (Son of Alphaeus).

Middle School

The Last Supper

Topical Bible Exercise

What is *unleavened bread*?

Nave's, page 499

Bible Dictionary Exercise

What were the *feasts* of Israel for?

Zondervan's, page 173

Concordance Exercise

What verse refers to Satan entering *Judas*?

Luke 22:3 (Cruden's, page 265)

Quest Question

Why do you think that some people seem to follow the Lord for a time and then at some point turn and appear to leave the Lord?

Answers will vary. Possibly they were never true believers, or like Judas, they are enticed by the things of the world. Matthew 13:1-9.

Timeline Review

Healed-Sick   Healed- Demon Possessed   Raised the Dead   Entered Jerusalem

Memory Verse Review

Matthew 21:9

Luke 9:1

Matthew 4:23

Luke 9:16

Memory Work: The Twelve Apostles: Andrew, Simon (Peter), Phillip, Matthew (Levi), James, John, Bartholomew, Thomas, James (Son of Alphaeus).

The Last Supper

Memory Verse: John 13:1

Jesus Warned of His Death

Read aloud: Matthew 26:1-5

Discuss Jesus Warned of His Death: During the week of Passover, Jesus warned His disciples that soon He was going to be killed. The chief priests, scribes, and elders gathered with the high priest to plot how to kill Jesus by devious means.

Draw and have students draw: Jesus, thinking of the cross and talking to a disciples.

Judas and the Chief Priest

Read aloud: Luke 22:1-6

Discuss Judas and the Chief Priest: As Passover drew near, Satan entered the apostle named Judas (Iscariot) in order to get Judas to betray Jesus. Judas met with the chief priests to arrange for the betrayal. Judas was paid for his part in the scheme.

Draw and have students draw: A chief priest handing Judas money.

Look up the following words in a Bible Dictionary:

Passover

New Covenant

betray

deny

stumble

Passover Preparations

Read aloud: Matthew 26:17-19

Discuss Passover Preparations: On the first day of the Feast of Passover, Jesus gave directions to His Disciples regarding the upcoming Passover meal.

Draw and have students draw: The disciples carrying supplies for the Passover meal.

Judas Was Identified as the Betrayer

Read aloud: Matthew 26:20-25

Discuss Judas Was Identified as the Betrayer: At the Last Supper, Jesus revealed Judas as the betrayer.

Map: Label the Upper Room.

Draw and have students draw: Jesus dipping His hand into a bowl with Judas.

Completed Student Page

Teacher Notes:

The Last Supper

Read aloud: Matthew 26:26-29

Discuss The Last Supper: Toward the end of the Last Supper, Jesus blessed the bread and the cup, instituting the New Covenant. After the meal, Jesus and His apostles sang a hymn and went to the Mount of Olives.

Draw and have students draw: Jesus at the Last Supper holding a cup and the bread.

Teacher Notes

Completed Student Page

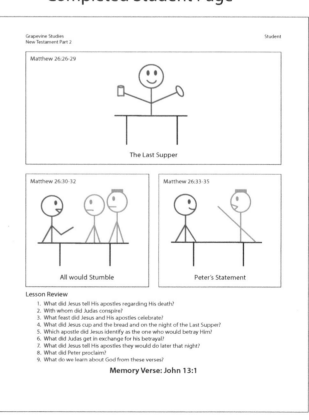

All Would Stumble

Read aloud: Matthew 26:30-32

Discuss All Would Stumble: Jesus warned the apostles and then quoted a prophecy which stated that all His "flock" would be scattered and would stumble because of the events which were about to take place.

Draw and have students draw: Jesus talking with the disciples.

Peter's Statement

Read aloud: Matthew 26:33-35

Discuss Peter's Statement: Peter denied that he would stumble, but Jesus told him that before the night was finished Peter would deny Him three times.

Draw and have students draw: Peter declaring he would not deny Jesus.

Lesson Review:

1. What did Jesus tell His apostles regarding His death? He would be killed.

2. With whom did Judas conspire? The chief priest, the captain, the scribes, and the Pharisees.

3. What feast did Jesus and His apostles celebrate? The Feast of Passover.

4. What did Jesus institute with the cup and the bread on the night of the Last Supper? The New Covenant.

5. Which apostle did Jesus identify as the one who would betray Him? Judas.

6. What did Judas get in exchange for his betrayal? Money.

7. What did Jesus tell His apostles they would do later that night? They would stumble and scatter.

8. What did Peter proclaim? He would not deny the Lord.

9. What do we learn about God from these verses? Jesus was committed to God's plan of bringing forth the New Covenant.

Memory Verse: John 13:1

Early Elementary and Elementary

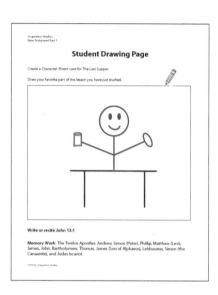

Information for the The Last Supper card:

- Jesus warned His Apostles that He would be killed.

- The chief priest plotted with Judas Iscariot for Jesus' arrest.

- Jesus ate the Passover Meal with all of His Apostles.

- Jesus warned His Apostles that they would all stumble.

Memory Verse: John 13:1

Memory Work: The Twelve Apostles: Andrew, Simon (Peter), Phillip, Matthew (Levi), James, John, Bartholomew, Thomas, James (Son of Alphaeus), Lebbaeus, Simon (the Canaanite), and Judas Iscariot.

Middle School

The Garden of Gethsemane

Topical Bible Exercise

Where is the Garden of *Gethsemane* located?

Nave's, page 172

Bible Dictionary Exercise

What are the five times that *angels* played a role in Jesus' earthly life?

Zondervan's, page 39

Concordance Exercise

In what two books of the Bible is *Gethsemane* mentioned?

Matthew and Mark (Cruden's, page 195)

Quest Question

What should we do when we face trials in life?

We should imitate Jesus and seek to do the Father's will and not our own.

Timeline Review

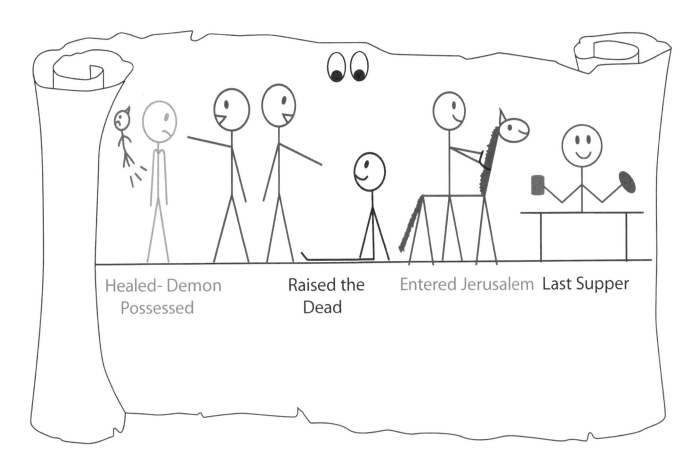

Healed- Demon
Possessed

Raised the
Dead

Entered Jerusalem Last Supper

Memory Verse Review

John 13:1

Matthew 21:9

Luke 9:1

Matthew 4:23

Memory Work: The Twelve Apostles: Andrew, Simon (Peter), Phillip, Matthew (Levi), James, John, Bartholomew, Thomas, James (Son of Alphaeus), Lebbaueus, Simon (the Canaanite), and Judas Iscariot.

The Garden of Gethsemane

Memory Verse: Mark 14:36

Jesus Went to Gethsemane

Read aloud: Mark 14:32-34; Luke 22:39-40

Discuss Jesus Went to Gethsemane: After the Passover meal, Jesus took His disciples and went to the Garden of Gethsemane, which was His custom. Upon arriving at the garden, Jesus took Peter, James, and John aside and asked them to watch and pray with Him.

Map: Label the Garden of Gethsemane.

Draw and have students draw: Jesus and two disciples.

Gethsemane

Not My Will But Yours

Read aloud: Mark 14:35-36; Luke 22:41-42

Discuss Not My Will But Yours: Jesus went a little farther into the garden and prayed not that His own will would be done but that the Father's will would be done.

Draw and have students draw: Jesus praying with His face to the ground. Label the garden of Gethsemane.

Look up the following words in a Bible Dictionary:

tempted

will

strengthened

I AM

Jesus Was Strengthened

Read aloud: Luke 22:43

Discuss Jesus Was Strengthened: While Jesus prayed, an angel appeared and strengthened Him.

Draw and have students draw: An angel with Jesus.

The Disciples Slept

Read aloud: Mark 14:37-42; Luke 22:44-46

Discuss The Disciples Slept: Jesus went a little farther into the garden and prayed not that His own will would be done but that the Father's will would be done.

Draw and have students draw: Jesus standing, one disciple sleeping, and the other disciple having just woken up.

Completed Student Page

Teacher Notes:

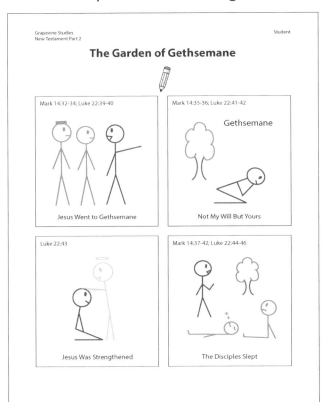

Judas Went to the Garden

Read aloud: John 18:1-9; Mark 14:43-46

Discuss Judas Went to the Garden: After leaving the Passover meal, Judas went to the chief priest. Judas took with him a great crowd (the chief priest, the elders, and the officers of the temple). He then went to the garden where He betrayed Jesus with a kiss.

Draw and have students draw: Judas pointing to Jesus.

Jesus Healed the Servant's Ear

Read aloud: Luke 22:49-51; John 18:10-11

Discuss Jesus Healed the Servant's Ear: Peter, in an attempt to defend Jesus, struck out with his sword and cut off the ear of the servant of the high priest. Jesus rebuked Peter and healed the servant's ear.

Draw and have students draw: Jesus healing the ear of a man.

Teacher Notes

Completed Student Page

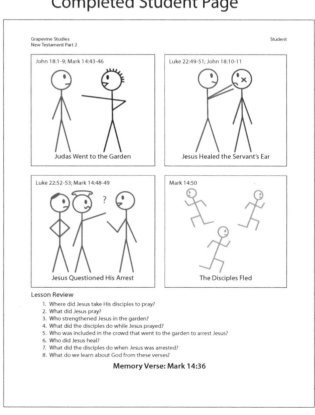

Jesus Questioned His Arrest

Read aloud: Luke 22:52-53; Mark 14:48-49

Discuss Jesus Questioned His Arrest: Jesus asked the crowd who they were looking for, and upon their response, He asked why they had waited to arrest Him when He had been regularly in the temple.

Draw and have students draw: Jesus questioning the chief priests.

The Disciples Fled

Read aloud: Mark 14:50

Discuss The Disciples Fled: When Jesus' disciples saw what was happening, they all fled.

Draw and have students draw: The disciples fleeing.

Lesson Review:

1. Where did Jesus take His disciples to pray? The Garden of Gethsemane.

2. What did Jesus pray? Not that His own will would be done but that the Father's will would be done.

3. Who strengthened Jesus in the garden? An angel.

4. What did the disciples do while Jesus prayed? They slept.

5. Who was included in the crowd that went to the garden to arrest Jesus? Judas, the chief priests, officers of the temple, and the elders.

6. Who did Jesus heal? The servant of the high priest.

7. What did the disciples do when Jesus was arrested? They fled.

8. What do we learn about God from these verses? God's will is to be done even when it is not our will.

Memory Verse: Mark 14:36

Early Elementary and Elementary

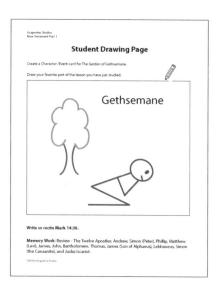

Information for The Garden of Gethsemane:

- After the Passover Meal, Jesus and the 11 Apostles went to the Garden.

- While Jesus prayed, the Apostles fell asleep.

- Jesus prayed not that His will be done but that the will of the Father would be done.

- Judas betrayed Jesus.

- After Peter cut off the ear of the servant, Jesus healed the servant's ear.

- When Jesus was arrested, the Apostles fled.

Memory Verse: Mark 14:36

Memory Work: Review - There are 66 books in the Bible: 39 books in the Old Testament and 27 books in the New Testament.

Middle School

The Trials of Jesus Part 1

Topical Bible Exercise

What is the *Sanhedrin*?

> Nave's, page 424

Bible Dictionary Exercise

Who was *Annas*?

> Zondervan's, page 46

Concordance Exercise

In what verse would we find reference to Jesus being *mocked*?

> Luke 22:63 (Cruden's, page 322)

Quest Question

Why did the Council or Sanhedrin want Jesus dead?

> Jesus was leading the people away from dependence upon the religious leaders of the day and pointing out their hypocrisy. Many Jews believed that Jesus was the long-awaited Messiah, but the Council refused to believe that fact and considered Jesus' words blasphemous and thus they wanted to have him put to death.

Timeline Review

Raised the Dead   Entered Jerusalem   Last Supper   Gethsemane

Memory Verse Review

Mark 14:36

John 13:1

Matthew 21:9

Luke 9:1

Memory Work: Review - There are 66 books in the Bible: 39 books in the Old Testament and 27 books in the New Testament.

The Trials of Jesus Part 1

Memory Verse: Matthew 26:57

Trial 1: Annas

Read aloud: John 18:12-14, 19-23

Discuss Trial 1: Annas: After Jesus was arrested, He was taken to Annas, the high priest, for His first trial. Annas asked him about His disciples and doctrine. Jesus responded that His teaching (doctrine) was always in the open and those who heard Him could bear witness to His teaching.

Draw and have students draw: Jesus before Annas.

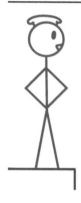 

Trial 2: Caiaphas, the High Priest

Read aloud: John 18:24

Discuss Trial 2: Caiaphas, the High Priest: Annas had Jesus bound and sent to Caiaphas for trial.

Map: Label the House of Caiaphas.

Draw and have students draw: Jesus before Caiaphas.

Look up the following words in a Bible Dictionary:

high priest

doctrine

mocked

blasphemous

Council/Sanhedrin

Peter Denied Jesus

Read aloud: Luke 22:54-62

Discuss Peter Denied Jesus: Peter followed Jesus and his captors to the home of the high priest. While Peter was standing in the courtyard, three people recognized him as one of the disciples of Jesus. Each time Peter denied their claim. Jesus looked at Peter just as he gave his third denial, and at that moment a rooster crowed.

Draw and have students draw: Peter saying "No!" when questioned.

Jesus Was Beaten and Mocked

Read aloud: Luke 22:63-65

Discuss Jesus Was Beaten and Mocked: As Jesus was held in the courtyard of the high priest's home, the men who held Him beat and mocked HIm.

Draw and have students draw: Jesus being beaten and mocked.

Completed Student Page

Teacher Notes:

Trial 3: Caiaphas and the Council

Read aloud: Mark 14:55-62

Discuss Trial 3: Caiaphas and the Council: Caiaphas had Jesus taken before the chief priests, the scribes, and the elders to be tried. False witnesses were brought to testify against Jesus, and finally the high priest asked Him if He was the Christ, to which Jesus responded that He was.

Map: Label the Temple. The Sanhedrin or council met in the chambers at the Temple.

Draw and have students draw: Jesus before Caiaphas and the Council.

Teacher Notes

Completed Student Page

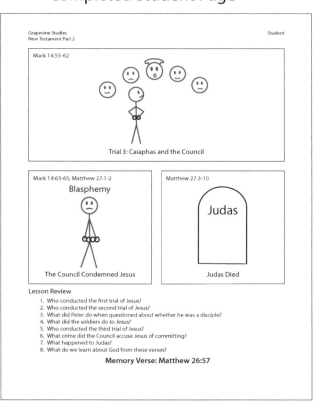

The Council Condemned Jesus

Blasphemy

Read aloud: Mark 14:63-65; Matthew 27:1-2

Discuss The Council Condemned Jesus: When Jesus told the Council that He was the Christ, the high priest tore his clothes and accused Jesus of speaking blasphemy. The Council then demanded that Jesus be put to death.

Draw and have students draw: Jesus in chains after being accused of blasphemy.

Judas Died

Read aloud: Matthew 27:3-10

Discuss Judas Died: When Judas heard that the Council had condemned Jesus to death, he was sorry. Judas sought to return the money to the priests. Judas then went and hanged himself. The chief priests consulted together and used the blood money to buy a field.

Draw and have students draw: Judas's grave.

Lesson Review:

1. Who conducted the first trial of Jesus? Annas.

2. Who conducted the second trial of Jesus? Caiaphas.

3. What did Peter do when questioned about whether he was a disciple? He denied it three times.

4. What did the soldiers do to Jesus? They beat and mocked Him.

5. Who conducted the third trial of Jesus? Caiaphas and the Council/the Sanhedrin.

6. What crime did the Council accuse Jesus of committing? Blasphemy.

7. What happened to Judas? He hanged himself.

8. What do we learn about God from these verses? God is with us even when our closest friends abandon us.

Memory Verse: Matthew 26:57

Early Elementary and Elementary

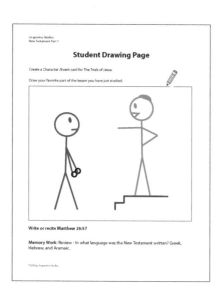

Information for the card for the Trials of Jesus:

- Jesus had three Religious Trials:

    1. Annas

    2. Caiaphas

    3. Caiaphas and the Council.

- Peter denied Jesus three times during these trials.

- Jesus was beaten and mocked.

- Jesus was condemned to death by the religious leaders on the charge of blasphemy.

Memory Verse: Matthew 26:57

Memory Work: Name the Gospels: Matthew, Mark, Luke, and John.

Middle School

The Trials of Jesus Part 2

Topical Bible Exercise

What is a *garrison*?

Nave's, page 169

Bible Dictionary Exercise

Define the names *Christ* and *Jesus*.

Zondervan's, page 106

How did the Romans *scourge* a man?

Zondervan's, page 528

Concordance Exercise

What verse states that Pilate *washed* his hands of the matters concerning Jesus?

Matthew 27:24 (Cruden's, page 532)

Quest Question

Pilate asked Jesus, "What is truth?" (John 18:38) How would you have answered that question?

Answers will vary. John 14:6.

Timeline Review

Jesus entered Jerusalem   Last Supper   Garden of Gethsemane   Jesus Arrested

Memory Verse Review

Matthew 26:57

Mark 14:36

John 13:1

Matthew 21:9

Memory Work: Name the Gospels: Matthew, Mark, Luke, and John.

The Trials of Jesus Part 2

Memory Verse: Matthew 27:26

Trial 4: Pilate

Read aloud: Luke 23:1-7

Discuss Trial 4: Pilate: After being tried by the Sanhedrin, the crowd took Jesus to Pilate (at the Antonia Fortress). At this point the accusations against Jesus changed from those related to the Jewish law to those related to Roman law. Pilate found no fault in Jesus, and when he learned that Jesus was from Galilee, Pilate sent Him to Herod.

Map: Label the Antonia Fortress.

Draw and have students draw: Jesus being questioned by Pilate.

Trial 5: Herod Antipas

Read aloud: Luke 23:8-12

Discuss Trial 5:Herod Antipas: Herod was pleased that Jesus was brought to him, for Herod had wanted to see Jesus, whom he had heard much about. Although Herod questioned Jesus, Jesus did not answer any of the questions. After questioning Jesus, he sent Him back to Pilate.

Map: Label the Herod's Palace.

Draw and have students draw: Jesus being questioned by Herod.

Look up the following words in a Bible Dictionary:

fault

Herod Antipas

governor

washing his hands

just

scourged

Trial 6: Pilate Questioned Jesus

Read aloud: Matthew 27:11-14

Discuss Trial 6: Pilate Questioned Jesus: After appearing before Herod, Jesus was returned to Pilate for His final trial. Pilate asked Jesus if He was the King of the Jews, and Jesus responded that He was the King of the Jews. The chief priests and the elders began accusing Him, but Jesus did not answer their accusations.

Draw and have students draw: Jesus before Pilate.

Barabbas or Jesus

Read aloud: Matthew 27:15-21; Mark 15:6-11

Discuss Barabbas or Jesus: Pilate had a tradition of releasing a prisoner at the Feast of Passover. When Pilate asked the crowd whom they wanted released, at the prompting of the chief priests and elders, the crowd asked for Barabbas. It is interesting to note that Pilate's wife warned him to have nothing to do with Jesus.

Draw and have students draw: Jesus and Barabbas before Pilate.

Completed Student Page

Teacher Notes:

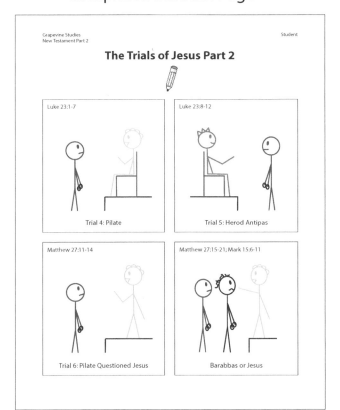

Pilate Washed His Hands

Read aloud: Matthew 27:22-25; Mark 15:12-14

Discuss Pilate Washed His Hands: When Pilate asked the crowd what he should do with Jesus, they demanded that Pilate should have Jesus crucified. Although Pilate did not think that Jesus was guilty, his desire was to please the crowd and prevent a riot.

Draw and have students draw: Pilate washing his hands.

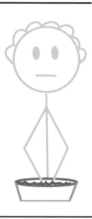

Jesus Was Scourged

Read aloud: Matthew 27:26; Mark 15:15

Discuss Jesus Was Scourged: Pilate released Barabbas and turned Jesus over to be scourged and then crucified.

Draw and have students draw: Jesus being scourged.

Teacher Notes

Completed Student Page

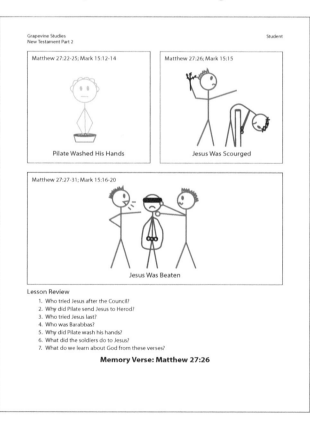

Jesus Was Beaten

Read aloud: Matthew 27:27-31; Mark 15:16-20

Discuss Jesus Was Beaten: After being scourged, Jesus was clothed in a scarlet/purple robe and had a crown of thorns placed on His head. After beating and spitting on Jesus, the soldiers removed the robe and dressed Him in His own clothes.

Draw and have students draw: Jesus wearing a crown of thorns and a purple robe with soldiers beating and mocking Him.

Lesson Review:

1. What did Jesus tell His apostles regarding His death? He would be killed.

2. With whom did Judas conspire? The chief priest, the captain, the scribes, and the Pharisees.

3. What feast did Jesus and His apostles celebrate? The Feast of Passover.

4. What did Jesus institute with the cup and the bread on the night of the Last Supper? The New Covenant.

5. Which apostle did Jesus identify as the one who would betray Him? Judas.

6. What did Judas get in exchange for his betrayal? Money.

7. What did Jesus tell His apostles they would do later that night? They would stumble and scatter.

8. What did Peter proclaim? He would not deny the Lord.

9. What do we learn about God from these verses? Jesus was committed to God's plan of bringing forth the New Covenant.

Memory Verse: Matthew 27:26

Early Elementary and Elementary

Student Drawing Page

Add to the Trials of Jesus card:

- Jesus had three Civil Trials:

    1. Pontius Pilate

    2. Herod Antipas

    3. Pontius Pilate

- Pilate declared Jesus innocent but condemned Him to death at the crowd's request.

- Barabbas was released instead of Jesus.

- Jesus was beaten and mocked with a robe and crown of thorns before being scourged.

Memory Verse: Matthew 27:26

New Testament Overview

~

Final Review

Final Review

1. What was Jesus doing when the tempest arose? He was sleeping.

2. How did Jesus calm the sea? By speaking to the wind and the waves, and it was so.

3. How did the disciples respond when Jesus calmed the sea? They marveled.

4. How did the disciples respond when they saw Jesus walking on the water? They thought He was a ghost.

5. Who got out of the boat to walk on the water with Jesus? Peter.

6. What did the disciples do when Jesus and Peter walked on the water? They worshipped Him and proclaimed Him to be the Son of God.

7. Recite Matthew 8:27.

8. When Jesus asked the disciples to feed the crowds, how did they respond? By telling Jesus that they didn't have enough food to feed the crowds.

9. What did Jesus do with the fish and loaves? He gave thanks and blessed the loaves and fish.

10. How many people did Jesus feed with five loaves and two fish? 5,000 men.

11. After feeding the 5,000, how many baskets of leftovers were gathered? 12.

12. How many people did Jesus feed with seven loaves and a few small fish? 4,000 men.

13. After feeding the 4,000, how many baskets of leftovers were gathered? 7.

14. Recite Luke 9:16.

15. What kinds of sicknesses and ailments did Jesus heal? The deaf, mute, blind, lepers, and those with palsy.

16. Where did Jesus heal? In various cities, on the roadways, and in homes.

17. What was the response of some of those who were healed? They thanked Jesus and worshipped and praised God.

18. How did the scribes respond to Jesus healing people and forgiving them of their sins? They questioned Jesus' authority to forgive sins.

19. Recite Matthew 4:23.

20. What is a demon? A spirit who seeks men who will worship it instead of the one true God.

21. What is an unclean spirit? Evil spirit who entices men to do evil and is opposed to God.

22. What did Jesus do when He encountered people who were possessed with an evil spirit? He rebuked and then cast out the demon/evil spirit.

23. What did the demons/unclean spirits say about Jesus? They called Him the Holy One of God and the Son of the Most High God.

24. To whom did Jesus give authority to cast out demons? His apostles and disciples.

25. What happened to the men who were not believers when they tried to cast out demons? They were attacked and publicly humiliated.

26. Recite Luke 9:1.

27. What did Jesus do to the widow's son? He raised him from the dead.

28. Why had Jairus come to Jesus? To request healing for his daughter.

29. What happened to Jairus's daughter? She died, and Jesus came and raised her from the dead.

30. Who sent for Jesus to tell Him that Lazarus was sick? His sisters, Mary and Martha.

31. Where was Lazarus when Jesus arrived in Bethany? In the tomb.

32. What happened to Lazarus? Jesus raised him from the dead.

33. How did the people respond when Jesus raised people from the dead? They glorified God, they questioned who Jesus was, and some believed in Jesus.

34. Recite Luke 7:15.

35. How did the chief priests respond to Lazarus's resurrection? They wanted to kill both Jesus and Lazarus.

36. How did the people respond to Lazarus's resurrection? The people believed in Jesus.

37. What was Jesus riding when He entered Jerusalem? A colt that had not been ridden before.

38. What did the people do when Jesus entered Jerusalem? They threw leafy branches and coats on the road and sang to Him.

39. What event brought Jesus to Jerusalem? The Feast of Passover.

40. What did Jesus do at the temple? He drove out the money changers and merchants, and then He taught and healed.

41. Why did the leaders hate Jesus? Because the people believed in Him and followed Him.

42. Recite Matthew 21:9.

43. What did Jesus tell His apostles regarding His death? He would be crucified.

44. With whom did Judas conspire? The chief priest, the captain, the scribes, and the Pharisees.

45. What feast did Jesus and His apostles celebrate? The Feast of Passover.

46. What did Jesus institute with the cup and the bread on the night of the Last Supper? The New Covenant.

47. Which apostle did Jesus identify as the one who would betray Him? Judas.

48. What did Judas get in exchange for his betrayal? Money.

49. What did Jesus tell His apostles they would do later that night? They would stumble and scatter.

50. What did Peter proclaim? He would not deny the Lord.

51. Recite John 13:1.

52. Where did Jesus take His disciples to pray? The Garden of Gethsemane.

53. What did Jesus pray? Not that His own will but would be done but the will of the Father.

54. Who strengthened Jesus in the garden? An angel.

55. What did the disciples do while Jesus prayed? They slept.

56. Who was included in the crowd that went to the garden to arrest Jesus? Judas, the chief priests, officers of the temple, and the elders.

57. Who did Jesus heal? The servant of the high priest.

58. What did the disciples do when Jesus was arrested? They fled.

59. Recite Mark 14:36.

60. Who conducted the first trial of Jesus? Annas.

61. Who conducted the second trial of Jesus? Caiaphas.

62. What did Peter do when questioned about whether he was a disciple? He denied it three times.

63. What did the soldiers do to Jesus? They beat and mocked him.

64. Who conducted the third trial of Jesus? Caiaphas and the Council/the Sanhedrin.

65. What crime did the Council/Sanhedrin accuse Jesus of committing? Blasphemy.

66. What happened to Judas? He hanged himself.

67. Recite Matthew 26:57.

68. Who tried Jesus after the Sanhedrin? Pontius Pilate.

69. Why did Pilate send Jesus to Herod? Jesus was from Herod's district.

70. Who tried Jesus last? Pontius Pilate.

71. Who was Barabbas? A criminal released by Pilate during the Feast of Passover.

72. Why did Pilate wash his hands? To make the statement that he was innocent in the death of Jesus.

73. What did the soldiers do to Jesus? They scourged Him, beat Him, put a scarlet/purple robe and a crown of thorns on Him, and then mocked Him.

74. Recite Matthew 27:26.

For Early Elementary and Elementary Levels:

75. How many books are in the Bible? 66.

76. In what language was the New Testament written? Greek, Hebrew, and Aramaic.

77. Name the Gospels. Matthew, Mark, Luke, and John.

78. Name the Twelve Apostles. Andrew, Simon (Peter), Phillip, Matthew (Levi), James, John, Bartholomew, Thomas, James (Son of Alphaeus), Lebbaueus, Simon (the Canaanite), and Judas Iscariot.

Jesus Healed the Sick/Lame

Jesus Fed the People

Matthew, Mark, Luke, and John

Jesus and the Seas

Jesus Entered Jerusalem

Jesus Raised the Dead

Matthew, Mark, Luke, and John

Jesus Healed the Demon-Possessed

The Last Supper

The Garden of Gethsemane

Jesus Arrested

The Trials

Matthew, Mark, Luke, and John

Map

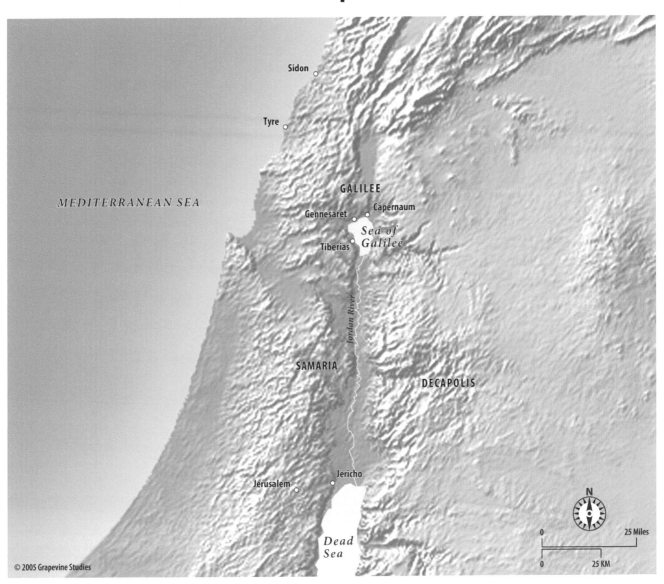

Label:

1. The Sea o f Galilee.

2. The Dead Sea.

3. The Jordan River.

4. The Mediterranean Sea.

5. The region of the Galilee.

6. The city of Gennesaret.

7. The city of Capernaum.

8. The city of Tyre.

9. The city of Sidon.

10. The region of the Decapolis.

11. The city of Jericho.

12. The region of Samaria.

Map

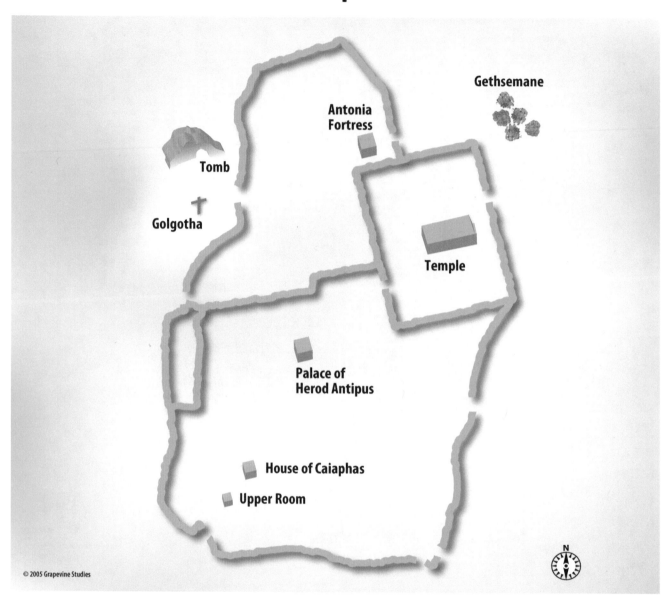

Label:

1. The Upper Room.

2. Gethsemane.

3. The House of Caiaphas.

4. The Temple.

5. The Antonia Fortress.

6. The Palace of Herod

New Testament Overview
~
Part 3

Jesus Crucified: At approximately 9:00 in the morning, Jesus was crucified between two thieves with a sign over His head reading, "Jesus, the King of the Jews." At about 3:00 in the afternoon, Jesus died. At the time of Jesus' death there were many amazing events: darkness and earthquake, the temple veil was torn top to bottom, and graves were opened and those who had been dead appeared to many.

Draw and have students draw: Jesus on the cross.

Jesus Died: After a Roman soldier verified that Jesus was indeed dead, He was taken down from the cross and buried in the borrowed tomb of Joseph of Arimathea.

Draw and have students draw: Jesus dead on the cross.

Jesus Rose: After three days Jesus conquered death and the grave by rising from the dead. On the third day when the women went to the tomb to anoint Jesus' body, an angel met them and told them of His resurrection.

Draw and have students draw: The tomb, with the stone rolled back and a purple arrow pointing out of the empty tomb and up.

The Gospel Symbol #3: At this point, the Gospel is completed, drawing the broken relationship between God and man being restored by Jesus' sacrifice on the cross and His resurrection from the dead.

Draw and have students draw: The purple God triangle connected to a man's heart with a cross.

The Eyes: Throughout the Old Testament, our eyes looked forward to the Messiah, but when Jesus is born we change the eyes to looking down. Now that Jesus has come we watch what He does.

Draw and have students draw: Eyes looking down.

Completed Student Page

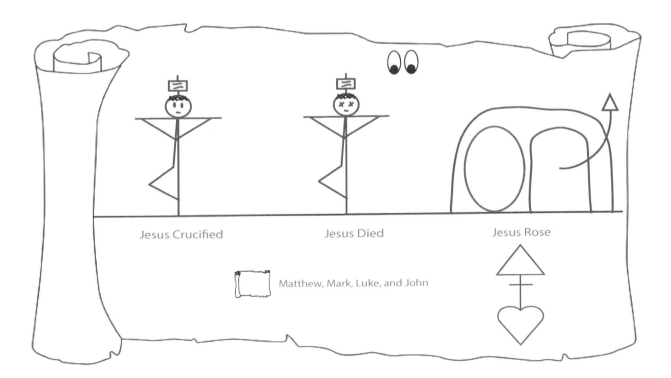

Jesus Appeared: After Jesus' resurrection He appeared many times and to many people, at one time appearing to a crowd numbering 500. Jesus met with His apostles on different occasions, verifying His resurrection and giving them final instructions.

Draw and have students draw: Jesus showing His Disciples His hands and side.

Jesus Ascended: At the end of forty days Jesus ascended to heaven, where He now sits at the right hand of the Father interceding for us. An angel appeared to the apostles when Jesus ascended and told them that when He returns, He will come in the same manner.

Draw and have students draw: Jesus on a cloud, with an arrow pointing up, showing His ascension.

My Notes:

The Holy Spirit: Fifty days after Jesus died on the cross, on the Feast of Pentecost, the Disciples were gathered in an upper room in Jerusalem as Jesus had commanded them. While they were praying the Holy Spirit came upon them in the form of tongues of fire.

Draw and have students draw: A man and woman praying as the Holy Spirit (purple dove) comes to them.

My Notes:

Completed Student Page

Jesus Appeared   Jesus Ascended   The Holy Spirit

Acts

Eyes: After the Ascension of Jesus we change the eyes. One set of eyes looks back to His first coming. The second set of eyes looks forward to His second coming.

Draw and have students draw: A set of eyes looking back and a set of eyes looking forward.

The Early Church: On the day of Pentecost, the day the Holy Spirit was given to the Church, Peter preached at the temple, and 3,000 men believed and were baptized. Many things marked the early Church including prayer, fellowship, the breaking of bread together, and following the apostles' teachings.

Draw and have students draw: A Disciple preaching about Jesus (cross).

The Persecution: Not long after the birth of the Church, the persecution of those who accepted Jesus as the Messiah began. The first man to die because of his faith in Jesus the Messiah, Stephen, was tried and stoned to death. Many other believers were also arrested and imprisoned during this time.

Draw and have students draw: Stephen under rocks.

Saul: While Stephen was being stoned a young man named Saul watched the coats of those doing the stoning. Saul became an aggressive persecutor of the followers of Jesus. While Saul was traveling to Damascus to persecute believers, he encountered Jesus and became a believer himself.

Draw and have students draw: Saul holding his hand up as Jesus talks to him.

My Notes:

Completed Student Page

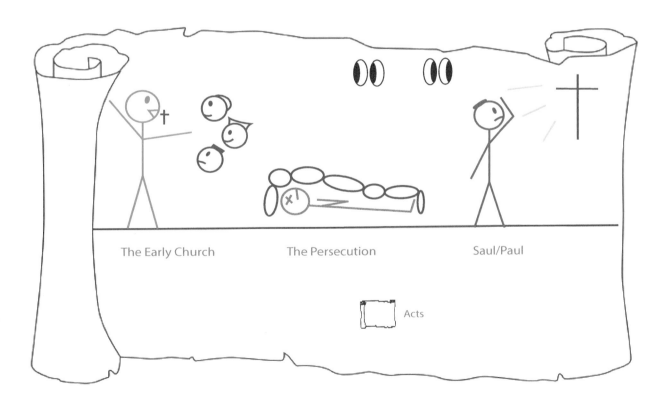

The Early Church   The Persecution   Saul/Paul

Acts

Lesson Goals and Key Points

THE CRUCIFIXION

The goal of this lesson is to establish the fact that Jesus was crucified and died.

Key Points:
- Simon carried Jesus' crossbeam to the place of execution.
- The inscription above Jesus read, "This is the King of the Jews."
- Jesus was crucified between two thieves.
- Jesus asked God to forgive those involved in His death.
- The soldiers cast lots for Jesus' clothing.
- The crowd mocked Jesus while He was on the cross

Memory Verse: Luke 23:33

THE DEATH OF JESUS

The goal of this lesson is to examine the events surrounding the death of Jesus.

Key Points:
- Jesus asked the apostle John to care for His mother.
- Jesus cried out to God and then died.
- When Jesus died three things happened:
    1. The temple veil was torn top to bottom.
    2. An earthquake struck.
    3. Saints were resurrected.
- A soldier pierced His side to confirm His death

Memory Verse: Luke 23:46

THE BURIAL AND RESURRECTION

The goal of this lesson is to understand the events that occurred at the burial and resurrection of Jesus.

Key Points:
- Jesus was buried by Joseph of Arimathea and Nicodemus.
- Jesus was buried in a new tomb.
- A guard was set at the tomb to ensure that the Disciples did not steal the body.
- After three days Jesus rose from the grave.
- Mary, Peter, and the Disciples verified the resurrection by confirming that the tomb was empty.

Memory Verse: John 19:41-42

THE ASCENSION

The goal of this lesson is to learn about the events that took place between the resurrection and the ascension.

Key Points:
- After the resurrection, Jesus appeared to various people and groups of people for a period of forty days.
    1. The two disciples who were traveling to Emmaus.
    2. The apostles, on three different occasions.
    3. As many as 500 at one time.
- Before His ascension Jesus gave His apostles final instructions to spread the gospel.
- Jesus ascended into the clouds and now sits at the right hand of the Father interceding for us

Memory Verse: Mark 16:19

WAS JESUS THE MESSIAH? PART 1

The goal of this lesson is to demonstrate that Jesus of Nazareth was the promised Messiah.

Key Points:
- Jesus was the Messiah, Hebrew for "the Anointed One."
- Jesus was the Christ, Greek for "the Anointed One."
- Jesus fulfilled all New Testament prophecies regarding the Messiah.
- The New Testament writers documented Jesus' life, death, and resurrection while many of the eyewitnesses to the events were alive

Memory Verse: John 1:14

Page intentionally left blank

Middle School

Quest Page

Topical Bible

What is a *tunic*?

Nave's, page 494

Bible Dictionary

Give three facts concerning the *cross*.

Answers may vary. (Zondervan's, page 119)

Concordance

How many times is the term *crucified* mentioned in Scripture?

28 (Cruden's, page 95)

Quest Question

Why did Jesus have to die?

Hebrews 9:22.

The Crucifixion

Memory Verse: Luke 23:33

Simon Carried the Cross

Read aloud: Luke 23:26-32

Discuss Simon Carried the Cross: After Jesus was scourged and beaten, He was led away to be crucified. Because of Jesus' weakened condition, He was unable to carry His cross, so Simon carried the crossbeam for Jesus. As Jesus was led through the multitude, He spoke to those that followed Him and warned them. Two other criminals were also led out with Jesus to be crucified.

Draw and have students draw: Simon walking behind Jesus and carrying Jesus' cross.

The Inscription

Read aloud: John 19:19-22

Discuss The Inscription: Above each crucified person an inscription was placed indicating the type of crime he had been charged with. Pilate wrote Jesus' inscription, and the chief priests protested, but Pilate refused to have the inscription changed.

Draw and have students draw: A sign stating King of the Jews.

King
of the
Jews

Look up the following words in a Bible Dictionary:

inscription

crucified

tunic

lots

mocked

Paradise

Jesus Was Crucified

Golgotha

Read aloud: Matthew 27:33-38; Mark 15:22-28; Luke 23:33; John 19:17-18 (Teacher note: You can opt to read some or all of the Scriptures listed.)

Discuss Jesus Was Crucified: Jesus was crucified around 9:00 A.M. at a place called Golgotha, outside the city of Jerusalem. I recommend that teachers do a personal study on this most important event to determine what their students should know.

Map: Label hill of Golgotha.

Draw and have students draw: Jesus crucified between two thieves.

Completed Student Page

Teacher Notes

Grapevine Studies
New Testament Part 3

Student

Luke 23:33-34

Forgiveness

John 19:23-24

The Soldiers

Matthew 27:39-44; Luke 23:35-37

The Crowd Mocked

Luke 23:39-43

The Thieves

Lesson Review
1. Who carried the cross for Jesus?
2. What inscription did Pilate have put above Jesus?
3. What happened to Jesus at Golgotha?
4. What did Jesus ask the Father to do to those who crucified Him?
5. Who cast lots for Jesus' tunic?
6. What did the crowd do to Jesus while He was on the cross?
7. What did Jesus promise the repentant thief on the cross?
8. What do we learn about God from these verses?

Memory Verse: Luke 23:33

Forgiveness

Read aloud: Luke 23:33-34

Discuss Forgiveness: On the cross, Jesus prayed that the Father would forgive those who had crucified Him.

Draw and have students draw: Jesus asking God to forgive His enemies.

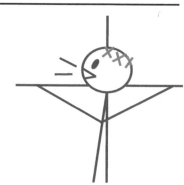

The Soldiers

Read aloud: John 19:23-24

Discuss The Soldiers: After Jesus was crucified the soldiers cast lots for His clothing, as had been prophesied.

Draw and have students draw: Two soldiers, one with a short straw and the winner with the long straw and tunic.

Teacher Notes

Completed Student Page

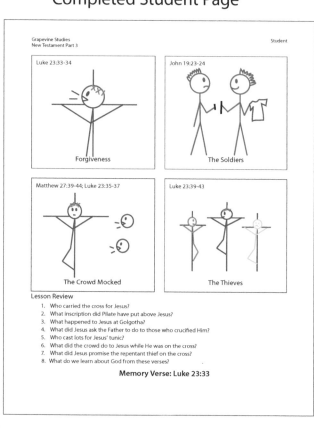

The Crowd Mocked

Read aloud: Matthew 27:39-44; Luke 23:35-37

Discuss The Crowd Mocked: The soldiers, thieves, chief priests, scribes, elders, and those passing by the cross mocked Jesus.

Draw and have students draw: The people mocking Jesus.

The Thieves

Read aloud: Luke 23:39-43

Discuss The Thieves: One of the crucified thieves mocked Jesus, while the other thief recognized his own sin and the innocence of Jesus. The repentant thief asked Jesus to remember him, and Jesus assured this thief that he would be with Jesus in Paradise.

Draw and have students draw: Jesus talking to one of the thieves.

Lesson Review

1. Who carried the cross for Jesus? Simon of Cyrene.

2. What inscription did Pilate have put above Jesus? Jesus of Nazareth, the King of the Jews.

3. What happened to Jesus at Golgotha? He was crucified.

4. What did Jesus ask the Father to do to those who crucified Him? Forgive them.

5. Who cast lots for Jesus' tunic? The soldiers who crucified Him.

6. What did the crowd do to Jesus while He was on the cross? They mocked Him.

7. What did Jesus promise the repentant thief on the cross? He would be with Jesus that day in Paradise.

8. What do we learn about God from these verses? God is a forgiving God, and Jesus suffered a great deal for the penalty of our sins.

Memory Verse: Luke 23:33

Early Elementary and Elementary

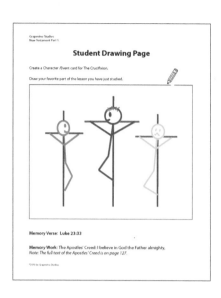

Information for the Crucifixion card:

- Simon carried the cross for Jesus.
- The inscription on the cross read, "This is the King of the Jews."
- Jesus was crucified between two thieves.
- Jesus asked God to forgive those involved in His death.
- The soldiers cast lots for Jesus' clothing.
- The crowd mocked Jesus on the cross

Memory Verse: Luke 23:33

Memory Work: *Note: The full text of the Apostles' Creed is on page 264.* The Apostles' Creed: I believe in God the Father almighty,

Middle School

The Death of Jesus

Topical Bible

What is the temple *veil*?

Nave's, page 502

Bible Dictionary

What was a *centurion*?

Zondervan's, page 102

Concordance

After Jesus died a soldier *pierced* His side. Find the verse that speaks about this event.

John 19:34 (Cruden's, page 364)

Quest Question

Many interesting events coincided with the death of Jesus on the cross. Name one and explain its significance. (To be done at the end of the lesson.)

Answers will vary.

Timeline Review

Jesus Arrested The Trials Jesus Crucified

Memory Verse Review

Luke 23:33

Matthew 27:26

Matthew 26:57

Memory Work: The Apostles' Creed: I believe in God the Father almighty,

The Death of Jesus

Memory Verse: Luke 23:46

Jesus, John, and Mary

Read aloud: John 19:25-27

Discuss Jesus, John, and Mary: While on the cross Jesus made provisions for His mother to be cared for by the Apostle John. According to church history, John took care of Mary until her death.

Draw and have students draw: Jesus talking to John and Mary who are standing at the foot of the cross.

Jesus Cried Out to God

Read aloud: Mark 15:33-36; Luke 23:44-46

Discuss Jesus Cried Out to God: From the sixth hour to the ninth hour, darkness covered the land. The last thing that Jesus did before He died was cry out to the Father.

Draw and have students draw: Jesus on the cross, crying out to God the Father.

Look up the following words in a Bible Dictionary:

sixth/ninth hour

finished

temple veil

fallen asleep

centurion

Jesus Died

Read aloud: John 19:28-30; Mark 15:37

Discuss Jesus Died: Jesus knew that He had accomplished all that needed to be completed, and then He stated, "It is finished," and gave up His spirit.

Draw and have students draw: Jesus dead on the cross. Note death with an X over each eye.

Completed Student Page

Teacher Notes:

The Temple Veil, the Earthquake, and the Graves

Read aloud: Matthew 27:50-53

Discuss The Temple Veil: Many important and interesting events surrounded the death of Jesus. The darkness lifted and the veil in the temple was torn top to bottom.

Map: Label the Temple.

Draw and have students draw: The temple veil torn in two.

Discuss The Earthquake: An earthquake struck Jerusalem.

Draw and have students draw: The ground broken open.

Discuss The Graves Opened: At the same time as the temple veil tore and the earth quaked, the graves of dead saints opened. Those who were resurrected appeared to many.

Draw and have students draw: An open grave and a man talking to a woman.

Teacher Notes

Completed Student Page

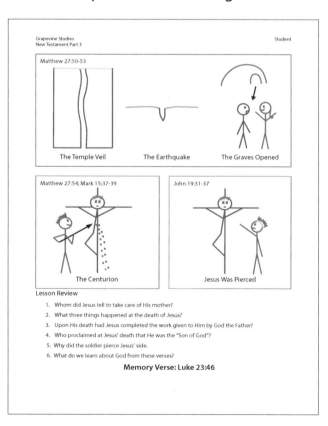

The Centurion

Read aloud: Matthew 27:54; Mark 15:37-39

Discuss The Centurion: After witnessing the death of Jesus and the events surrounding His death, the centurions and guards were very afraid and proclaimed that Jesus must have been the "Son of God."

Draw and have students draw: The centurion standing by the cross of Jesus after He died.

Jesus Was Pierced

Read aloud: John 19: 31-37

Discuss Jesus Was Pierced: As evening approached it was necessary to remove the bodies from the crosses in order to bury them before sundown. To hasten the death of those being crucified, the legs of both thieves were broken. However, when they came to break Jesus' legs it was discovered that He was already dead. To ensure that He was dead, a spear was thrust into His side, bringing forth water and blood.

Draw and have students draw: A Roman soldier piercing Jesus' side and both water and blood coming out.

Lesson Review

1. Whom did Jesus tell to take care of His mother? John.

2. What three things happened at the death of Jesus? (1) The temple veil was torn in two, (2) an earthquake struck, and (3) the graves of the saints were opened and they appeared to many.

3. Upon His death had Jesus completed the work given to Him by God the Father? Yes.

4. Who proclaimed at Jesus' death that He was the "Son of God"? The centurion.

5. Why did the soldier pierce Jesus' side? To make sure He was dead.

6. What do we learn about God from these verses? Jesus fulfilled all of the things prophesied about the Messiah, and He completed the work given to Him by God.

Memory Verse: Luke 23:46

Early Elementary and Elementary

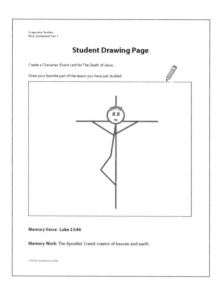

Information for the Death of Jesus card:

- Jesus asked John to care for His mother.

- Jesus cried out to God and then died.

- When Jesus died three things happened:

  1. The Temple Veil was torn from the top to bottom.

  2. An earthquake struck.

  3. Saints were resurrected.

- A soldier pierced Jesus side to confirm that He was dead.

Memory Verse: Luke 23:46

Memory Work: The Apostles' Creed: creator of heaven and earth.

Middle School

The Burial and Resurrection

Topical Bible

What is a *tomb*?

Nave's, pages 488-489

Bible Dictionary

What does the term *resurrection* mean?

Zondervan's, page 497

Concordance

Look up one reference to *resurrection* and write out the main point of the verse.

Answers will vary. (Cruden's page 406)

Quest Question

Why is the resurrection of Jesus so important to the Christian faith?

Answers will vary. I Corinthians 15:12-19.

Timeline Review

Jesus Arrested   The Trials   Jesus Crucified   Jesus Died

Memory Verse Review

Luke 23:46

Luke 23:33

Matthew 27:26

Matthew 26:57

Memory Work: The Apostles' Creed: creator of heaven and earth.

The Burial and Resurrection

Memory Verse: John 19:41-42

Jesus Was Buried

Read aloud: Matthew 27:57-61; Mark 15:42-47; Luke 23:50-56; John 19:38-42

Discuss Jesus Was Buried: Joseph of Arimathea went to Pilate and received permission to take the body of Jesus. Joseph and Nicodemus wrapped Jesus' body in linen and laid him in Joseph's new tomb, which was near the place of execution. The women present noted the place of burial so that they could return at a later time and finish preparing the body.

Map: Label the Tomb of Jesus.

Draw and have students draw: Jesus in the tomb, covered by a cloth.

Pilate Set a Guard

Read aloud: Matthew 27:62-66

Discuss Pilate Set a Guard: The chief priests and the Pharisees were worried that the disciples would steal Jesus' body. They asked Pilate for a guard to be set around His tomb, and he gave them their request. The chief priests sealed the stone entrance to the tomb and set a guard there.

Draw and have students draw: Roman guard.

Look up the following words in a Bible Dictionary:

tomb

seal

linen cloths

peace

The Empty Tomb

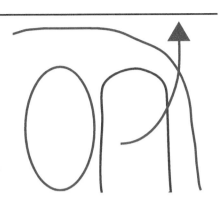

Read aloud: Matthew 28:1-8; Luke 24:1-8

Discuss The Empty Tomb: After the Sabbath, the women came to Jesus' tomb to finish preparing His body for burial. Upon arriving they were greeted by an angel, who informed them that Jesus had risen from the dead and gave them instructions to tell the disciples.

Draw and have students draw: The open tomb with an arrow coming out and pointing upward.

Peter at the Tomb

Read aloud: Luke 24:9-12; John 20:1-9

Discuss Peter at the Tomb: When the women returned and told the disciples that Jesus was not in the tomb, Peter and John ran to the tomb. Upon arriving they found it empty and the linen burial cloths folded up. Then Peter left the tomb and marveled at what he had seen.

Draw and have students draw: Peter looking into the empty tomb.

Completed Student Page

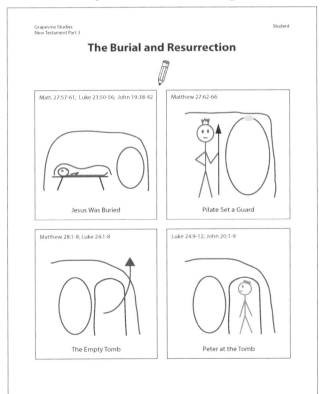

Teacher Notes:

Mary and Jesus

Read aloud: John 20:11-18

Discuss Mary and Jesus: Mary returned to the empty tomb to find two angels sitting where Jesus' body had been placed, and they asked why she was weeping. Mary responded that she wanted to know the location of His body. Turning around, she encountered Jesus, whom she mistook as the gardener.

Draw and have students draw: Mary kneeling before Jesus.

Jesus and Ten Disciples

Read aloud: John 20:19-23

Discuss Jesus and the Disciples: On Sunday evening ten of the disciples were gathered together when Jesus appeared to them, showing them His nail-scarred hands and side. Jesus also gave them instructions during this visit.

Draw and have students draw: Jesus showing His hands and side to His disciples.

Teacher Notes

Completed Student Page

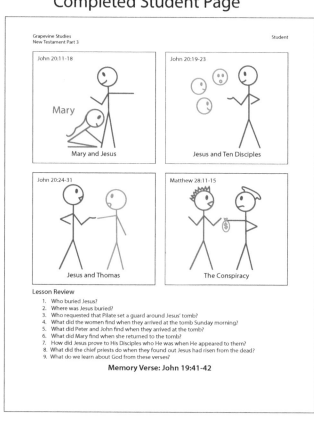

Jesus and Thomas

Read aloud: John 20:24-31

Discuss Jesus and Thomas: The disciple Thomas, who was not present when Jesus appeared to the other disciples, questioned whether they had really seen Him. Eight days later, all eleven of the disciples were together, including Thomas; when Jesus appeared again to them. This time Jesus showed Thomas His hands and His side and Thomas believed.

Draw and have students draw: Jesus showing Thomas His hands and side.

The Conspiracy

Read aloud: Matthew 28:11-15

Discuss The Conspiracy: When the soldiers who had guarded Jesus' tomb returned with the report of the events that had taken place, the chief priests came up with a plan. The soldiers were told to say that the disciples had stolen the body of Jesus. In return the soldiers were given protection and paid to perpetuate this lie.

Draw and have students draw: A chief priest giving money to a soldier.

Lesson Review

1. Who buried Jesus? Joseph of Arimathea and Nicodemus.
2. Where was Jesus buried? In Joseph of Arimathea's new tomb in a garden near the place of the crucifixion.
3. Who requested that Pilate set a guard around Jesus' tomb? The chief priests and Pharisees.
4. What did the women find when they arrived at the tomb Sunday morning? An empty tomb and an angel.
5. What did Peter and John find when they arrived at the tomb? An empty tomb and the burial clothes neatly folded.
6. What did Mary find when she returned to the tomb? An angel and then the risen Jesus.
7. How did Jesus prove to His disciples who He was when He appeared to them? By showing them His hands and side.
8. What did the chief priests do when they found out Jesus had risen from the dead? They paid the guards to spread the lie that Jesus' disciples had stolen his body.
9. What do we learn about God from these verses? Jesus did rise from the dead, proving His power over death and the grave.

Memory Verse: John 19:41-42

Early Elementary and Elementary

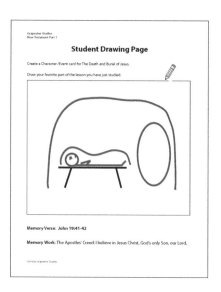

Information for the Burial and Resurrection card:

• Jesus was buried by Joseph of Arimathea and Nicodemus.

• Jesus was buried in a new tomb.

• A guard was set at the tomb to ensure that the disciples did not steal His body.

• After three days Jesus rose from the grave.

• Mary, Peter and the Disciples verified the resurrection by confirming the tomb was empty.

Memory Verse: John 19:41-42

Memory Work: The Apostles' Creed: I believe in Jesus Christ, God's only Son, our Lord,

Middle School

Jesus Ascended

Topical Bible

What is *Emmaus*?

Nave's, page 138

Bible Dictionary

Define the *gospel*.

Zondervan's page 203

Concordance

"Go into the world and preach the gospel to every creature." Where is this verse found?

Mark 16:15 (Cruden's page 212)

Quest Question

What do you learn about Jesus' return from Acts 1:9-11?

When Jesus returns, He will come in the clouds, in the same manner that He left the disciples at the ascension.

Timeline Review

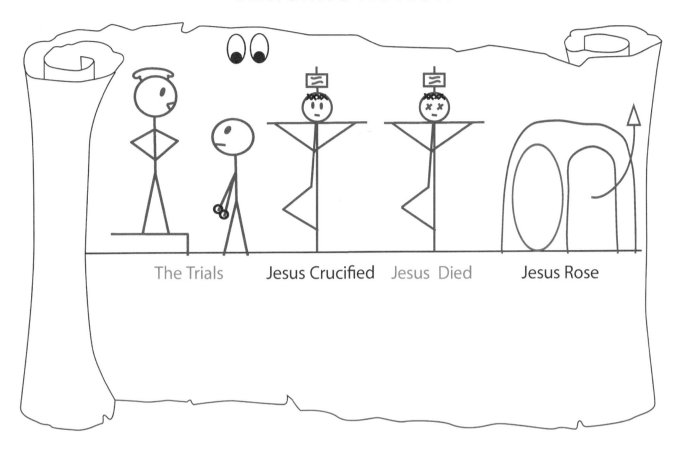

The Trials   Jesus Crucified   Jesus Died   Jesus Rose

Memory Verse Review

John 19:41-42

Luke 23:46

Luke 23:33

Matthew 27:26

Memory Work: The Apostles' Creed: I believe in Jesus Christ, God's only Son, our Lord,

Jesus Ascended

Memory Verse: Mark 16:19

Road to Emmaus

Read aloud: Luke 24:13-27

Discuss Road to Emmaus: Two of Jesus' disciples (not apostles) were traveling to Emmaus and were discussing the events that had recently happened in Jerusalem. Jesus appeared and walked with them and expressed the desire to know what they were discussing. Jesus began explaining from the Scriptures all the things the prophets had said about the coming Messiah.

Draw and have students draw: Jesus talking to two disciples as they walked to Emmaus.

Jesus Revealed

Read aloud: Mark 16:12-13; Luke 24:28-35

Discuss Jesus Revealed: The disciples did not know that it was Jesus who talked with them until Jesus broke the bread. When they recognized Jesus, He left them. These disciples immediately returned to Jerusalem to tell the eleven apostles about what had happened.

Draw and have students draw: Jesus breaking bread with the two disciples.

Look up the following words in a Bible Dictionary:

disciples

baptizing

teaching

gospel

ascend

Jesus at the Sea

Read aloud: John 21:1-14

Discuss Jesus at the Sea : In obedience to Jesus' command (Matt. 28:7), the disciples went to Galilee. While waiting in Galilee, some of the disciples decided to go fishing. After an unsuccessful night, Jesus greeted them and told them where to put down their nets. The catch was so large that the boat threatened to capsize. At that point they realized it was Jesus and went ashore to meet Him.

Draw and have students draw: Jesus by a fire and a disciple in a boat with fish in his net.

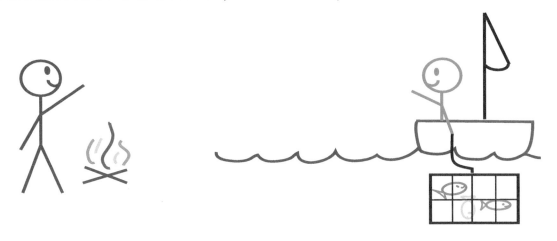

Completed Student Page

Teacher Notes:

Jesus Appeared to Many

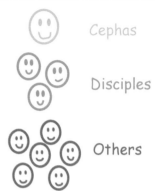

Read aloud: I Corinthians 15:3-7

Discuss Jesus Appeared to Many: After His resurrection, Jesus was seen by many people, including His disciples. Many of those who saw Him alive lived during the writing of what we call the New Testament.

Draw and have students draw: Cephas, Disciples, and others.

Final Instructions

Read aloud: Matthew 28:16-20; Mark 16:14-18

Discuss Final Instructions: On Sunday evening ten of the disciples were gathered together when Jesus appeared to them, showing them His nail-scarred hands and side. Jesus also gave them instructions during this visit.

Draw and have students draw: Jesus talking to His disciples.

Teacher Notes

Completed Student Page

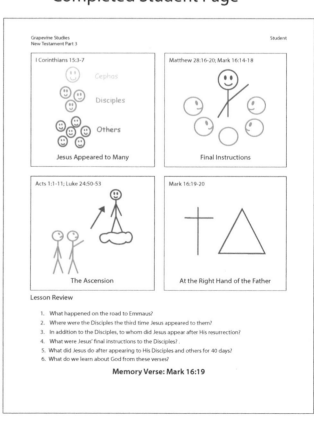

The Ascension

Read aloud: Acts 1:1-11; Luke 24:50-53

Discuss The Ascension: : At the end of forty days Jesus ascended into heaven. The angel reminded the disciples that one day Jesus would return in the same manner He left.

Draw and have students draw: Jesus ascending into heaven as two disciples watch.

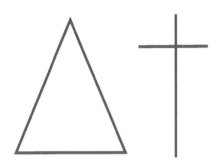

At the Right Hand of the Father

Read aloud: Mark 16:19-20

Discuss At the Right Hand of the Father: Jesus ascended and now sits at the right hand of the Father, praying for us.

Draw and have students draw: Jesus (the cross) at the right of God the Father (purple triangle).

Lesson Review:

1. What happened on the road to Emmaus? Jesus appeared and talked with two disciples.

2. Where were the disciples the third time Jesus appeared to them? The Sea of Galilee/Tiberius.

3. In addition to the Disciples, to whom did Jesus appear after His resurrection? The two disciples on the road to Emmaus and as many as 500 people at once.

4. What were Jesus' final instructions to the disciples? To go, preach the gospel, make disciples, baptize believers, and teach them to obey what He had taught them.

5. What did Jesus do after appearing to His disciples and others for 40 days? He ascended into at sit at the right hand of the Father.

6. What do we learn about God from these verses? God raised Jesus from the dead, and the proof of that was evident to the disciples and to the many people He appeared to after the resurrection.

Memory Verse: Mark 16:19

Early Elementary and Elementary

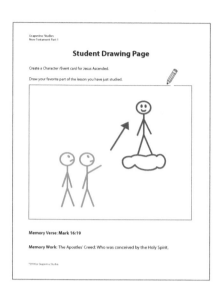

Information for the Jesus Ascended card:

- After the resurrection, Jesus made appearances over a period of 40 days.

  1. The two disciples on the road to Emmaus.

  2. The Apostles

  3. As many as 500 people at one time.

- Before His ascension Jesus gave His Apostles final instructions to spread the gospel.

- Jesus ascended into the clouds and now sits at the right hand of the Father interceding for us

Memory Verse: Mark 16:19

Middle School

Was Jesus the Messiah? Part 1

Topical Bible

What does *Messiah* mean?

Nave's, page 313

Bible Dictionary

What does the term *Christ* mean?

Zondervan's, page 106

What does the term *genealogy* mean?

Zondervan's, page 192

Concordance

Give a Bible verse that refers to Jesus of *Nazareth*.

Matthew 21:11, Mark 14:67, Acts 3:6, and others (Cruden's, page 335)

Quest Question

Why was it important for two of the four Gospel writers to note the genealogy of Jesus?

To establish that Jesus was of the lineage of Abraham and the lineage of David.

Timeline Review

| Jesus Crucified | Jesus Died | Jesus Rose | Jesus Appeared |

Memory Verse Review

Mark 16:19

John 19:41-42

Luke 23:46

Luke 23:33

Memory Work: The Apostles' Creed: Who was conceived by the Holy Spirit,

Was Jesus the Messiah? Part 1

Memory Verse: John 1:14

Messiah

Discuss Messiah: The word Messiah is a Hebrew word and means the "anointed one."

Write and have students write: Messiah Hebrew for Anointed One.

Messiah

Hebrew for

Anointed One

Christ

Greek for

Anointed One

Christ

Discuss Christ: The word Christ is a Greek word and means the "anointed one."

Write and have students write: Christ Greek for Anointed One.

Look up the following words in a Bible Dictionary:

Messiah

Christ

anointed

prophecy

Genealogy of Jesus

Read aloud: Matthew 1:1-17; Luke 3:23-38

Discuss John Pointed to Jesus: Two of the gospel writers mention the genealogy of Jesus: Matthew and Luke. Matthew follows Joseph's line, sometimes called the "royal lineage," and Luke follows the line of Mary, sometimes called the "common lineage." Although Joseph was not Jesus' biological father, the author of Matthew deemed his genealogy to be important. Between Adam and Jesus there were sixty-two generations.

Chart and have students chart: Counting the generations between Adam and Jesus.

Adam (10) Noah (10) Abraham (14) David (14) Babylon (14) Jesus

Babylonian Captivity

Completed Student Page

Teacher Notes:

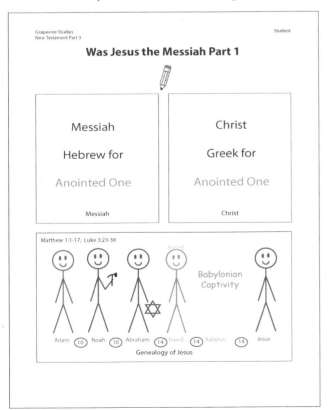

Born of Woman

Read aloud: Genesis 3:15; Matthew 1:18; Galatians 4:4

Discuss Born of Woman: The Old Testament prophesied that the Messiah would be born of a woman, and we know her as Mary.

Draw and have students draw: Mary holding Jesus.

Born of a Virgin

Read aloud: Isaiah 7:14; Luke 1:27

Discuss Born of a Virgin: The Old Testament prophesied that the Messiah would be born of a woman who had not known a man, and Mary was a virgin at Jesus' birth.

Draw and have students draw: Mary.

Born in Bethlehem

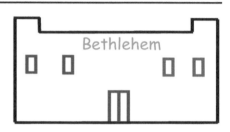

Read aloud: Micah 5:2; Luke 2:4-7

Discuss Born in Bethlehem: The Old Testament prophesied that the Messiah would be born in Bethlehem of Judea, and He was.

Draw and have students draw: The town of Bethlehem.

Teacher Notes

Completed Student Page

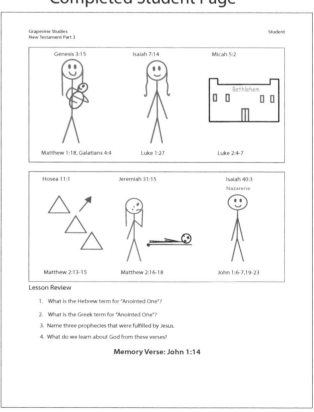

Out of Egypt

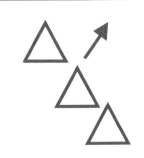

Read aloud: Hosea 11:1; Matthew 2:13-15

Discuss Born of Woman: The Old Testament prophesied that the Messiah would be called out of Egypt.

Draw and have students draw: Three pyramids (representing Egypt) and a purple arrow pointing out.

Death of the Children

Read aloud: Jeremiah 31:15; Matthew 2:16-18

Discuss Death of the Children: The Old Testament prophesied that the coming of Messiah would be associated with the death of children.

Draw and have students draw: A mother weeping over her dead child.

Called a Nazarene

Nazarene

Read aloud: Matthew 2:23

Discuss Born in Bethlehem: The Old Testament prophesied that the Messiah would be born in Bethlehem of Judea, and He was.

Draw and have students draw: Jesus, noting He was a Nazarene.

Lesson Review:

1. What is the Hebrew term for "Anointed One"? Messiah

2. What is the Greek term for "Anointed One"? Christ.

3. Name three prophecies that were fulfilled by Jesus. Jesus was born of a woman, born of a virgin, and born in the city of Bethlehem.

4. What do we learn about God from these verses? Jesus fulfilled Old Testament prophecies about the birth of the Messiah.

Memory Verse: John 1:14

Early Elementary and Elementary

Student Drawing Page

Information for Jesus the Messiah card:

• Jesus was the Messiah, Hebrew for the Anointed One.

• Jesus was the Christ, Greek for the Anointed One.

• Jesus fulfilled all Old Testament prophecies regarding the Messiah.

• The New Testament writers documented Jesus' life, death and resurrection while many of the eye witnesses to the events were still living.

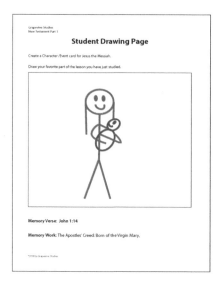

Memory Verse: John 1:14

Memory Work: The Apostles' Creed: Born of the Virgin Mary,

New Testament Part 3
~
Section Review

Section Review

1. Who carried the cross for Jesus? Simon of Cyrene.

2. What inscription did Pilate have put above Jesus? Jesus of Nazareth, the King of the Jews.

3. What happened to Jesus at Golgotha? He was crucified.

4. What did Jesus ask the Father to do to those who crucified Him? Forgive them.

5. Who cast lots for Jesus' tunic? The soldiers who crucified Him.

6. What did the crowd do to Jesus while He was on the cross? They mocked Him.

7. What did Jesus promise the repentant thief on the cross? He would be with Jesus that day in Paradise.

8. Recite Luke 23:33.

9. Whom did Jesus tell to take care of His mother? John.

10. What three things happened at the death of Jesus? (1) The temple veil was torn in two, (2) an earthquake struck, and (3) the graves of the saints were opened and they appeared to many.

11. Upon His death had Jesus completed the work given to Him by God the Father? Yes.

12. Who proclaimed at Jesus' death that He was the "Son of God"? The centurion.

13. Why did the soldier pierce Jesus' side? To make sure He was dead.

14. Recite Luke 23:46.

15. Who buried Jesus? Joseph of Arimathea and Nicodemus.

16. Where was Jesus buried? In Joseph of Arimathea's new tomb in a garden near the place of the crucifixion.

17. Who requested that Pilate set a guard around Jesus' tomb? The chief priests and Pharisees.

18. What did the women find when they arrived at the tomb Sunday morning? An empty tomb and an angel.

19. What did Peter and John find when they arrived at the tomb? An empty tomb and the burial clothes neatly folded.

20. What did Mary find when she returned to the tomb? An angel and then the risen Jesus.

21. How did Jesus prove to His disciples who He was when He appeared to them? By showing them His hands and side.

22. What did the chief priests do when they found out Jesus had risen from the dead? They paid the guards to spread the lie that Jesus' disciples had stolen his body.

23. Recite John 19:41-42.

24. What happened on the road to Emmaus? Jesus appeared and talked with two disciples.

25. Where were the disciples the third time Jesus appeared to them? The Sea of Galilee/Tiberius.

26. In addition to the Disciples, to whom did Jesus appear after His resurrection? The two disciples on the road to Emmaus and as many as 500 people at once.

27. What were Jesus' final instructions to the disciples? To go, preach the gospel, make disciples, baptize believers, and teach them to obey what He had taught them.

28. What did Jesus do after appearing to His disciples and others for 40 days? He ascended into heaven to sit at the right hand of the Father.

29. Recite Mark 16:19.

30. What is the Hebrew term for "Anointed One"? Messiah

31. What is the Greek term for "Anointed One"? Christ.

32. Name three prophecies that were fulfilled by Jesus. Jesus was born of a woman, born of a virgin, and born in the city of Bethlehem.

33. Recite John 1:14.

34. Recite John 20:30-31.

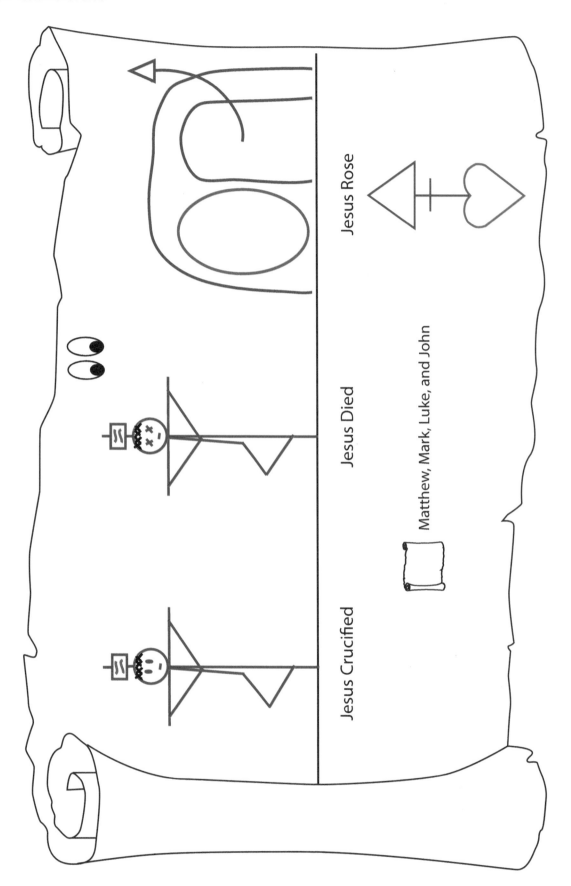

Jesus Rose

Jesus Died

Jesus Crucified

Matthew, Mark, Luke, and John

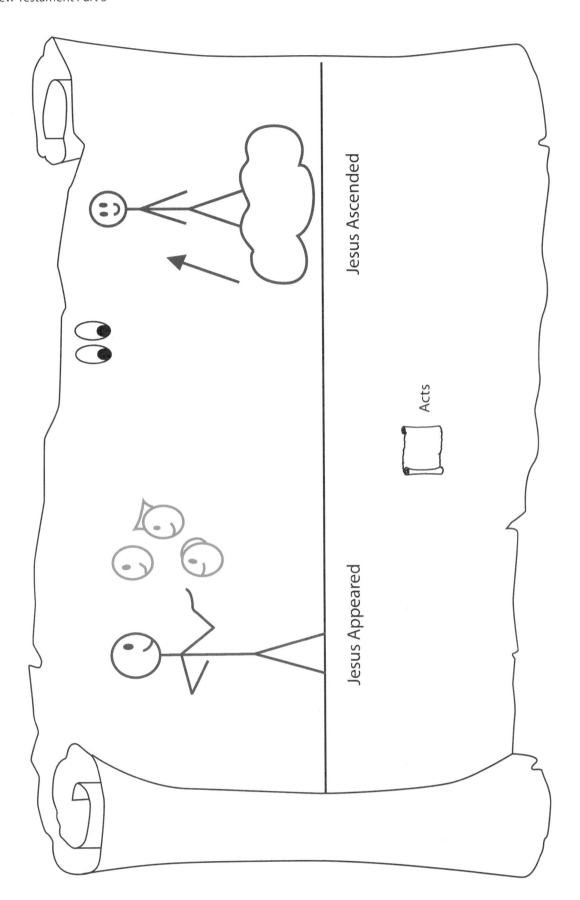

Lesson Goals and Key Points

WAS JESUS THE MESSIAH? PART 2

The goal of this lesson is to demonstrate that Jesus of Nazareth was the promised Messiah.

Key Points:
- Jesus was the Messiah, Hebrew for "the Anointed One."
- Jesus was the Christ, Greek for "the Anointed One."
- Jesus fulfilled all New Testament prophecies regarding the Messiah.
- The New Testament writers documented Jesus' life, death, and resurrection while many of the eyewitnesses to the events were alive.

Memory Verse: John 20:30-31

THE HOLY SPIRIT

The goal of this lesson is to understand what took place at the giving of the Holy Spirit on the day of Pentecost.

Key Points:
- Before Jesus ascended, He commanded His apostles to go to Jerusalem and wait for the gift from the Father.
- While in Jerusalem, the apostles, other disciples, and women met in the upper room for prayer.
- The apostles replaced Judas with a man named Matthais.
- On the Feast of Pentecost, 50 days after the Feast of Passover, when the apostles, other disciples, and women were together in the upper room, the Holy Spirit was given.
- Once filled with the Holy Spirit, the apostles were able to preach in various languages to those gathered for Pentecost

Memory Verse: Acts 1:8

THE EARLY CHURCH

The goal of this lesson lesson is to establish the facts surrounding the growth of the Early Church.

Key Points:
- The early Church began in the upper Room on the day of Pentecost.
- Peter preached on Pentecost, and 3,000 men repented and were baptized.
- The early Church:
    1. Learned the Apostles' doctrine.
    2. Fellowshipped together.

- The early Church continued:
    3. Broke bread together.
    4. Prayed with one another.
    5. Gave to those in need.
    6. Worshipped in the temple.
    7. Added new believers.

Memory Verse: Acts 2:42

THE PERSECUTION

The goal of this lesson is to examine the events associated with the persecution of the Early Church.

Key Points:
- Peter and John were arrested for healing a lame man in the name of Jesus. After being warned not to preach in Jesus' name, they were released.
- Peter and John continued to preach in Jesus' name.
- The apostles were arrested, but an angel released them from prison and they returned to preaching in Jesus' name.
- Stephen was the first recorded martyr of Christianity.

Memory Verse: Acts 7:59

SAUL

The goal of this lesson is to introduce students to the man Saul, also known as Paul.

Key Points:
- Saul was present at the stoning of Stephen.
- Saul was a persecutor of the early Church.
- Jesus appeared to Saul on the road to Damascus, and from that point on Saul believed that Jesus was the Messiah.

Memory Verse: Acts 9:15-16

Middle School

Quest Page

Topical Bible

What is a *parable*?

Nave's, page 352

Bible Dictionary

Define *transgression*.

Zondervan's, page 592

Concordance

Give a Bible verse that refers to "*Messiah* which is the Christ."

John 1:41 (Cruden's, page 318)

Quest Question

Why is it important to know that Jesus of Nazareth fulfilled New Testament prophecy regarding the Messiah?

If Jesus had not fulfilled every prophecy in every detail, He would not have been the Messiah.

Timeline Review

| Jesus Died | Jesus Rose | Jesus Appeared | Jesus Ascended |

Memory Verse Review

John 1:14

Mark 16:19

John 19:41-42

Luke 23:46

Memory Work: The Apostles' Creed: Born of the Virgin Mary,

Was Jesus the Messiah Part 2

Memory Verse: John 20:30-31

Messiah

Discuss Messiah: The word Messiah is a Hebrew word and means the "anointed one."

Write and have students write: Messiah Hebrew for Anointed One.

Messiah

Hebrew for

Anointed One

Christ

Greek for

Anointed One

Christ

Discuss Christ: The word Christ is a Greek word and means the "anointed one."

Write and have students write: Christ Greek for Anointed One.

Look up the following words in a Bible Dictionary:

parable

rejected

accused

garment

transgressor

pierced

Healed the Sick, Spoke in Parables, Rejected by the People

Read aloud: Isaiah 53:4; Matthew 8:15-17; Psalm 78:2; Matthew 13:34-35; Psalm 118:22-23; Matthew 21:42-46

Discuss Healed the Sick, Spoke in Parables, Rejected by the People: Jesus healed the sick, lame, deaf, and mute just as Isaiah foretold. Jesus taught by using parables. Even though Jesus performed miracles and spoke the truth, many still rejected Him as Messiah.

Chart and have students chart: Jesus healing, Jesus telling a parable, and a man rejecting Jesus.

Completed Student Page

Teacher Notes:

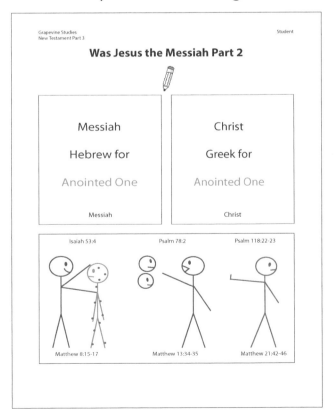

Falsely Accused

Read aloud: Psalm 27:12; Matthew 26:60

Discuss Falsely Accused: The Old Testament prophesied that the Messiah would be falsely accused.

Draw and have students draw: Jesus in chains.

Garments Divided

Read aloud: Psalm 22:18; Luke 23:34

Discuss Garments Divided: The Old Testament prophesied that the Messiah's garments would be divided.

Draw and have students draw: A Roman soldier holding a garment and straw.

Numbered Among Transgressors

Read aloud: Isaiah 53:12; Luke 23:32-33

Discuss Numbered Among Transgressors: The Old Testament prophesied that the Messiah would be numbered among criminals.

Draw and have students draw: Jesus with a criminal.

Teacher Notes

Completed Student Page

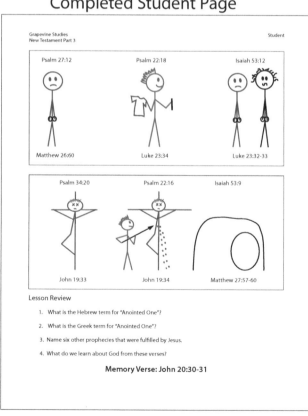

No Bones Broken

Read aloud: Psalm 34:20; John 19:33

Discuss No Bones Broken: The Old Testament prophesied that no bones of the Messiah would be broken.

Draw and have students draw: Jesus on the cross.

Pierced

Read aloud: Psalm 22:16; John 19:34

Discuss Pierced: Jesus' body was pierced after His death.

Draw and have students draw: Jesus, dead on the cross, as a Roman soldier pierced His side.

Connected with the Rich in Death

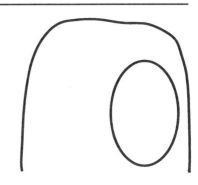

Read aloud: Isaiah 53:9; Matthew 27:57-60

Discuss Born in Bethlehem: Jesus was buried in the new tomb of Joseph of Arimathea, who was a rich man.

Draw and have students draw: A new tomb.

Lesson Review:

1. What is the Hebrew term for "Anointed One"? Messiah

2. What is the Greek term for "Anointed One"? Christ.

3. Name other prophecies that were fulfilled by Jesus. Jesus healed the sick, spoke in parables, was rejected by others, was falsely accused, His garments were divided, He was numbered among transgressors, none of His bones were broken, He was pierced, and his burial was connected with the rich.

4. What do we learn about God from these verses? Jesus fulfilled Old Testament prophecies about the Messiah.

Memory Verse: John 20:30-31

Early Elementary and Elementary

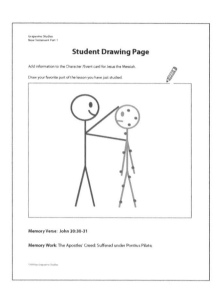

Add information to the Jesus the Messiah Card:

- Record the other important fulfillments you deem important to your students.

Memory Verse: John 20:30-31

Memory Work: The Apostles' Creed: Suffered under Pontius Pilate,

Middle School

The Holy Spirit

Topical Bible

What do you learn about the *tongues of fire*?

Nave's, page 489

Bible Dictionary

Who is the *Holy Spirit*?

Zondervan's, page 231

Concordance

Give three verses in which *tongues* are mentioned.

Answers will vary. (Cruden's, page 506)

Quest Question

What is the role of the Holy Spirit in the life of a believer? Give Scriptural references to defend your answers.

Scriptures and answers will vary.

Timeline Review

Jesus Died   Jesus Rose   Jesus Appeared   Jesus Ascended

Teacher Note: The timeline review is the same as the last lesson because we have two lessons on Jesus the Messiah.

Memory Verse Review

John 20:30-31

John 1:14

John 19:41-42

Luke 23:46

Memory Work: The Apostles' Creed: Suffered under Pontius Pilate,

The Holy Spirit

Memory Verse: Acts 1:8

The Command

Read aloud: Acts 1:1-11

Discuss The Command: Before Jesus ascended into heaven, He commanded the apostles to wait in Jerusalem until they received the promise from the Father. After they received this promise, they would be His witnesses throughout all the earth.

Map: Label the city of Jerusalem.

Draw and have students draw: Jesus telling his followers to wait and be a witness for Him.

The Upper Room

Read aloud: Acts 1:12-14

Discuss The Upper Room: In obedience to Jesus' command, the apostles, the women, Jesus' mother, and Jesus' brothers returned to Jerusalem and gathered in the Upper Room to pray.

Draw and have students draw: A man worshipping and a woman praying in the Upper Room.

Look up the following words in a Bible Dictionary:

promise

baptize

lots

one accord

tongues

devout

Choosing a New Apostle

Read aloud: Acts 1:15-22

Discuss Choosing a New Apostle: While in Jerusalem awaiting the promise of God, the apostles decided to replace Judas. The qualifications for the new apostle would be that the man had been with them from the time of Jesus' baptism and had been a witness of His resurrection.

Draw and have students draw: John baptizing Jesus with an arrow pointing to the tomb with the resurrection arrow coming out.

Matthias

Read aloud: Acts 1:23-26

Discuss Matthias: The apostles drew lots between two men, Justus and Matthais, to become one of the twelve apostles.

Draw and have students draw: Two apostles casting lots.

Completed Student Page

Teacher Notes:

The Holy Spirit

Read aloud: Acts 2:1-4

Discuss The Holy Spirit: On the day of Pentecost (Lev. 23:15-22 Feast of Pentecost/Weeks), when they (apostles, Disciples, and the women) were in the upper room and all in one accord, they were filled with the Holy Spirit and spoke in other tongues as the Spirit enabled them.

Draw and have students draw: Men and women with tongues of fire above them and the Holy Spirit (purple bird) coming.

Teacher Notes

Completed Student Page

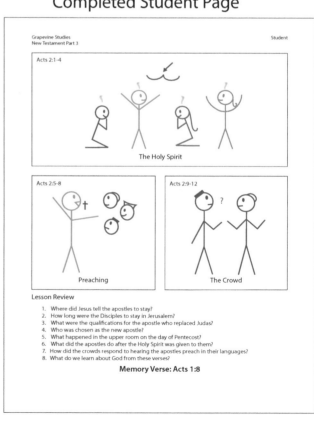

Preaching

Read aloud: Acts 2:5-8

Discuss Preaching: The apostles began to preach in the native languages of those gathered in Jerusalem from all over the known world to celebrate the Feast of Pentecost/Weeks.

Draw and have students draw: An apostle preaching.

The Crowd

Read aloud: Acts 2:9-12

Discuss The Crowd: When these men heard the apostles preaching in their native languages, they marveled and asked what this meant.

Draw and have students draw: Two men questioning one another.

Lesson Review

1. Where did Jesus tell the apostles to stay? Jerusalem.

2. How long were the Disciples to stay in Jerusalem? Until they received the gift from the Father.

3. What were the qualifications for the apostle who replaced Judas? He had to be a witness of Jesus' baptism and His resurrection.

4. Who was chosen as the new apostle? Matthais.

5. What happened in the upper room on the day of Pentecost? The Holy Spirit came upon the people in the room in the form of tongues of fire.

6. What did the apostles do after the Holy Spirit was given to them? They preached to those in Jerusalem.

7. How did the crowds respond to hearing the apostles preach in their languages? They were amazed and asked what it meant.

8. What do we learn about God from these verses? When the Holy Spirit was given, He indwelt and empowered the apostles to fulfill what Jesus had commissioned them to do.

Memory Verse: Acts 1:8

Early Elementary and Elementary

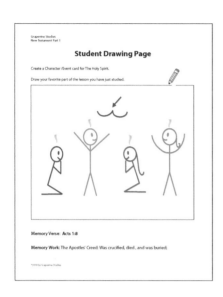

Information for the Holy Spirit card:

- Jesus commanded the Apostles to go to Jerusalem where they would receive a gift from the Father.
- The Apostles, women, and other disciples prayed in the Upper Room.
- On Pentecost, the Holy Spirit came on all those in the Upper Room.
- After being filled with the Holy Spirit, the Apostles preached to those in Jerusalem in their own native languages

Memory Verse: Acts 1:8

Memory Work: The Apostles' Creed: Was crucified, died , and was buried;

Middle School

The Early Church

Topical Bible

What is the *Church*?

Nave's, page 83

Bible Dictionary

Define *repentance*.

Zondervan's, page 495

Concordance

Give two verses in which you find the word *believers*.

Acts 5:14 and I Timothy 4:12 (Cruden's, page 30)

Quest Question

What actions should mark a believer?

Study of God's Word, fellowship, baptism, communion, prayer, giving, and worship. Acts 2:41-47.

Timeline Review

Jesus Rose   Jesus Appeared   Jesus Ascended   The Holy Spirit

Memory Verse Review

Acts 1:8

John 20:30-31

John 1:14

John 19:41-42

Memory Work: The Apostles' Creed: Was crucified, died , and was buried;

The Early Church

Memory Verse: Acts 2:42

Passover in Jerusalem

Read aloud: Acts 2:5-8, 12-36

Discuss Passover in Jerusalem: On the day of Pentecost, after the Holy Spirit had filled the believers in the upper room, the apostles began to preach to the men in Jerusalem. Peter stood up and reminded the men present of the promises of the New Testament concerning the Christ and revealed that Jesus was the Christ.

Draw and have students draw: Peter preaching to men from different countries.

Look up the following words in a Bible Dictionary:

Hades

repent

remission

doctrine

saved

The Response

Read aloud: Acts 2:37-40

Discuss The Response: When the men in Jerusalem heard Peter's message, they asked what they should do. Peter responded by calling them to repent and be baptized in the name of Jesus Christ, and as a result they would receive the Holy Spirit.

Draw and have students draw: A man praying.

The Baptisms

Read aloud: Acts 2:41

Discuss The Baptisms: After hearing Peter's message, many of the men of Jerusalem repented, and that day 3,000 of them were baptized.

Draw and have students draw: A new believer being baptized.

Completed Student Page

Teacher Notes:

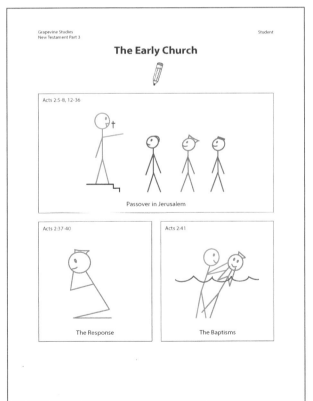

Apostles' Doctrine

Read aloud: Acts 2:42-47

Discuss Apostles' Doctrine: The early church were taught by the apostles.

Draw and have students draw: An apostle teaching a man.

Fellowship

Discuss Fellowship: It was important for the early church to get together for fellowship.

Draw and have students draw: Two women talking.

Broke Bread Together

Discuss Broke Bread Together: The early church broke bread together.

Draw and have students draw: Broken bread.

Teacher Notes

Completed Student Page

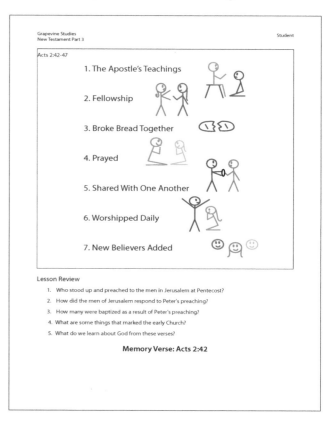

Prayed

Discuss Prayed: The early church prayed individually and together.

Draw and have students draw: Two people praying.

Gave and Shared

Discuss Gave and Shared: It was important for the early church to help those in need in the church.

Draw and have students draw: A man giving something to another man.

Worshipped

Discuss Worshipped: The early church met often at the temple to worship together.

Draw and have students draw: Two people worshipping.

New Believers Added

Discuss New Believers Added: The early church grew quickly.

Draw and have students draw: New believers.

Lesson Review:

1. Who stood up and preached to the men in Jerusalem at Pentecost? Peter and the apostles.

2. How did the men of Jerusalem respond to Peter's preaching? They were "cut to the heart" and wanted to know what they should do.

3. How many were baptized as a result of Peter's preaching? 3,000.

4. What are some things that marked the early Church? They continued in the Apostles' doctrine, fellowship, breaking of bread, prayer, giving, and worship, and new believers were added to the Church every day.

5. What do we learn about God from these verses? God changes men's lives through the Word and through believers.

Memory Verse: Acts 2:42

Early Elementary and Elementary

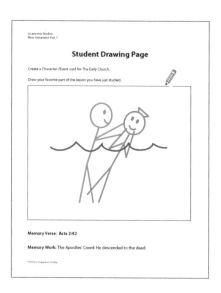

Add to The Early Church card:

- The Church began on the day of Pentecost when the Holy Spirit was given to believers in the Upper Room.

- The Early Church
  1. Learned the Apostles' doctrine.
  2. Fellowshipped.
  3. Broke bread together.
  4. Prayed for one another.
  5. Gave to those in need.
  6. Worshipped in Temple.
  7. New believers were added.

Memory Verse: Acts 2:42

Memory Work: The Apostles' Creed: He descended to the dead.

Middle School

The Persecution

Topical Bible

What does *preaching* mean?

Nave's, page 379

Bible Dictionary

Under what condition would someone be punished by *stoning*?

Zondervan's, page 567

Concordance

If you were researching *persecution* against the Church, in what verse would you begin?

Acts 8:1 (Cruden's, page 362)

Quest Question

Give an example of someone who has given his life because of his faith in Jesus.

Teachers, please encourage your students to become more aware of the persecution against Christians going on throughout the world today. Voice of the Martyrs is a good resource.

Timeline Review

Jesus Appeared   Jesus Ascended   The Holy Spirit   The Early Church

Memory Verse Review

Acts 2:42

Acts 1:8

John 20:30-31

John 1:14

Memory Work: The Apostles' Creed: He descended to the dead.

The Persecution

Memory Verse: Acts 7:59

The Lame Man Was Healed

Read aloud: Acts 3:1-8

Discuss The Lame Man Was Healed: One day, as Peter and John went to the temple at the hour of prayer, they encountered a man lame from birth. Instead of giving him alms, they healed in the name of Jesus Christ. The man then went into the temple leaping and praising God.

Draw and have students draw: A man jumping for joy after being healed.

Peter Preached

Read aloud: Acts 3:9-16

Discuss Peter Preached: When the people saw the lame man healed, they were amazed. Peter then took the opportunity to tell the people about Jesus and how faith in Jesus had healed the lame man.

Draw and have students draw: Peter preaching to a group of people.

Look up the following words in a Bible Dictionary:

lame

alms

Sadducees

Peter and John Were Arrested

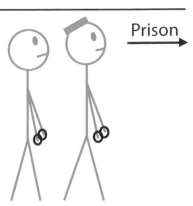

Read aloud: Acts 4:1-14

Discuss Peter and John Were Arrested: After the religious leaders heard the sermon Peter had preached, they had Peter and John arrested because they spoke of the resurrection of Jesus. When Peter and John were questioned, the leaders were amazed with their answers. The religious leaders also remembered these men had been with Jesus.

Draw and have students draw: Peter and John in chains.

Peter and John Were Released

Read aloud: Acts 4:18-31

Discuss Peter and John Were Released: The religious leaders released Peter and John but commanded them not to speak in the name of Jesus. Peter and John stated that they must obey God. After their release they prayed for courage, boldness, and opportunity.

Draw and have students draw: Two men praying with the Holy Spirit over them.

Completed Student Page

Teacher Notes:

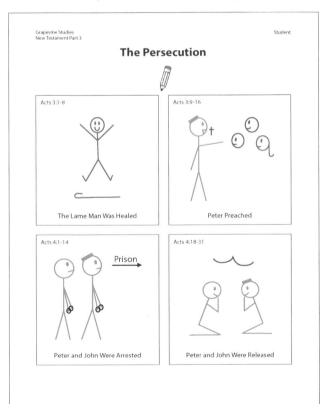

The Apostles Were Arrested

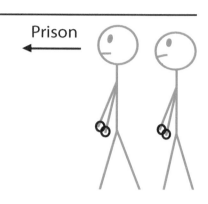

Prison

Read aloud: Acts 5:12-18

Discuss The Apostles Were Arrested: The apostles continued to preach the gospel, heal the sick, and perform miracles, which led the religious leaders to put them in prison.

Draw and have students draw: Two apostles going to prison.

The Angel

Read aloud: Acts 5:19-20

Discuss The Angel: That night, an angel of the Lord went to the prison where the apostles were being held and released them. The angel told them to return to the temple and teach the people.

Write and have students write: An angel at the prison door.

Teacher Notes

Completed Student Page

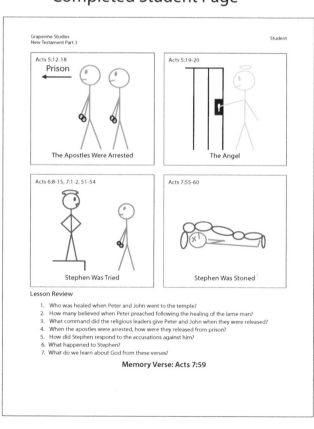

Stephen was Tried

Read aloud: Acts 6:8-15, 7:1-2, 51-54

Discuss Stephen was Tried: Stephen was great in faith and was being used of God. Stephen's enemies falsely accused him and had him arrested. When he was on trial he gave a speech showing that Jesus was the Christ. Stephen then pointed out the sins of the religious leaders, which made them very angry.

Draw and have students draw: Stephen in chains before a priest.

Stephen was Stoned

Read aloud: Acts 7:55-60

Discuss The Crowd: After Stephen's speech, the religious leaders stoned Stephen to death.

Draw and have students draw: Stephen dead under a pile of stones.

Lesson Review

1. Who was healed when Peter and John went to the temple? A man lame from birth.

2. How many believed when Peter preached following the healing of the lame man? 5,000.

3. What command did the religious leaders give Peter and John when they were released? Not to speak or teach in Jesus' name.

4. When the apostles were arrested, how were they released from prison? An angel of the Lord released them.

5. How did Stephen respond to the accusations against him? He reminded the religious leaders of the prophecies concerning the Messiah and then pointed out their failure to recognize that these prophecies had been fulfilled in Jesus.

6. What happened to Stephen? He was falsely accused and stoned to death.

7. What do we learn about God from these verses? God takes care of His people, whether it is in life or in death.

Memory Verse: Acts 7:59

Early Elementary and Elementary

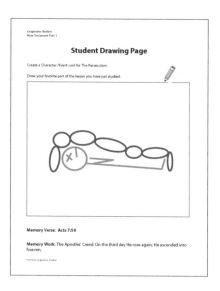

Middle School

Topical Bible

What is *Tarsus*?

Nave's, page 473

Bible Dictionary

Define the term *Christian*.

Zondervan's, page 108

Concordance

What is the first mention of the term *Christian* in the Bible?

Acts 11:26 (Cruden's, page 72)

Quest Question

What are some of the various ways that God draws people to Himself?

Answers will vary. Christian family and friends, preaching, the Word of God, or direct contact with the living God as in Paul's case.

Information for The Persecution card:

- Peter and John were arrested for healing a lame man in the name of Jesus. After warning Peter and John not to preach in Jesus' name, they were released.
- Peter and John continued to preach in Jesus' name.
- The Apostles were arrested but an angel released them from prison and they returned to preaching in Jesus' name.
- Stephen was the first recorded martyr of Christianity.

Memory Verse: Acts 7:59

Memory Work: On the third day He rose again; He ascended into heaven,

Saul

Timeline Review

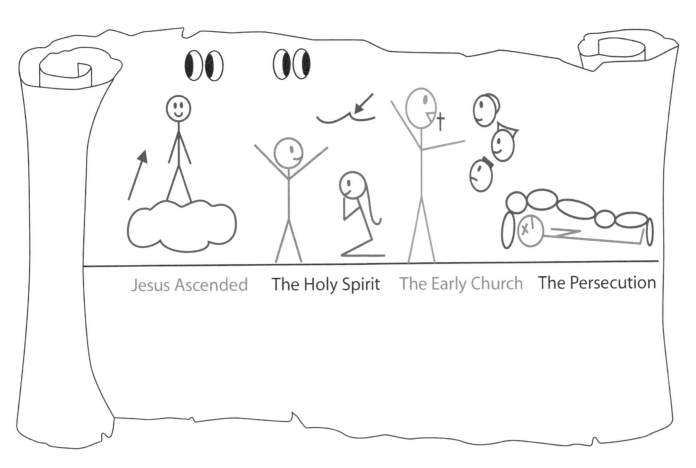

Jesus Ascended   The Holy Spirit   The Early Church   The Persecution

Memory Verse Review

Acts 7:59

Acts 2:42

Acts 1:8

John 20:30-31

Memory Work: On the third day He rose again; He ascended into heaven,

Saul

Memory Verse: Acts 9:15-16

Saul at Stephen's Death

Read aloud: Acts 7:57-60

Discuss Saul at Stephen's Death: Saul was present at the stoning of Stephen. He watched over the coats of those who were stoning Stephen.

Draw and have students draw: Saul standing with two coats on the ground.

Saul Persecuted the Church

Read aloud: Acts 8:1-4

Discuss Saul Persecuted the Church: The death of Stephen marked an escalation in the persecution of the Church. Saul joined in actively persecuting the Church, which caused the believers to scatter throughout the area. They preached the Gospel wherever they went.

Draw and have students draw: Saul pointing to a man and woman who are running away.

Look up the following words in a Bible Dictionary:

The Way

Hellenists

Christian

Jesus Spoke to Saul

Read aloud: Acts 9:1-8

Discuss Jesus Spoke to Saul: Saul's pursuit of believers pointed him to Damascus. Saul began a journey that would forever change his life. On the road to Damascus, the Lord Jesus Christ appeared to Saul and convinced him that Jesus was the Messiah. The appearance left Saul blind so that he had to be led into Damascus by his traveling companions.

Draw and have students draw: Jesus appearing to Saul.

Ananias

Read aloud: Acts 9:9-16

Discuss Ananias: After entering Damascus, Saul fasted for three days. The Lord appeared to Ananias and told him to pray for Saul. The Lord assured him that Saul was indeed chosen by God for a special assignment.

Draw and have students draw: Jesus speaking to Ananias about Saul.

Completed Student Page

Teacher Notes:

Saul Was Baptized

Read aloud: Acts 9:17-19

Discuss Saul Was Baptized: Ananias prayed for Saul. Saul received his sight and was baptized. Saul then remained in Damascus with the disciples there.

Draw and have students draw: Saul being baptized.

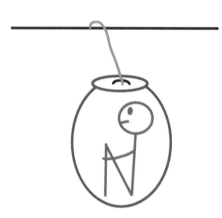

Saul Escaped

Read aloud: Acts 9:20-25

Discuss Saul Escaped: After Saul was baptized, he immediately began to preach that Jesus was the Christ to the Jews in the synagogue. The Jews were amazed by what he said and could not disprove what Saul said in regard to Jesus being the Messiah. The Jews then sought to kill Saul, but the disciples helped him to escape the city.

Write and have students write: Saul hiding in a basket.

Teacher Notes

Completed Student Page

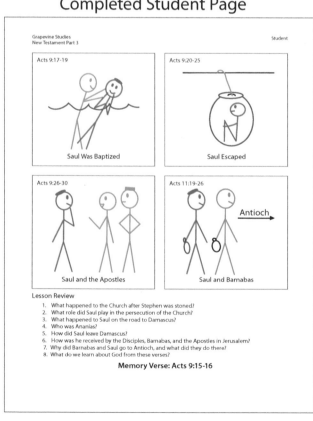

Saul and the Apostles

Read aloud: Acts 9:26-30

Discuss Saul and the Apostles: Saul returned from Damascus to Jerusalem, where he attempted to unite with believers. The Disciples were skeptical of his conversion, but a Disciple named Barnabas took Saul to the apostles. Saul remained in Jerusalem and preached to the Jews. When Saul's life was in danger he was sent to Tarsus.

Draw and have students draw: Saul talking to the Apostles.

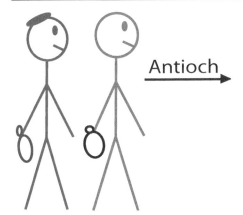

Saul and Barnabas

Read aloud: Acts 11:19-26

Discuss Saul and Barnabas: When the Church was scattered by persecution, some of the believers settled in Antioch and preached the Gospel. Many people believed. When word reached Jerusalem, Barnabas and Saul were chosen to go to Antioch and verify the account. Barnabas and Saul remained in Antioch for a year.

Draw and have students draw: Saul and Barnabas walking to Antioch.

Lesson Review

1. **What happened to the Church after Stephen was stoned?** The Church entered a time of persecution, which caused the believers to scatter and preach the gospel in new areas.
2. **What role did Saul play in the persecution of the Church?** Saul was one of the main persecutors of the early Church.
3. **What happened to Saul on the road to Damascus?** The Lord appeared to Saul, and he was struck blind and believed that Jesus was the Messiah.
4. **Who was Ananias?** A believer from Damascus. The Lord spoke to him, and he prayed for Saul to receive his sight. Saul's sight was restored.
5. **How did Saul leave Damascus?** In a basket which was let down over the city wall.
6. **How was he received by the Disciples, Barnabas, and the Apostles in Jerusalem?** The Disciples doubted his conversion, while Barnabas and the apostles believed that Saul had truly become a believer.
7. **Why did Barnabas and Saul go to Antioch, and what did they do there?** They went to verify the fact that many Jews had become believers there, and they stayed to teach the people.
8. **What do we learn about God from these verses?** God can use persecution to move believers and to spread the Gospel.

Memory Verse: Acts 9:15-16

Early Elementary and Elementary

Student Drawing Page

Information for the Jesus Prayed card:

- Saul was present at the stoning of Stephen.

- Saul was a persecutor of the early Church.

- Jesus appeared to Saul on the road to Damascus, and from that point on Saul believed that Jesus was the Messiah.

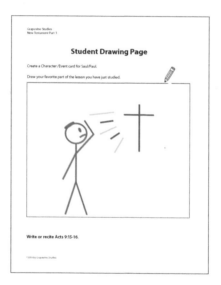

Memory Verse: Acts 9:15-16

Final Review

1. Who carried the cross for Jesus? Simon of Cyrene.

2. What inscription did Pilate have put above Jesus? Jesus of Nazareth, the King of the Jews.

3. What happened to Jesus at Golgotha? He was crucified.

4. What did Jesus ask the Father to do to those who crucified Him? Forgive them.

5. Who cast lots for Jesus' tunic? The soldiers who crucified Him.

6. What did the crowd do to Jesus while He was on the cross? They mocked Him.

7. What did Jesus promise the repentant thief on the cross? He would be with Jesus that day in Paradise.

8. Recite Luke 23:33.

9. Whom did Jesus tell to take care of His mother? John.

10. What three things happened at the death of Jesus? (1) The temple veil was torn in two, (2) an earthquake struck, and (3) the graves of the saints were opened and they appeared to many.

11. Upon His death had Jesus completed the work given to Him by God the Father? Yes.

12. Who proclaimed at Jesus' death that He was the "Son of God"? The centurion.

13. Why did the soldier pierce Jesus' side? To make sure He was dead.

14. Recite Luke 23:46.

15. Who buried Jesus? Joseph of Arimathea and Nicodemus.

16. Where was Jesus buried? In Joseph of Arimathea's new tomb in a garden near the place of the crucifixion.

17. Who requested that Pilate set a guard around Jesus' tomb? The chief priests and Pharisees.

18. What did the women find when they arrived at the tomb Sunday morning? An empty tomb and an angel.

19. What did Peter and John find when they arrived at the tomb? An empty tomb and the burial clothes neatly folded.

20. What did Mary find when she returned to the tomb? An angel and then the risen Jesus.

21. How did Jesus prove to His Disciples who He was when He appeared to them? By showing them His hands and side.

22. What did the chief priests do when they found out Jesus had risen from the dead? They paid the guards to spread the lie that Jesus' Disciples had stolen his body.

23. Recite John 19:41-42.

24. What happened on the road to Emmaus? Jesus appeared and talked with two Disciples.

25. Where were the Disciples the third time Jesus appeared to them? The Sea of Galilee/Tiberius.

26. In addition to the Disciples, to whom did Jesus appear after His resurrection? The two Disciples on the road to Emmaus and as many as 500 people at once.

27. What were Jesus' final instructions to the Disciples? To go, preach the gospel, make Disciples, baptize believers, and teach them to obey what He had taught them.

28. What did Jesus do after appearing to His Disciples and others for 40 days? He ascended into heaven to sit at the right hand of the Father.

29. Recite Mark 16:19.

30. What is the Hebrew term for "Anointed One"? Messiah

31. What is the Greek term for "Anointed One"? Christ.

32. Name five prophecies that were fulfilled by Jesus. Jesus was born of a woman, born of a virgin, born in the city of Bethlehem, Jesus healed the sick, spoke in parables, was rejected by others, was falsely accused, His garments were divided, He was numbered among transgressors, none of His bones were broken, He was pierced, and his burial was connected with the rich in burial.

33. Recite John 1:14.

34. Recite John 20:30-31.

35. Where did Jesus tell the apostles to stay? Jerusalem.

36. How long were the Disciples to stay in Jerusalem? Until they received the gift from the Father.

37. What were the qualifications for the apostle who replaced Judas? He had to be a witness of Jesus' baptism and His resurrection.

38. Who was chosen as the new apostle? Matthias.

39. What happened in the upper room on the day of Pentecost? The Holy Spirit came upon the people in the room in the form of tongues of fire.

40. What did the apostles do after the Holy Spirit was given to them? They preached to those in Jerusalem.

41. How did the crowds respond to hearing the apostles preach in their languages? They were amazed and asked what it meant.

42. Recite Acts 1:8.

43. Who stood up and preached to the men in Jerusalem at Pentecost? Peter and the apostles.

44. How did the men of Jerusalem respond to Peter's preaching? They were "cut to the heart" and wanted to know what they should do.

45. How many were baptized as a result of Peter's preaching? 3,000.

46. What are some things that marked the early Church? They continued in the Apostles' doctrine, fellowship, breaking of bread, prayer, giving, and worship, and new believers were added to the Church every day.

47. Recite Acts 2:42.

48. Who was healed when Peter and John went to the temple? A man lame from birth.

49. How many believed when Peter preached following the healing of the lame man? 5,000.

50. What command did the religious leaders give Peter and John when they were released? Not to speak or teach in Jesus' name.

51. When the apostles were arrested, how were they released from prison? An angel of the Lord released them.

52. How did Stephen respond to the accusations against him? He reminded the religious leaders of the prophecies concerning the Messiah and then pointed out their failure to recognize that these prophecies had been fulfilled in Jesus.

53. What happened to Stephen? He was falsely accused and stoned to death.

54. Recite Acts 7:59.

55. What happened to the Church after Stephen was stoned? The Church entered a time of persecution, which caused the believers to scatter and preach the gospel into new areas.

56. **What role did Saul play in the persecution of the Church?** Saul was one of the main persecutors of the early Church.

57. **What happened to Saul on the road to Damascus?** The Lord appeared to Saul, and he was struck blind and believed that Jesus was the Messiah.

58. **Who was Ananias?** A believer from Damascus. The Lord spoke to him, and he prayed for Saul to receive his sight. Saul's sight was restored.

59. **How did Saul leave Damascus?** In a basket which was let down over the city wall.

60. **How was he received by the Disciples, Barnabas, and the Apostles in Jerusalem?** The Disciples doubted his conversion, while Barnabas and the apostles believed that Saul had truly become a believer.

61. **Why did Barnabas and Saul go to Antioch, and what did they do there?** They went to verify the fact that many Jews had become believers there, and they stayed to teach the people.

62. Recite Acts 9:15-16.

For Early Elementary and Elementary Levels:

63. **How many books are in the Bible?** 66.

64. **In what language was the New Testament written?** Greek.

65. **Name the Gospels.** Matthew, Mark, Luke, and John.

66. **Name the Book of Church History.** Acts.

67. **Name the Epistles?** Romans, I & II Corinthians, Galatians, Ephesians, Philippians, Colossians, I & II Thessalonians, I & II Timothy, Titus, Philemon, Hebrews, James, I & II Peter, I, II, & III John, Jude and Revelation.

68. **Name the Twelve Apostles:** Andrew, Simon (Peter), Phillip, Matthew (Levi), James, John, Bartholomew, Thomas, James (Son of Alhpaeus), Lebbaueus, Simon (the Canaanite), and Judas Iscariot.

69. **Recite the first part of the Apostles Creed.**

I believe in God, the Father Almighty,
Creator of heaven and earth.
I believe in Jesus Christ, God's only Son, our Lord,
Who was conceived by the Holy Spirit,
Born of the Virgin Mary,
Suffered under Pontius Pilate,
Was crucified, died, was buried;
On the third day He rose again;
He ascended into heaven,

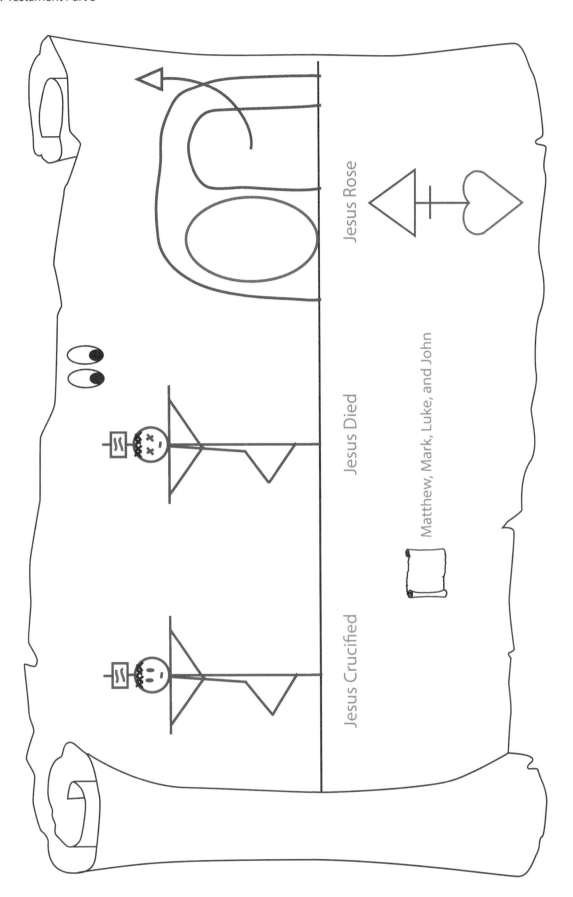

Jesus Rose

Jesus Died

Jesus Crucified

Matthew, Mark, Luke, and John

The Apostles' Creed

I believe in God, the Father Almighty,

Creator of heaven and earth.

I believe in Jesus Christ, God's only Son, our Lord,

Who was conceived by the Holy Spirit,

Born of the Virgin Mary,

Suffered under Pontius Pilate,

Was crucified, died, was buried;

On the third day He rose again;

He ascended into heaven,

He is seated at the right hand of the Father,

and He will come again to judge the living and the dead.

I believe in the Holy Spirit,

the holy catholic church,

the communion of saints,

the forgiveness of sins,

the resurrection of the body,

and life everlasting.
Amen.

Map

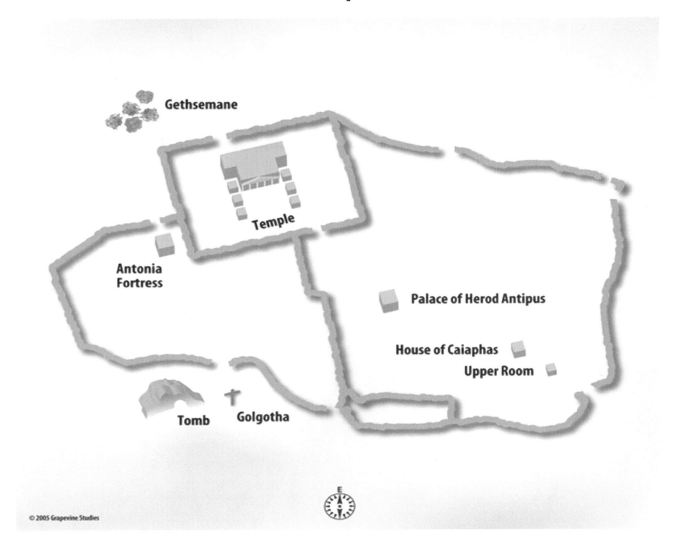

Review:

    1. The Upper Room.

    2. Gethsemane.

    3. House of Caiaphas.

    4. The Temple.

    5. Palace of Herod Antipas.

    6. The Antonia Fortress.

Label:

    1. The hill of Golgotha.

    2. The Tomb of Jesus.

Page intentionally left blank

New Testament Overview

~

Part 4

Paul: God changed Saul's name to Paul, and through Paul the gospel spread to the Gentiles. Paul helped to start many of the early churches. Many of his letters to those churches are in the New Testament.

Draw and have students draw: We use the same picture for Saul and Paul.

God

The Church

Letters to the Churches: Many of the books of the New Testament are letters written to Churches established by the eleven apostles and Paul. These letters cover a great number of topics related to living the Christian life.

Draw and have students draw: An envelope indicating the letter is from God to The Church.

The Eyes: After the Ascension of Jesus we change the eyes. One set of eyes looks back to His first coming. The second set of eyes looks forward to His second coming.

Draw and have students draw: A set of eyes looking back and a set of eyes looking forward.

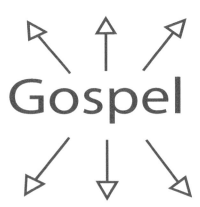

The Gospel: After the giving of the Holy Spirit, the Church continued to grow and will eventually spread throughout the world.

Draw and have students draw: Write the word Gospel and have arrows around it going out, representing the Gospel going out.

My notes:

Completed Student Page

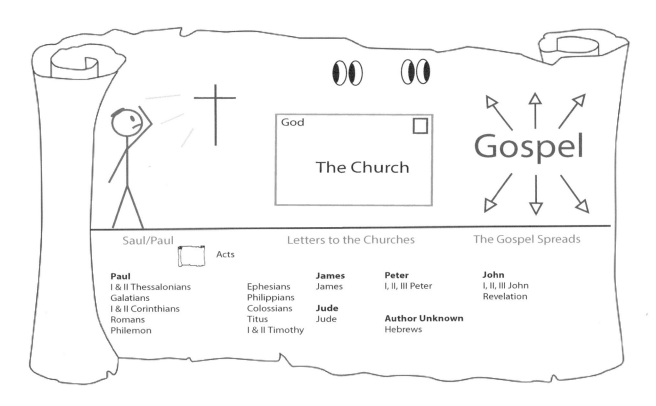

Note to Teachers: There is much debate about the events recorded in the book of Revelation. I have purposely left this timeline as open as we can to enable you, the teacher, to give your perspective on the events recorded in this book.

Great Tribulation

The Great Tribulation: There is a time of great tribulation marked by three judgments: the seven seal judgments, seven trumpet judgments, and the seven bowl judgments.

Write and have students write: Great Tribulation.

Jesus Returns: At the end of the Great Tribulation Jesus will return to earth. When He returns, every eye will see Him! Jesus will return riding on a white horse.

Draw and have students draw: Jesus on a cloud, with an arrow pointing down, showing His return.

My Notes:

Millennium

The Millennium: At the beginning of the millennium, Satan will be chained to the bottomless pit and will be unchained at the end of the millennium. The millennium is a 1,000-year period of time in which Jesus reigns sovereign.

Draw and have students draw: Satan chained, then unchained with the word Millennium written between the two Satan drawings.

My Notes:

Completed Student Page

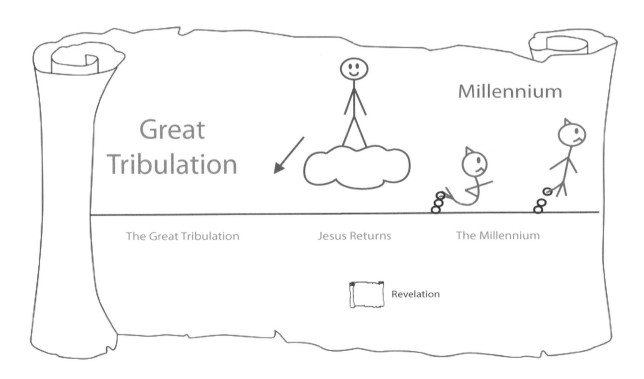

The Judgment: At the White Throne Judgment, all mankind will kneel before God and be judged.

Draw and have students draw: Men from every tribe, nation and language kneeling before God.

Hell: Hell was originally designed as a place of judgment for the devil and his angels, but it will also contain those who have rejected Jesus the Messiah.

Draw and have students draw: Satan in hell.

My Notes:

Heaven: Heaven awaits those who have put their faith and trust in Jesus the Messiah . Finally, heaven will be a place where God dwells among His people.

Draw and have students draw: A man worshipping God from heaven.

My Notes:

Completed Student Page

Lesson Goals and Key Points

PAUL

The goal of this lesson is to see what happened to Saul and how he became known as Paul.

Key Points:
- Saul and Paul are the same man.
- Paul's mission in life was to preach the Gospel to the Gentiles, the Jews, and kings.
- Paul wrote many of the New Testament epistles.

Memory Verse: Acts 9:15-16

LETTERS TO THE CHURCHES

The goal of these lessons is for the students to see that in the fullness of time God sent His Son into the world.

Key Points:
- The New Testament epistles/letters were written to Churches and individuals.
- The epistles were meant to correct, encourage, exhort, and teach.
- There are twenty-two New Testament epistles.
- Paul wrote thirteen of the epistles.

Memory Verse: II Timothy 4:7-8 & Romans 15:4

THE GOSPEL

The goal of this lesson is to show how the Gospel can be taught with stick figures and Scripture.

Key Points:
- The main points of the Gospel are:
  1. Creation
  2. Sin
  3. The Promise
  4. The Messiah
  5. Sinless Life
  6. Died
  7. Buried
  8. Rose
  9. Ascended
  10. Restored
  11. Coming Again
  12. Judgment

Memory Verse: Matthew 24:14

SHARING THE GOSPEL

The goal of this lesson is to learn a simple method for sharing the Gospel and to learn ways that believers can grow in their faith.

Key Points:

- The main points of understanding the Gospel are:
    1. I am a sinner.
    2. Jesus died for me.
    3. I need to repent.
    4. I can receive God's forgiveness.

- I can grow in my faith by:
    1. Learning and obeying the Bible.
    2. Fellowshipping with other believers.
    3. Praying.
    4. Celebrating communion.
    5. Being baptized.
    6. Sharing the Gospel

Memory Verse: James 1:22

NOTES

Page intentionally left blank

Middle School

Quest Page
Topical Bible

Names were important in Bible times, and their meanings often described the person. What does the name *Barnabas* mean?

Nave's, page 49

Bible Dictionary

What do the names *Saul* and *Paul* mean?

Zondervan's, page 526 and 437

Concordance

In what verse do we find Saul first being called Paul?

Acts 13:9 (Cruden's, page 356)

Quest Question

How should Christians view suffering for the name of Jesus?

Answers will vary, but I recommend a word study on biblical references to suffering.

Paul

Memory Verse: II Timothy 4:7-8

Paul's Mission

Read aloud: Acts 9:15

 Jews

 Kings

 Gentiles

Discuss Paul's Mission: When God spoke to Ananias regarding Paul, the Lord told him that Paul would bear His name to the Gentiles, to kings, and to the Jews. God also said Paul would suffer for His name.

Draw and have students draw: Paul preaching Jesus (purple cross) to the Jews, kings, and Gentiles.

Saul and Paul

Saul = Paul

Read aloud: Acts 13:9

Discuss Zacharias and the Angel: At this time in history it was not uncommon to be known by two names. Saul was possibly the Hebrew name while Paul was the Roman version.

Write and have students write: Saul = Paul.

Look up the following words in a Bible Dictionary:

priest , righteous, walking, blameless

altar of incense

make ready

mute

prophesied

strong, manifestation

Paul Preached to the Gentiles

Read aloud: Acts 13:42-49

Discuss Paul Preached to the Gentiles: Upon leaving the synagogue in Antioch, Paul and Barnabas were approached by Gentiles who requested that they preach to them. When Paul preached to the Gentiles, some of the Jews opposed Paul, but the Gentiles received the Word of God.

Draw and have students draw: Paul preaching to the "Gentiles."

Gentiles

Jews

Paul Preached to the Jews

Read aloud: Acts 18:1-11

Discuss Paul Preached to the Jews: As Paul went out to preach the Gospel he would spend his Sabbaths in synagogues reasoning with the Jews. While he was in Corinth, some of the Jews opposed Paul, but many believed, including the ruler of the synagogue.

Draw and have students draw: Paul preaching to the "Jews."

Completed Student Page

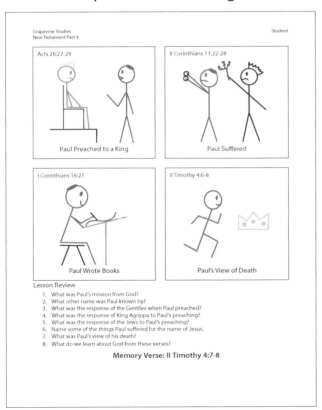

Teacher Notes

Paul Preached to a King

Read aloud: Acts 26:27-29

Discuss Paul Preached to a King: While in Caesarea, Paul had an opportunity to testify before King Agrippa, who was king of the northern part of Israel. King Agrippa responded that Paul had almost persuaded him to become a Christian.

Draw and have students draw: Paul preaching to a king.

Paul Suffered

Read aloud: II Corinthians 11:22-28

Discuss Paul: Just as the Lord had said, Paul suffered many things for the name of Jesus Christ. His sufferings included being stoned, beaten, and shipwrecked.

Draw and have students draw: Paul being beaten.

Teacher Notes

Completed Student Page

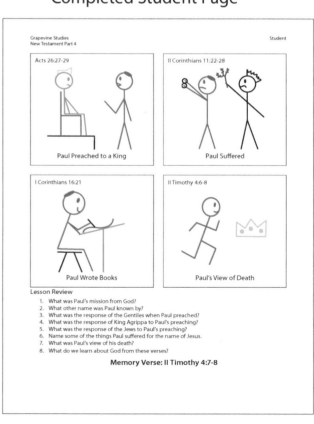

Paul Wrote Books

Read aloud: I Corinthians 16:21

Discuss Paul Wrote Books: As Paul traveled, he often began churches in the cities where he stayed. Paul would later write letters to these Churches to encourage, exhort, correct, and teach them the ways of the Lord. Paul also wrote letters to individuals and churches.

Draw and have students draw: Paul writing a letter.

Paul's View of Death

Read aloud: II Timothy 4:6-8

Discuss Paul's View of Death: As Paul wrote his last letter before his death, he told Timothy that he had done what the Lord had called him to do and that he looked forward to his crown of righteousness.

Draw and have students draw: A man running toward a crown.

Lesson Review

1. What was Paul's mission from God? To preach the Gospel to the Gentiles, to kings, and to the Jews.

2. What other name was Paul known by? Saul.

3. What was the response of the Gentiles when Paul preached? Many received the Word with gladness and glorified the Lord.

4. What was the response of King Agrippa to Paul's preaching? He was almost persuaded.

5. What was the response of the Jews to Paul's preaching? Some opposed but some believed, including the ruler of the synagogue.

6. Name some of the things Paul suffered for the name of Jesus. Stoning, shipwreck, and beatings.

7. What was Paul's view of his death? He looked forward to the crown of righteousness.

8. What do we learn about God from these verses? God desires that all Gentiles, kings, and Jews come to believe.

Memory Verse: II Timothy 4:7-8

Early Elementary and Elementary

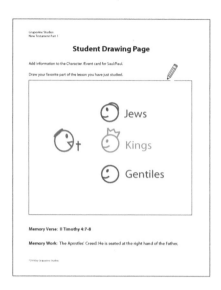

Add information for the Saul/Paul card:

- Saul and Paul are the same man.

- Paul's mission in life was to preach the gospel to the Gentiles, Jews, and kings.

- Paul wrote many of the New Testament epistles.

Memory Verse: II Timothy 4:7-8

Memory Verse: *Note: For the complete version of the Apostles' Creed - see page 350.* The Apostles' Creed: He is seated at the right hand of the Father,

Middle School

Letter to the Churches Part 1

Topical Bible

Name three people who are named in the Bible as writing *letters*.

Answers will vary. (Nave's, page 290)

Bible Dictionary

What is an *epistle*?

A letter. (Zondervan's, page 156)

Concordance

What is the first mention of a *letter* in the Bible?

II Samuel 11:14 (Cruden's, page 287)

Quest Question

Why were the New Testament letters important to the early Church?

To confirm the New Testament prophecies that Jesus would be born of the lineage of Abraham and David.

Timeline Review

| The Early Church | The Persecution | Saul/Paul |

Memory Verse Review

II Timothy 4:7-8

Acts 9:15-16

Acts 7:59

Acts 2:42:59

Memory Work: The Apostles' Creed: He is seated at the right hand of the Father,

Letters to the Churches Part 1

Memory Verse: II Timothy 3:16-17

Letters to the Churches

Read aloud: II Timothy 3:16

Discuss Letters to the Churches: We will cover the books of the New Testament in the order that they appear in our Bibles. In the top left corner of the "envelope" I have listed the author and the biblical "address." In the center of the envelope I have listed to whom the letter was written and the biblical address. I recommend locating the Churches on a map. This is a great opportunity to explain to your students how the canon of scripture was developed and why some books were chosen and others rejected.

Draw and have students draw: Paul writing letters that Teach, Exhort, Correct, and Encourage believers.

Teach
Exhort
Correct
Encourage

Romans

Read aloud: Romans 1:1, 1:7

Discuss Romans: The book of Romans was written by Paul to the church in Rome.

Map: Label the city of Rome.

Draw and have students draw: An envelope, noting the letter is from Paul and to the Church in Rome.

Paul
Romans 1:1

Rome
Romans 1:7

Look up the following words in a Bible Dictionary:

teach

exhort

correct

encourage

I & II Corinthians

Read aloud: I Corinthians 1:1-2, II Corinthians 1:1
Discuss I & II Corinthians: Paul wrote two letters to the church in Corinth.
Map: Label the city of Corinth.
Draw and have students draw: Two envelopes, noting the letters are from Paul and to the Church in Corinth.

Galatians

Read aloud: Galatians 1:1-2
Discuss Colossians: The book of Galatians was written by Paul to the church at Galatia.
Map: Label the region of Galatia.
Draw and have students draw: An envelope noting the letter is from Paul to the Church in Galatia.

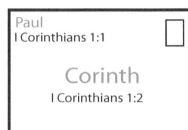
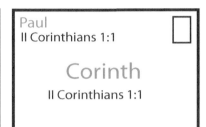

Completed Student Page	Teacher Notes

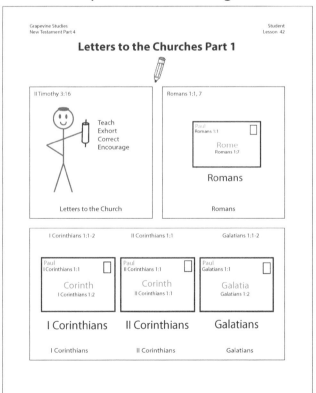

Ephesians, Philippians, and Colossians

Read aloud: Ephesians 1:1-2

Discuss Ephesians: The book of Ephesians was written by Paul to the church in Ephesus.

Map: Label the city of Ephesus.

Draw and have students draw: An envelope noting the letter is from Paul to the Church in Ephesus.

Read aloud: Philippians 1:1

Discuss Philippians: The book of Philippians was written by Paul to the church in Philippi.

Map: Label the city of Philippi.

Draw and have students draw: An envelope noting the letter is from Paul to the Church in Philippi.

Read aloud: Colossians 1:1-2

Discuss Colossians: The book of Colossians was written by Paul to the church in Colosse.

Map: Label the city of Colossi.

Draw and have students draw: An envelope noting the letter is from Paul to the Church in Colosse.

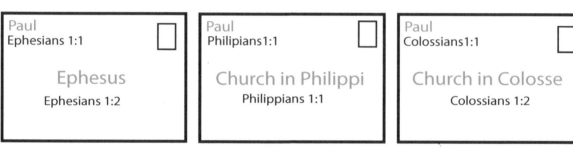

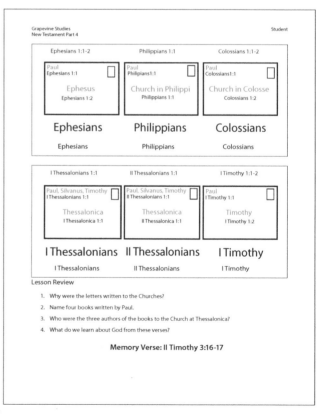

I & II Thessalonians

Read aloud: I Thessalonians 1:1; II Thessalonians 1:1

Discuss I Thessalonians: Paul wrote two letters to the church in Thessalonica.

Map: Label the city of Thessalonica.

Draw and have students draw: Two envelopes, noting the letters are from Paul and to the Church in Thessalonica.

I Timothy

Read aloud: I Timothy 1:1-2

Discuss Colossians: The book of I Timothy was written by Paul to his young disciple, Timothy.

Draw and have students draw: An envelope noting the letter is from Paul to Timothy.

Paul, Silvanus, Timothy ☐	Paul, Silvanus, Timothy ☐	Paul ☐
I Thessalonians 1:1	II Thessalonians 1:1	I Timothy 1:1
Thessalonica	Thessalonica	Timothy
I Thessalonica 1:1	II Thessalonica 1:1	I Timothy 1:2

Lesson Review

1. Why were the letters written to the Churches? To teach, exhort, correct and encourage believers.

2. Name four books written by Paul. See lesson.

3. Who were the three authors of the books to the Church at Thessalonica? Paul, Silvanus, and Timothy.

4. What do we learn about God from these verses? God had righteous men write books to help teach new believers how to live a life pleasing to God.

Memory Verse: II Timothy 3:16-17

Early Elementary and Elementary

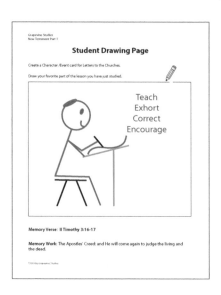

Information for the Letters to the Churches card:

- The New Testament epistles/letters were written to Churches and individuals.

- The epistles were meant to correct, encourage, exhort and teach.

Memory Verse: II Timothy 3:16-17

Memory Work: The Apostles' Creed: and He will come again to judge the living and the dead.

Middle School

Letters to the Churches Part 2

Letter to a New Believer

Write a letter to a new believer; be sure to include at least one Christian doctrine you would want him to know.

Teachers, since we are studying the letters to the Churches, we are doing something a little different with this Middle School.

Timeline Review

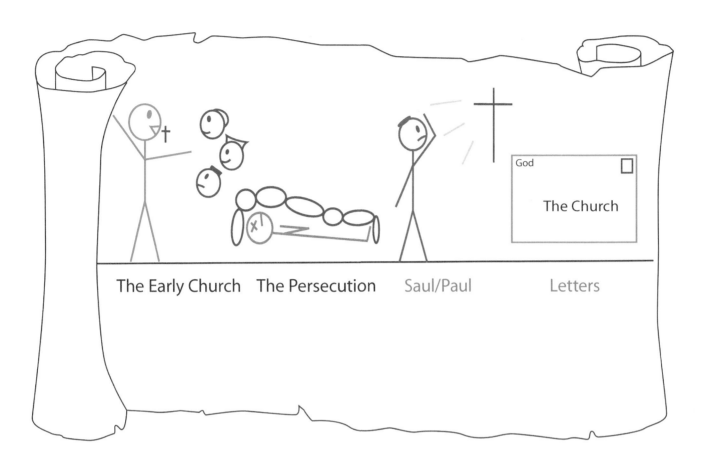

The Early Church   The Persecution   Saul/Paul   Letters

Memory Verse Review

II Timothy 3:16-17

II Timothy 4:7-8

Acts 9:15-16

Acts 7:59

Memory Work: The Apostles' Creed: and He will come again to judge the living and the dead.

Letters to the Churches Part 2

Memory Verse: Romans 15:4

II Timothy

Read aloud: II Timothy 1:2

Discuss II Timothy: The book of II Timothy was written by Paul to his young friend Timothy.

Draw and have students draw: An envelope noting the letter is from Paul to Timothy.

Titus

Read aloud: Titus 1:1, 4

Discuss Titus: The book of Titus was written by Paul to Titus.

Draw and have students draw: An envelope noting the letter is from Paul to Titus.

Philemon

Read aloud: Philemon 1:1

Discuss Philemon: The book of Philemon was written by Paul to Philemon.

Draw and have students draw: An envelope noting the letter is from Paul to Philemon.

Paul II Timothy 1:2	Paul Titus 1:1	Paul Philemon 1:1
Timothy II Timothy 1:2	Titus Titus 1:4	Philemon Philemon 1:1

Look up the following words in a Bible Dictionary:

learning

patience

comfort

hope

pilgrim

Hebrews

Read aloud: Hebrews 13:22

Discuss Hebrews: The book of Hebrews was written to the Jews by an unknown author.

Draw and have students draw: An envelope noting the author of the book of Hebrews is unknown.

James

Read aloud: James 1:1

Discuss James: The book of James was written by James to the Twelve Tribes who were scattered.

Draw and have students draw: An envelope noting the letter is from James to the Twelve Tribes.

I Peter

Read aloud: I Peter 1:1

Discuss I Peter: The book of I Peter was written by Peter to the pilgrims/ believers who were scattered in Pontus, Glatia, Cappadcias, Asia and Bithynia.

Draw and have students draw: An envelope noting the letter is from Peter to the Pilgrims.

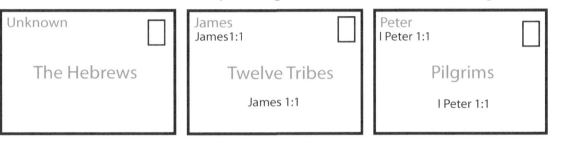

Teacher Notes

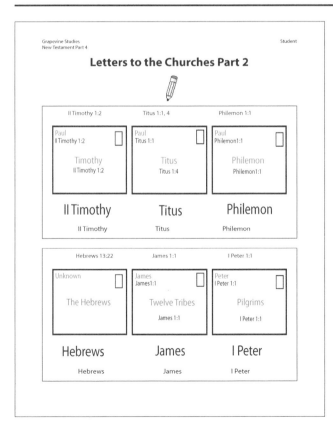

II Peter

Read aloud: II Peter 1:1

Discuss II Peter: The book of II Peter was written by Peter to the Church at large.

Draw and have students draw: An envelope noting the letter is from Peter to the Church at large.

I John 1:1

Read aloud: No Verse

Discuss James: The book of I John is a general letter to the Church.

Draw and have students draw: An envelope noting the letter is from John to Church at large.

II John

Read aloud: II John 1:1

Discuss I Peter: The book of II John was written by John to the elect lady and her children.

Draw and have students draw: An envelope noting the letter is from The elder to the elect lady and her children.

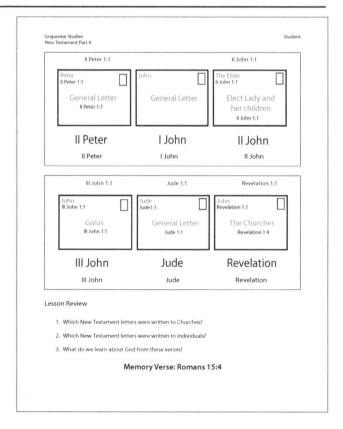

III John 1:1

Read aloud: III John 1:1

Discuss III John 1:1: The book of III John was written by John to Gaius.

Draw and have students draw: An envelope noting the author of the book of Hebrews is unknown.

Jude

Read aloud: Jude 1:1

Discuss Jude: The book of Jude was written by Jude to the Church at large.

Draw and have students draw: An envelope noting the letter is from Jude to The Church.

Revelation

Read aloud: Revelation 1:1, 4

Discuss Revelation: The book of Revelation was written by John to the seven Churches.

Draw and have students draw: An envelope noting the letter is from John to The 7 Churches.

John III John 1:1	Jude Jude1:1	John Revelation 1:1
Gaius III John 1:1	General Letter Jude 1:1	The Churches Revelation 1:4

Lesson Review

1. Which New Testament letters were written to Churches? Romans, I & II Corinthians, Galatians, Ephesians, Philippians, Colossians, I & II Thessalonians, Hebrews, I & II Peter, I John, Jude, and Revelation.

2. Which New Testament letters were written to individuals? I & II Timothy, Titus, Philemon, II & III John.

3. What do we learn about God from these verses? God desires for us to know and serve Him, and He has given us those instructions in the Bible.

Memory Verse: Romans 15:4

Early Elementary and Elementary

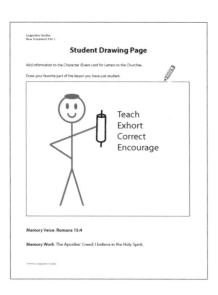

Add information for the Letters to the Churches card:

- There are twenty-two New Testament epistles.

- Paul wrote thirteen of the New Testament epistles.

Memory Verse: Romans 15:4

Memory Work: The Apostles' Creed: I believe in the Holy Spirit,

Middle School

The Gospel in Stick Figures

Topical Bible

What is the *sin* nature?

Nave's, page 450

Bible Dictionary

Define the term *propitiation.*

Zondervan's page 476

Concordance

What are two verses you would use to begin a study on the *Gospel*?

Answers will vary. (Cruden's, page 212)

Quest Question

What is the Gospel of Jesus Christ?

I Corinthians 15:1-6. I recommend that you cover this question at the end of the lesson.

Timeline Review

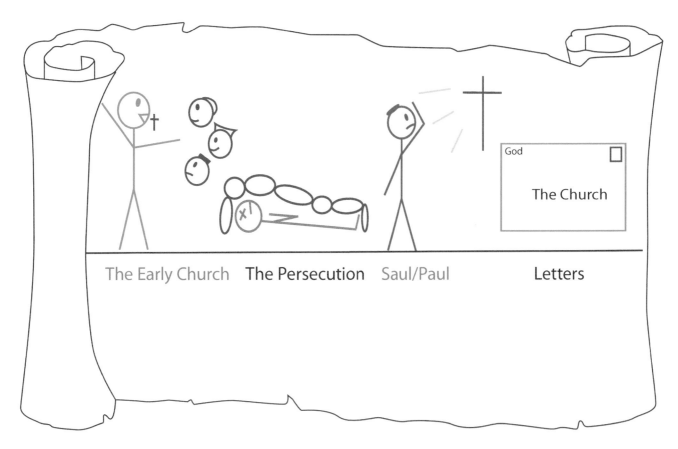

The Early Church   The Persecution   Saul/Paul   Letters

Teacher Note: The timeline review is the same as the last lesson because both lessons are on the Letters to the Church.

Memory Verse Review

Romans 15:4

II Timothy 3:16-17

II Timothy 4:7-8

Acts 9:15-16

Memory Work: The Apostles' Creed: I believe in the Holy Spirit,

The Gospel in Stick Figures

Memory Verse: Matthew 24:14

Note to Teachers: During this lesson, we would like to review the Gospel from Creation to Judgment. I have given only one verse at each point, with the desire that teachers and students would add their own verses to this outline.

Creation

Read aloud: Genesis 1:31

Discuss Creation: The purple triangle represents God. The solid line represents the perfect relationship between God and man as it was at Creation. The heart represents man.

Draw and have students draw: The purple God triangle connected to a man's (red) heart with a solid line.

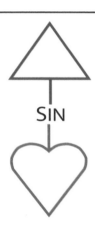

Sin

Read aloud: Genesis 3:6

Discuss Sin: The second symbol in the Gospel is the purple God triangle with a broken line to man's heart. Sin caused Adam and Eve's relationship with God to be broken.

Draw and have students draw: The purple God triangle with a broken line to man's heart. Note that the line is broken by sin.

Look up the following words in a Bible Dictionary:

gospel

sin

propitiation

tempted

ascend

The Promise

Read aloud: Genesis 3:15

Discuss The Promise: Although God punished Adam and Eve for their sin, He did not leave them without the promise that the Messiah would come and restore the broken relationship between God and man.

Draw and have students draw: Eyes looking forward to the Messiah coming.

Jesus Was Born

Read aloud: Galatians 4:4-5

Discuss Jesus Was Born: In the fullness of time Messiah was born, and His name was Jesus.

Draw and have students draw: Jesus in a manger.

A Sinless Life

Read aloud: Hebrews 4:15

Discuss A Sinless LIfe: When Jesus lived on earth He was tempted, just as we are, yet lived His life without sin.

Draw and have students draw: The word sin with a red circle and line through it.

Completed Student Page

Teacher Notes:

Grapevine Studies
New Testament Part 4

Student

The Gospel in Stick Figures

Genesis 1:31

Creation

Genesis 3:6

SIN

Sin

Genesis 3:15

The Promise

Galatians 4:4-5

Jesus Was Born

Hebrews 4:15

A Sinless Life

Died and Was Buried

Read aloud: Matthew 27:50, 59-60

Discuss Died and Was Buried: Scripture records that Jesus was scourged, beaten, and then crucified. After Jesus died, He was buried.

Draw and have students draw: Jesus in the tomb dead.

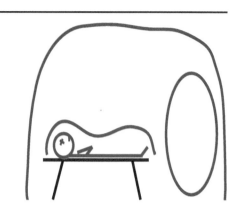

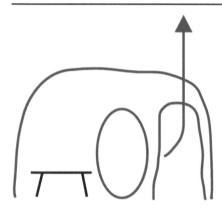

Rose and Ascended

Read aloud: Matthew 28:5-6; I Corinthians 15:1-5

Discuss Rose and Ascended: Three days after Jesus died and was buried, He rose from the grave. After appearing to many people, He ascended to Heaven, where He sits at the right hand of God interceding for us.

Draw and have students draw: A purple arrow going out and up from the empty tomb.

Teacher Notes

Completed Student Page

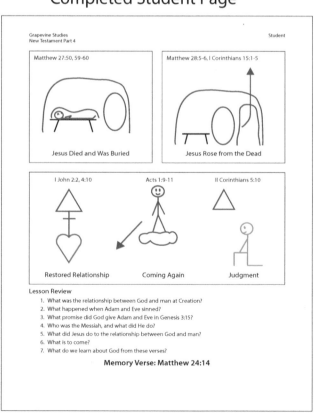

Restored Relationship

Read aloud: I John 2:2, 4:10

Discuss Restored Relationship: Through Jesus' death, burial, and resurrection, the relationship between God and man can be restored.

Draw and have students draw: Eyes looking forward to the Messiah coming.

Coming Again

Read aloud: Acts 1:9-11

Discuss Jesus Was Born: Scripture tells us that Jesus will come again, and when He does, everyone will see Him.

Draw and have students draw: Jesus coming again.

Judgment

Read aloud: II Corinthians 5:10

Discuss Judgment: All men will one day stand before God to be judged.

Draw and have students draw: A man kneeling before God.

Lesson Review:

1. What was the relationship between God and man at Creation? Perfect and complete.

2. What happened when Adam and Eve sinned? The relationship between God and man was broken.

3. What promise did God give Adam and Eve in Genesis 3:15? That one day a Messiah would be born who would restore the broken relationship between God and man.

4. Who was the Messiah, and what did He do? He was Jesus of Nazareth. He was born, lived a sinless life, was crucified, buried, rose again after three days, and ascended to heaven.

5. What did Jesus do to the relationship between God and man? Through His death and payment for our sins, Jesus provided a way for us to be forgiven and for our relationship with God to be restored.

6. What is to come? One day Jesus will come again, and all men will be judged.

7. What do we learn about God from these verses? God sent Jesus to restore the broken relationship between God and man.

Memory Verse: Matthew 24:14

Early Elementary and Elementary

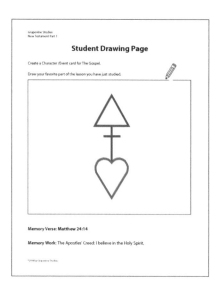

Information for The Gospel card:

The main points of the Gospel:

1. Creation
2. Sin
3. The Promise
4. The Messiah
5. Sinless Life
6. Died
7. Buried
8. Rose
9. Ascended
10. Restored
11. Coming Again
12. Judgment

Memory Verse: Matthew 24:14

Memory Work: The Apostles' Creed: I believe in the Holy Spirit,

Middle School

Sharing the Gospel

Topical Bible

What is *faith*?

Nave's, page 149

Bible Dictionary

Define the term *confession*.

Zondervan's, page 116

Concordance

Give the reference for this verse: "God helps those who help themselves."

I Hesitations 2:1 Phony verse, used to illustrate that not everything that sounds scriptural is biblical.

Quest Question

Are there different gospels or different ways to get to heaven? Scripturally defend your answer.

John 14:16. Defenses will vary.

Timeline Review

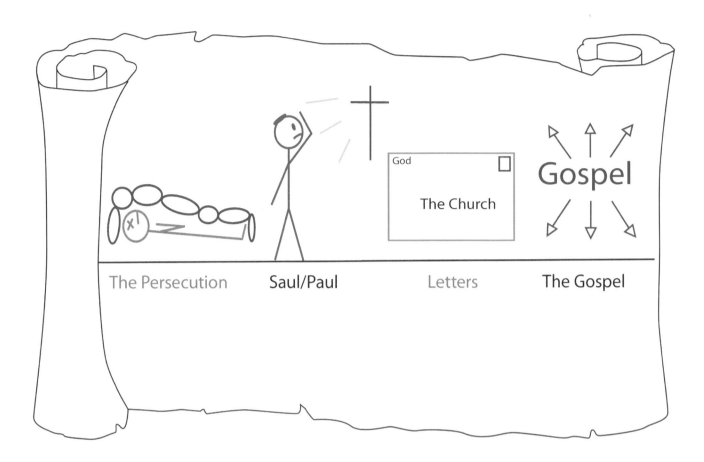

Memory Verse Review

Matthew 24:14

Romans 15:4

II Timothy 3:16-17

II Timothy 4:7-8

Memory Work: The Apostles' Creed: I believe in the Holy Spirit,

Sharing the Gospel

Memory Verse: James 1:22

Note to Teachers: During this lesson I would like to continue the Gospel, showing how to make it personal. I have given only one verse at each point, with the desire that teachers and students would add their own verses to this outline.

I Am a Sinner

Read aloud: I Corinthians 15:22; Romans 3:23

Discuss I Am a Sinner: It is important for each of us to understand and acknowledge that we are all sinners.

Draw and have students draw: Yourself acknowledging that you are a sinner.

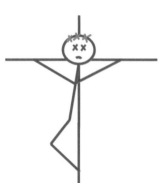

Jesus Died for Me

Read aloud: John 3:16

Discuss Jesus Died for Me: When Jesus died on the cross, the debt for my sins was paid in full.

Draw and have students draw: Jesus dead on the cross.

Look up the following words in a Bible Dictionary:

glory of God

only begotten son

perish

everlasting

repent

doctrine

I Need to Repent

Read aloud: Acts 17:30, 3:19

Discuss I Need to Repent: Repent means to agree with God about my sin. We do this initially when we first ask Jesus into our lives, and then daily after becoming believers.

Draw and have students draw: Yourself repenting.

I Can Receive God's Forgiveness

Read aloud: I John 1:9

Discuss I Can Receive God's Forgiveness: As a sinner, when I sincerely repent, God has promised that I will be forgiven.

Draw and have students draw: The purple God triangle and yourself asking God's forgiveness.

Completed Student Page

Teacher Notes:

Grapevine Studies
New Testament Part 4

Student

Sharing the Gospel

I Corinthians 15:22; Romans 3:23

I Am a Sinner

John 3:16

Jesus Died for Me

Acts 17:30, 3:19

I Need to Repent

I John 1:9

I Can Receive God's Forgiveness

Growing in My Faith

Read aloud: Acts 2:42, 38

Discuss Growing in My Faith: We will look at some of the things the early Church did as an expression of their new faith that helped them to grow to be strong Christians.

Learn and Obey Biblical Doctrine

Discuss Learn and Obey Biblical Doctrine: It is important that we not only learn the Word of God but also be obedient to those things we are taught.

Draw and have students draw: One man teaching another.

Continue Fellowship with Other Believers

Discuss Continue Fellowship with Other Believers: Fellowship is a necessary part of growing in the Lord. Through fellowship we learn, we are challenged, and we are corrected.

Draw and have students draw: Two women talking.

Teacher Notes

Completed Student Page

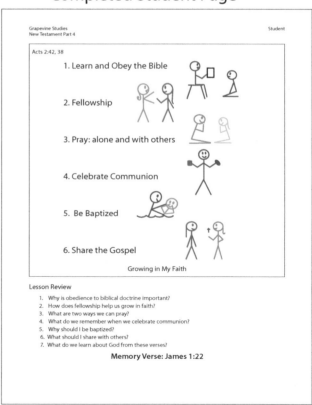

Grapevine Studies
New Testament Part 4

Student

Acts 2:42, 38

1. Learn and Obey the Bible

2. Fellowship

3. Pray: alone and with others

4. Celebrate Communion

5. Be Baptized

6. Share the Gospel

Growing in My Faith

Lesson Review
1. Why is obedience to biblical doctrine important?
2. How does fellowship help us grow in faith?
3. What are two ways we can pray?
4. What do we remember when we celebrate communion?
5. Why should I be baptized?
6. What should I share with others?
7. What do we learn about God from these verses?

Memory Verse: James 1:22

Pray in Private and with Other Believers

Discuss Pray in Private and with Other Believers: Communicating with our God is essential to growth.

Draw and have students draw: A man and woman praying.

Celebrate Communion

Discuss Celebrate Communion: In the fullness of time Messiah was born, and His name was Jesus.

Draw and have students draw: A man holding a cup and bread.

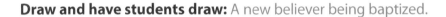

Be Baptized

Discuss Be Baptized: Baptism is an important public acknowledgement of our faith.

Draw and have students draw: A new believer being baptized.

Share the Gospel

Discuss Share the Gospel: Find effective ways to communicate the love of God to our family, friends, and others.

Draw and have students draw: One woman sharing the Gospel with another woman.

Lesson Review:

1. Why is obedience to biblical doctrine important? Obedience shows our love for God.
2. How does fellowship help us grow in faith? Through encouragement, correction, and exhortation.
3. What are two ways we can pray? In private and with others.
4. What do we remember when we celebrate communion? The Lord's death and the New Covenant in His blood.
5. Why should I be baptized? In obedience to the Lord.
6. What should I share with others? The Gospel.
7. What do we learn about God from these verses? God wants us to accept the Gospel and then grow in our faith.

Memory Verse: James 1:22

Early Elementary and Elementary

Student Drawing Page

Information for the Sharing the Gospel card:

- The main points of understanding the Gospel are:

    1. I am a sinner.
    2. Jesus died for me.
    3. I need to repent.
    4. I can receive God's forgiveness.

- I can grow in my faith by:

    1. Learning and obeying the Bible.
    2. Fellowshipping with other believers.
    3. Praying.
    4. Celebrating Communion.
    5. Being Baptized.
    6. Sharing the Gospel.

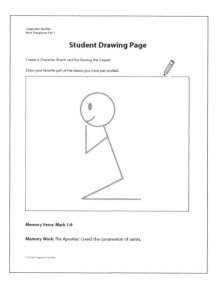

Memory Verse: Mark 1:9

Memory Work: The Apostles' Creed: the communion of saints,

Section Review

1. What was Paul's mission from God? To preach the Gospel to the Gentiles, to kings, and to the Jews.

2. What other name was Paul known by? Saul.

3. What was the response of the Gentiles when Paul preached? Many received the Word with gladness and glorified the Lord.

4. What was the response of King Agrippa to Paul's preaching? He was almost persuaded.

5. What was the response of the Jews to Paul's preaching? Some opposed but some believed, including the ruler of the synagogue.

6. Name some of the things Paul suffered for the name of Jesus. Stoning, shipwreck, and beatings.

7. What was Paul's view of his death? He looked forward to the crown of righteousness.

8. Recite II Timothy 4:7-8.

9. Why were the letters written to the Churches? To teach, exhort, correct and encourage believers.

10. Name four books written by Paul. See lesson.

11. Who were the three authors of the books to the Church at Thessalonica? Paul, Silvanus, and Timothy.

12. Recite II Timothy 3:16-17.

13. Which New Testament letters were written to Churches? Romans, I & II Corinthians, Galatians, Ephesians, Philippians, Colossians, I & II Thessalonians, Hebrews, I & II Peter, I John, Jude, and Revelation.

14. Which New Testament letters were written to individuals? I & II Timothy, Titus, Philemon, II & III John.

15. Recite Romans 15:4.

16. What was the relationship between God and man at Creation? Perfect and complete.

17. What happened when Adam and Eve sinned? The relationship between God and man was broken.

18. **What promise did God give Adam and Eve in Genesis 3:15?** That one day a Messiah would be born who would restore the broken relationship between God and man.

19. **Who was the Messiah, and what did He do?** He was Jesus of Nazareth. He was born, lived a sinless life, was crucified, buried, rose again after three days, and ascended to heaven.

20. **What did Jesus do to the relationship between God and man?** Through His death and payment for our sins, Jesus provided a way for us to be forgiven and for our relationship with God to be restored.

21. **What is to come?** One day Jesus will come again, and all men will be judged.

22. **Recite Matthew 24:44.**

23. **Why is obedience to biblical doctrine important?** Obedience shows our love for God.

24. **How does fellowship help us grow in faith?** Through encouragement, correction, and exhortation.

25. **What are two ways we can pray?** In private and with others.

26. **What do we remember when we celebrate communion?** The Lord's death and the New Covenant in His blood.

27. **Why should I be baptized?** In obedience to the Lord.

28. **What should I share with others?** The Gospel.

29. **Recite James 1:22.**

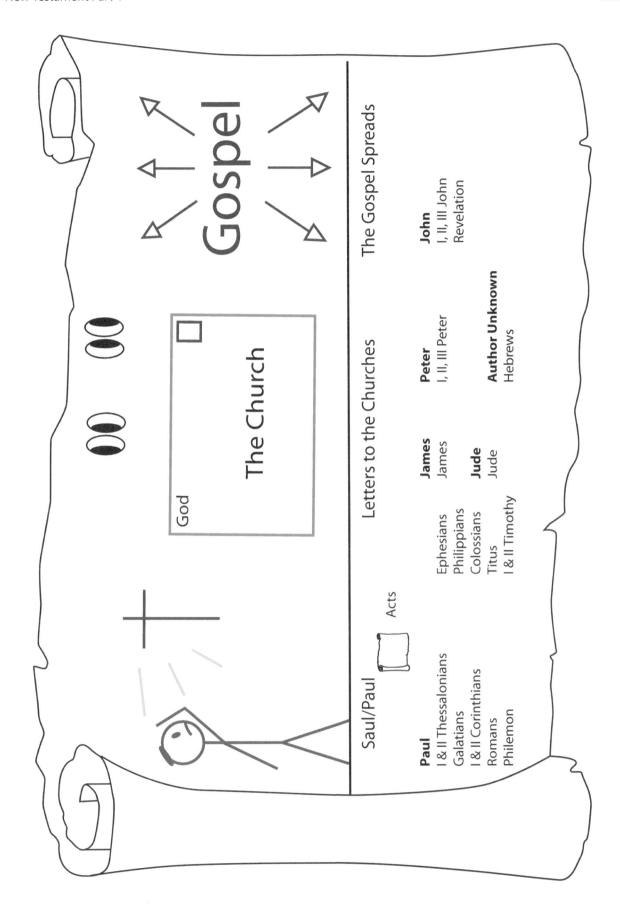

Gospel

God

The Church

The Gospel Spreads

John
I, II, III John
Revelation

Peter
I, II, III Peter

Author Unknown
Hebrews

Letters to the Churches

James
James

Jude
Jude

Ephesians
Philippians
Colossians
Titus
I & II Timothy

Saul/Paul

Acts

Paul
I & II Thessalonians
Galatians
I & II Corinthians
Romans
Philemon

Lesson Goals and Key Points

REVELATION

The goal of these lessons is to briefly introduce students to some of the events that will take place during the time known as the Great Tribulation.

Key Points:
- Mankind and Creation will experience great tribulation when:
    1. The seven seals are opened.
    2. The seven bowls are poured out.
    3. The seven trumpets are sounded.
- During the Great Tribulation, men will refuse to repent.

Memory Verse: Revelation 5:9 and Revelation 9:20

THE SECOND COMING

The goal of this lesson is to show what events will surround the second coming of Jesus Christ.

Key Points:
- Kings will gather their men to Armageddon to fight against God.
- Jesus will return and defeat the armies gathered against Him.
- Satan will be bound in the bottomless pit for the Millennium.
- During the Millennium, Jesus will reign over the earth.
- At the end of the Millennium, Satan will be released and will deceive mankind again.
- Jesus will defeat all His enemies at the final battle

Memory Verse: Revelation 1:7

NOTES

HELL

The goal of this lesson is to look at the facts regarding the place called Hell.

Key Points:
- All men will be judged.
- At the Great White Throne Judgment, the books will be opened.
- Anyone whose name is not found in the Book of Life will be thrown into the lake of fire and brimstone.
- Jesus will separate the believers from the unbelievers at the end of time.
- Hell was originally a place prepared for Satan and his demons.

Memory Verse: Revelation 20:15

HEAVEN

The goal of this lesson is to study some of the teachings of Jesus.

Key Points:
- Jesus taught that outward sins (actions) are a result of inward sins (thoughts and motives).
- When Jesus was asked what the greatest command was, He responded by saying to love God completely and also to love your neighbor as yourself.

Memory Verse: Revelation 21:3

NOTES

Middle School

Quest Page

Topical Bible

What is a *seal*?

Nave's, page 429

Bible Dictionary

Define *peace*.

Zondervan's, page 443

Concordance

Give three Old Testament references to *tribulation*.

Deuteronomy 4:30, Judges 10:14, I Samuel 26:24 (Cruden's, page 511)

Quest Question

Do you think you will live to see any part of the Great Tribulation?

Answers will vary.

Timeline Review

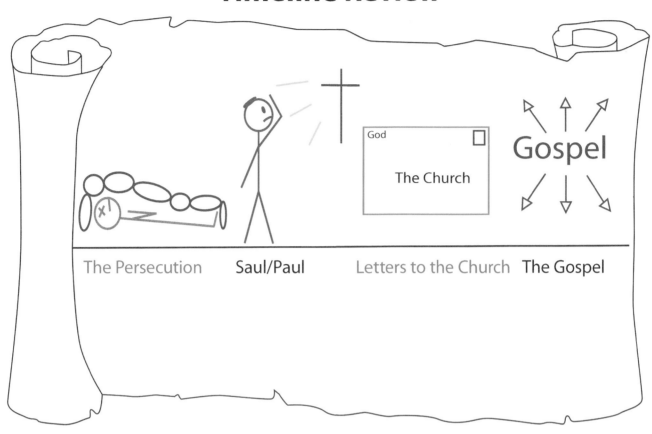

Teacher Note: The timeline review is the same as the last lesson because both lessons are on the Gospel.

Memory Verse Review

James 1:22

Matthew 24:14

Romans 15:4

II Timothy 3:16-17

Memory Work: The Apostles' Creed: the communion of saints,

Revelation Part 1

Memory Verse: Revelation 5:9

The Lamb and the Scroll

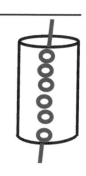

Read aloud: Revelation 5:1-7

Discuss The Lamb and the Scroll: John sees a scene in heaven in which there is a scroll at the right hand of God, but no one is worthy to open the scroll except Jesus.

Draw and have students draw: A scroll with seven seals.

Seal 1

Read aloud: Revelation 6:1-2

Discuss Seal 1: The first seal is a white horse with a rider who is given a crown and has a bow.

Draw and have students draw: A crown and a bow.

Seal 2

Read aloud: Revelation 6:3-4

Discuss Seal 2: The second seal is a fiery red horse whose rider is given a great sword and is sent to take peace from the earth.

Draw and have students draw: A sword.

Look up the following words in a Bible Dictionary:

seal

scroll

peace

scale

mountain

censer

Seal 3

Read aloud: Revelation 6:5-6

Discuss Seal 3: The third seal is a black horse whose rider is holding a pair of scales.

Draw and have students draw: A scale.

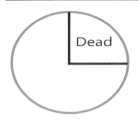

Seal 4

Read aloud: Revelation 6:7-8

Discuss Seal 4: The fourth seal is represented by a pale horse whose rider is death, followed by Hades, and power is given to kill one fourth of the earth.

Draw and have students draw: The earth, noting one fourth is "dead."

Seal 5

Read aloud: Revelation 6:9-11

Discuss Seal 5: When the fifth seal is opened, the souls of those who had been martyred are seen crying out and asking how long until God judges.

Draw and have students draw: A martyr crying out to God.

Teacher Notes:

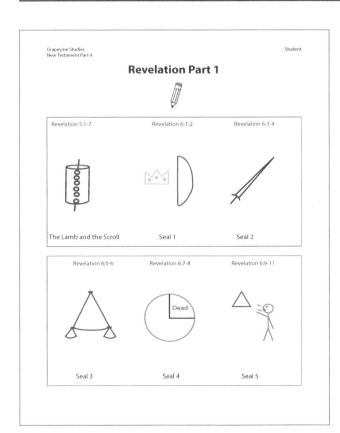

Seal 6

Read aloud: Revelation 6:12-17

Discuss Seal 6: At the breaking of the sixth seal there is a great earthquake, the sun becomes like sackcloth, the moon, like blood, and the stars fall from heaven.

Draw and have students draw: A blood moon, darkened son and falling stars.

Seal 7

Read aloud: Revelation 8:1-5

Discuss Seal 7: When the final seal is broken there is silence in heaven and seven angels are given seven trumpets. Another angel throws a censor to earth and as a result there is noise, lightning, thunder and an earthquake.

Draw and have students draw: Lightning and thunder, note there was silence.

Trumpet 1

Read aloud: Revelation 8:6-7

Discuss Trumpet 1: The first trumpet sounds, and fire and hail fall to the earth and burn up 1/3 of the trees and all the grass of the earth.

Draw and have students draw: A tree and grass with one third of them on fire.

Teacher Notes

Completed Student Page

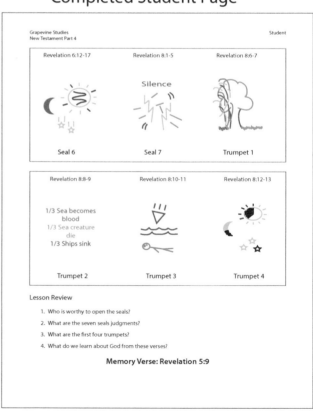

Trumpet 2

Read aloud: Revelation 8:8-9

Discuss Trumpet 2: The second trumpet sounds, and a mountain-like object is thrown into the sea causing 1/3 of the sea to become blood, killing 1/3 of the sea creatures and destroying 1/3 of the ships.

Write and have students write: 1/3 sea becomes blood, 1/3 sea creatures die, and 1/3 ships sink.

1/3 Sea becomes blood
1/3 Sea creature die
1/3 Ships sink

Trumpet 3

Read aloud: Revelation 8:10-11

Discuss Trumpet 3: The third trumpet sounds, and a great star falls from heaven and makes 1/3 of the rivers and springs bitter, causing men to die.

Draw and have students draw: A star/mountain falling into the sea and a dead man.

Trumpet 4

Read aloud: Revelation 8:12-13

Discuss Trumpet 4: The fourth trumpet sounded and 1/3 of the sun, moon, and stars go dark.

Draw and have students draw: One third of the sun, moon and stars darkened.

Lesson Review:

1. Who is worthy to open the seals? Jesus, the Lamb of God.

2. What are the seven seals judgments? 1) White horse; 2) Red horse; 3) Black horse; 4) Pale Horse; 5) Martyrs crying out; 6) Sun, moon and stars darkened and the earth quakes; 7) Silence in heaven and then noise and lightning.

3. What are the first four trumpets? 1) 1/3 of the trees and grass burn; 2) 1/3 of the sea becomes blood, 1/3 of the sea creatures die, and 1/3 of the ships sink. 3) 1/3 of the waters become bitter; 4) 1/3 of the sun, moon and stars are darkened.

4. What do we learn about God from these verses? During the great tribulation men and creation will be affected.

Memory Verse: Revelation 5:9

Grapevine Studies
New Testament Part 4

Teacher

Early Elementary and Elementary

Information for the Revelation:

- Mankind and creation will experience great tribulation when the:

    1. The seven Seals are opened.

    2. The seven Trumpets are sounded.

Memory Verse: Revelation 5:9

Memory Work: The Apostles' Creed: the forgiveness of sins,

Middle School

Revelation Part 2

Topical Bible

What is *revelation*?

Nave's, page 408

Bible Dictionary

Define *tribulation*.

Zondervan's, page 593

Concordance

Where would you begin a study on the *"mark* of the beast"?

Revelation 16:2 (Cruden's, page 311)

Quest Question

How will men respond when God demonstrates His great power during the Great Tribulation?

They will blaspheme, curse God, and remain unrepentant. Revelation 16.

®2019 by Grapevine Studies

318

Timeline Review

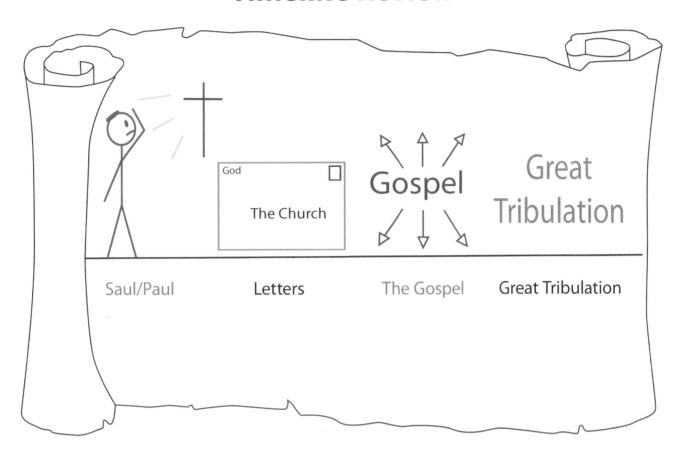

Memory Verse Review

Revelation 5:9

James 1:22

Matthew 24:14

Romans 15:4

Memory Work: The Apostles' Creed: the forgiveness of sins,

Revelation Part 2

Memory Verse: Revelation 20:10

Trumpet 5

Read aloud: Revelation 9:1-5

Discuss Trumpet 5: The fifth trumpet sounds and the bottomless pit is opened. Out of the pit come smoke and locusts. These locusts are given instructions not to harm those who have the seal of God on their foreheads but to torment men for five months.

Draw and have students draw: A man running from locust from the pit.

Trumpet 6

Read aloud: Revelation 9:13-19

Discuss Trumpet 6: The sixth trumpet releases four angels who kill 1/3 of mankind.

Draw and have students draw: Draw two people alive and one dead.

No Repentance

Read aloud: Revelation 9:20-21

Discuss No Repentance: Although many plagues have been sent upon mankind and the earth in judgment, men still refuse to repent of their wicked deeds.

Draw and have students draw: A man turning away from God.

Look up the following words in a Bible Dictionary:

revelation

tribulation

mark of the beast

signs

wrath

blasphemy

Trumpet 7

Read aloud: Revelation 11:15-16, 19

Discuss Trumpet 7: The last trumpet begins with heavenly worship. Then the temple of God in heaven is opened. This event is accompanied by lightning, thunder, earthquake, noise, and large hail.

Draw and have students draw: The Ark in heaven, lightning, and noise.

Mark of the Beast

Read aloud: Revelation 13:11-18

Discuss Mark of the Beast: The beast performs many convincing signs and miracles. He also makes all of mankind receive a mark in order to buy or sell.

Draw and have students draw: A mark on the forehead and hand.

Bowl 1

Read aloud: Revelation 15:7-8, 16:1-2

Discuss Bowl 1: The first bowl is poured out, causing sores on all those who have the mark of the beast or who worship him.

Draw and have students draw: A man with boils on his face.

Completed Student Page

Teacher Notes:

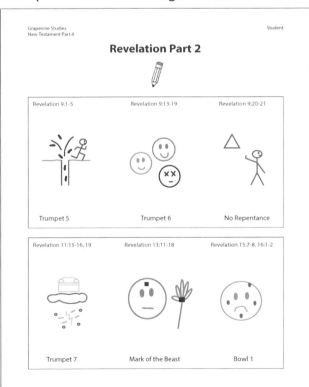

Bowl 2

Read aloud: Revelation 16:3

Discuss Bowl 2: The second bowl is poured out, the sea turns to blood, and all the sea creatures die.

Draw and have students draw: Two dead sea creatures in a bloody sea.

Bowl 3

Read aloud: Revelation 16:4-7

Discuss Bowl 3: The third bowl is poured out, and the rivers and springs turn to blood.

Draw and have students draw: A bloody river and spring.

Bowl 4

Read aloud: Revelation 16:8-9

Discuss Bowl 4: When the fourth bowl is poured out, men are scorched with heat but blaspheme God and still refuse to repent.

Draw and have students draw: A man shaking his fists at God.

Teacher Notes

Completed Student Page

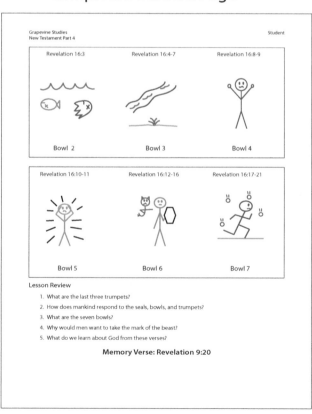

Bowl 5

Read aloud: Revelation 16:10-11

Discuss Bowl 5: The fifth bowl strikes the throne of the beast and causes darkness and pain to men, but men respond by blaspheming God.

Draw and have students draw: A man surrounded by darkness.

Bowl 6

Read aloud: Revelation 16:12-16

Discuss Bowl 6: The sixth bowl is poured out causing the Euphrates River to dry up. Out of the river come demon creatures, who gather men from all over the world to battle in a place called Armageddon.

Draw and have students draw: A soldier with a demon pointing.

Bowl 7

Read aloud: Revelation 16:17-21

Discuss Bowl 7: The last bowl begins with the proclamation "It is done." Thunders, lightning, and earthquakes more powerful than any before strike. Mountains and islands flee away and giant hailstones fall.

Draw and have students draw: A man running and hail falling.

Lesson Review:

1. What are the last three trumpets? 5) locust from the pit, 6) 1/3 mankind die, 7) lightnings and noise.

2. How does mankind respond to the seals, bowls, and trumpets? They blaspheme God and refuse to repent of their sins.

3. What are the seven bowls? 1) boils, 2) all sea creatures die, 3) rivers and springs turn to blood, 4) scorching heat, 5) darkness and pain, 6) gathering of an army, 7) earthquakes and hail.

4. Why would men want to take the mark of the beast? To be able to buy and sell.

5. What do we learn about God from these verses? There will come a time when God's stored-up wrath will be released.

Memory Verse: Revelation 9:20

Early Elementary and Elementary

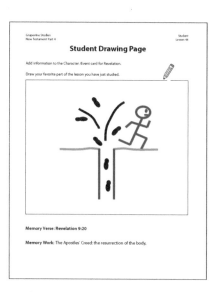

Add information to the Revelation card:

- Mankind and creation will experience great tribulation when:

    3. The seven Bowls are poured out.

- During The Great Tribulation men will refuse to repent.

Memory Verse: Revelation 9:20

Memory Work: The Apostles' Creed: the resurrection of the body,

Middle School

The Second Coming of Jesus

Topical Bible

What is *Armageddon*?

Nave's, page 33

Bible Dictionary

Define the *bottomless pit*.

Zondervan's, page 93

Concordance

The Bible teaches that the saints will reign with Jesus Christ for a *thousand* years. Where is this verse found?

Revelation 20:4 (Cruden's, page 501)

Quest Question

Will Jesus come again? Give scriptural references.

Yes, see lesson.

Timeline Review

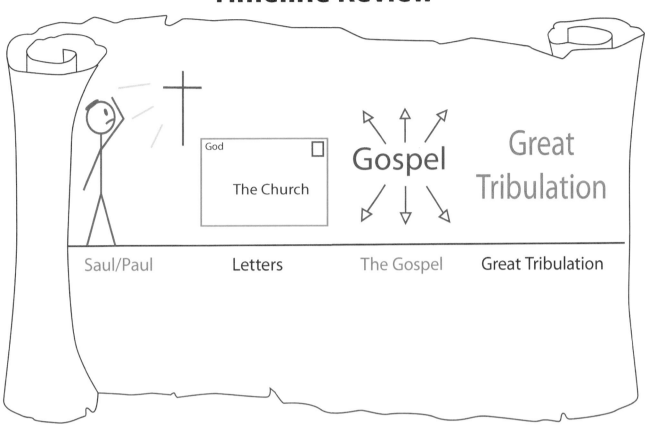

Teacher Note: The timeline review is the same as the last lesson because both lessons are on the Great Tribulation.

Memory Verse Review

Revelation 9:20

Revelation 5:9

James 1:22

Matthew 24:14

Memory Work: The Apostles' Creed: the resurrection of the body,

The Second Coming of Jesus

Memory Verse: Revelation 1:7

Armageddon

Read aloud: Revelation 16:12-16

Discuss Armageddon: During the last two lessons we have studied the events often called the "Great Tribulation." One of the events we looked at, the sixth bowl, sets the stage for the coming of Jesus. Demonic forces are unleashed and gather the kings of the earth and their armies to a place called Armageddon.

Draw and have students draw: A king and two soldiers.

Jesus Returns

Read aloud: Revelation 1:7, 19:11-16

Discuss Jesus Returns: This passage is a stunning description of Jesus as He comes to exercise judgment against the nations.

Draw and have students draw: Jesus on a cloud, with an arrow pointing down, showing His return.

Look up the following words in a Bible Dictionary:

signs

Armageddon

judges

bottomless pit

millennium

saints

The World Armies Are Defeated

Read aloud: Revelation 19:17-21

Discuss The World Armies Are Defeated: When Jesus returns, those who are gathered to fight against Him are completely destroyed.

Draw and have students draw: Jesus on a horse and two dead soldiers.

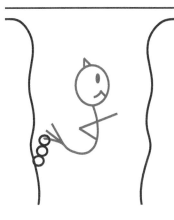

Satan Is Chained

Read aloud: Revelation 20:1-3

Discuss Satan Is Chained: The return of Jesus culminates with Satan being chained by an angel and thrown into the bottomless pit, where he will remain for 1,000 years.

Draw and have students draw: Satan chained to the bottomless pit.

Completed Student Page   Teacher Notes:

The Millennium

Read aloud: Revelation 20:4-6

Discuss The Millennium: During the Millennium (or 1,000 years), after the return of Jesus Christ, the saints reign with Him over the earth.

Draw and have students draw: Jesus sitting on His throne.

Satan Is Released

Read aloud: Revelation 20:7-8

Discuss Satan Is Released: When the Millennium is completed, Satan will be released from the bottomless pit to deceive mankind once more.

Draw and have students draw: Satan deceiving a man.

Teacher Notes

Completed Student Page

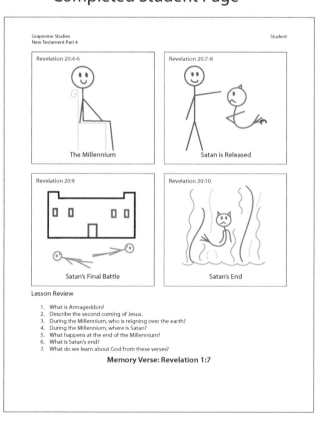

Satan's Final Battle

Read aloud: Revelation 20:9

Discuss Satan's Final Battle: Once Satan is released, he will deceive the nations and gather men for battle. When Satan's army surrounds the "camp of the saints" and the "beloved city," God will respond by sending fire from heaven to destroy them all.

Draw and have students draw: Two men dead in front of a city.

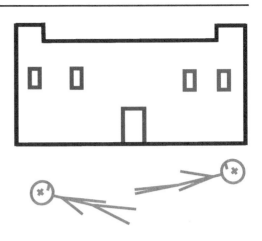

Satan's End

Read aloud: Revelation 20:10

Discuss Satan's End: Satan's end is in the lake of fire, where he will remain for eternity.

Draw and have students draw: Satan in the lake of fire.

Lesson Review:

1. What is Armageddon? A battlefield located in northern Israel in which the kings of the earth will gather their armies and be defeated at the coming of Jesus Christ.

2. Describe the second coming of Jesus. When Jesus returns every eye will see Him.

3. During the Millennium, who is reigning over the earth? Jesus and the saints.

4. During the Millennium, where is Satan? Chained to the bottomless pit.

5. What happens at the end of the Millennium? Satan is released and deceives man again.

6. What is Satan's end? The lake of fire for eternity.

7. What do we learn about God from these verses? Jesus will demonstrate with His return and throughout the Millennium that His power and justice are absolute.

Memory Verse: Revelation 1:7

Early Elementary and Elementary

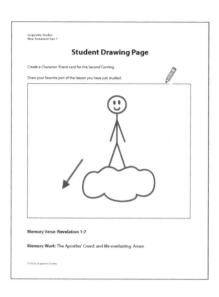

Information for The Second Coming card:

- Kings will gather their men to Armageddon to fight against God.
- Jesus will return and defeat the armies gathered against Him.
- Satan will be bound in the bottomless pit for the Millennium.
- During the Millennium, Jesus will reign over the earth.
- At the end of the Millennium, Satan will be released and will deceive mankind again.
- Jesus will defeat all His enemies at the final battle.

Memory Verse: Revelation 1:7

Memory Work: The Apostles' Creed: and life everlasting. Amen

Middle School

Hell

Topical Bible

Judgment: who will be judged?

Nave's, page 274

Bible Dictionary

Describe *hell*.

Zondervan's, page 223

Concordance

What are some different *books* mentioned in the Bible?

Cruden's, page 40

Quest Question

Is your name written in the Book of Life? How do you know for sure?

Answers will vary. Refer to the lesson on the Gospel.

Timeline Review

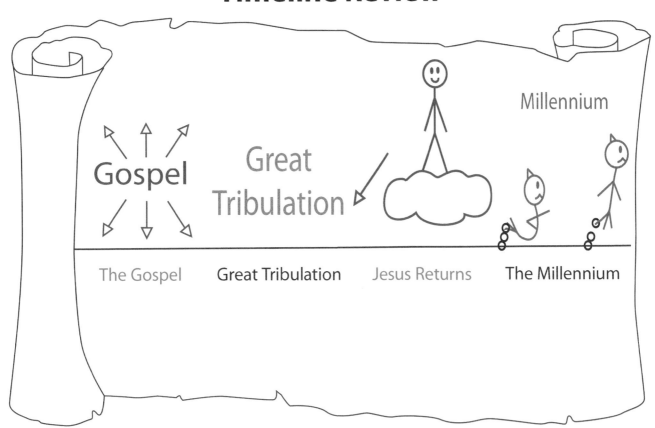

Memory Verse Review

Revelation 1:7

Revelation 9:20

Revelation 5:9

James 1:22

Memory Work: The Apostles' Creed: and life everlasting. Amen

Hell

Memory Verse: Revelation 20:15

All Mankind Will Be Judged

Read aloud: Romans 14:10-12; II Corinthians 5:10

Discuss All Mankind Will Be Judged: These two passages make it clear that each person will be judged, whether believer or unbeliever..

Draw and have students draw: A man kneeling before Jesus.

The Great White Throne Judgment

Read aloud: Revelation 20:11-15, 21:8

Discuss The Great White Throne Judgment: At the Great White Throne Judgment, the books will be opened, and those not recorded in the Book of Life will be thrown into the lake of fire.

Draw and have students draw: A book open with names written in it, a man who is sad because his name in not in the book, and the lake of fire.

Look up the following words in a Bible Dictionary:

judgment

account

Book of Life

hades

second death

Abraham's bosom

Separating the Sheep and the Goats

Read aloud: Revelation 19:17-21, 21:1-3; Matthew 25:31-34, 41, 46

Discuss Separating the Sheep and the Goats: While Jesus was on the earth, He described what Judgment would be like. The sheep represent believers, and the goats represent unbelievers. The believers will go to eternal life in the presence of God, but the unbelievers will be condemned to eternal punishment.

Draw and have students draw: A man praising God, with the word "sheep" over him. Jesus in the center. A sad man walking away with the word "goat" over him.

Sheep   Goat

Completed Student Page

Teacher Notes:

The Rich Man and Lazarus

Read aloud: Hebrews 9:27; Luke 16:19-31

Discuss The Rich Man and Lazarus: After the death of every man comes judgment. The story of the rich man and Lazarus is an example of the finality of this judgment.

Draw and have students draw: The rich man reaching up from hell and Lazarus in heaven.

Teacher Notes

Completed Student Page

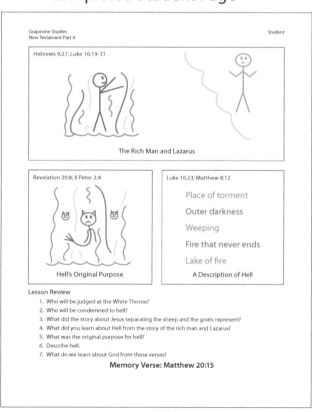

Hell's Original Purpose

Read aloud: Revelation 20:8; II Peter 2:4

Discuss Hell's Original Purpose: Hell was designed as a place of punishment for the devil and his angels. Even the demons are aware that their judgment awaits them.

Draw and have students draw: Satan and his demons in the Lake of Fire.

Place of torment

Outer darkness

Weeping

Fire that never ends

Lake of fire

A Description of Hell

Read aloud: Luke 16:23; Matthew 8:12

Discuss A Description of Hell: A place of torment, outer darkness, weeping, gnashing of teeth, fire that is never quenched, lake of fire and brimstone.

Write and have students write: Place of torment, outer darkness, weeping, fire that never ends, and lake of fire.

Lesson Review:

1. Who will be judged at the White Throne? All mankind.

2. Who will be condemned to hell? Anyone whose name is not found written in the Book of Life.

3. What did the story about Jesus separating the sheep and the goats represent? How God will separate believers from unbelievers at the end of time.

4. What did you learn about Hell from the story of the rich man and Lazarus? All men will be judged after death; judgment is final; there is no crossing over from hell to heaven or back to earth after judgment.

5. What was the original purpose for hell? A place of punishment for Satan and his angels.

6. Describe hell. A place of torment and weeping. Outer darkness, where the fire never ends.

7. What do we learn about God from these verses? God will judge every man, and woe to those who are not found recorded in the Book of Life.

Memory Verse: Revelation 20:15

Early Elementary and Elementary

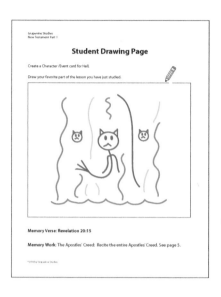

Information for the Hell card:

- All men will be judged.
- At the Great White Throne Judgment, the books will be opened.
- Anyone whose name is not found in the Book of Life will be thrown into the lake of fire and brimstone.
- Jesus will separate the believers from the unbelievers at the end of time.
- Hell was originally a place prepared for Satan and his demons.

Memory Verse: Revelation 20:15

Memory Work: The Apostles' Creed: Recite the entire Apostles' Creed. See page 350.

Middle School

Heaven

Topical Bible

What is *heaven*?

Nave's, page 199

Bible Dictionary

What is *holiness*?

Zondervan's, page 230

Concordance

Give one Old Testament verse referring to God *dwelling* among His people.

II Kings 4:13 and others (Cruden's, page 133)

Quest Question

How does Scripture describe heaven?

Answers will vary. Revelation 21:4, 5:9, 7:15-17

Timeline Review

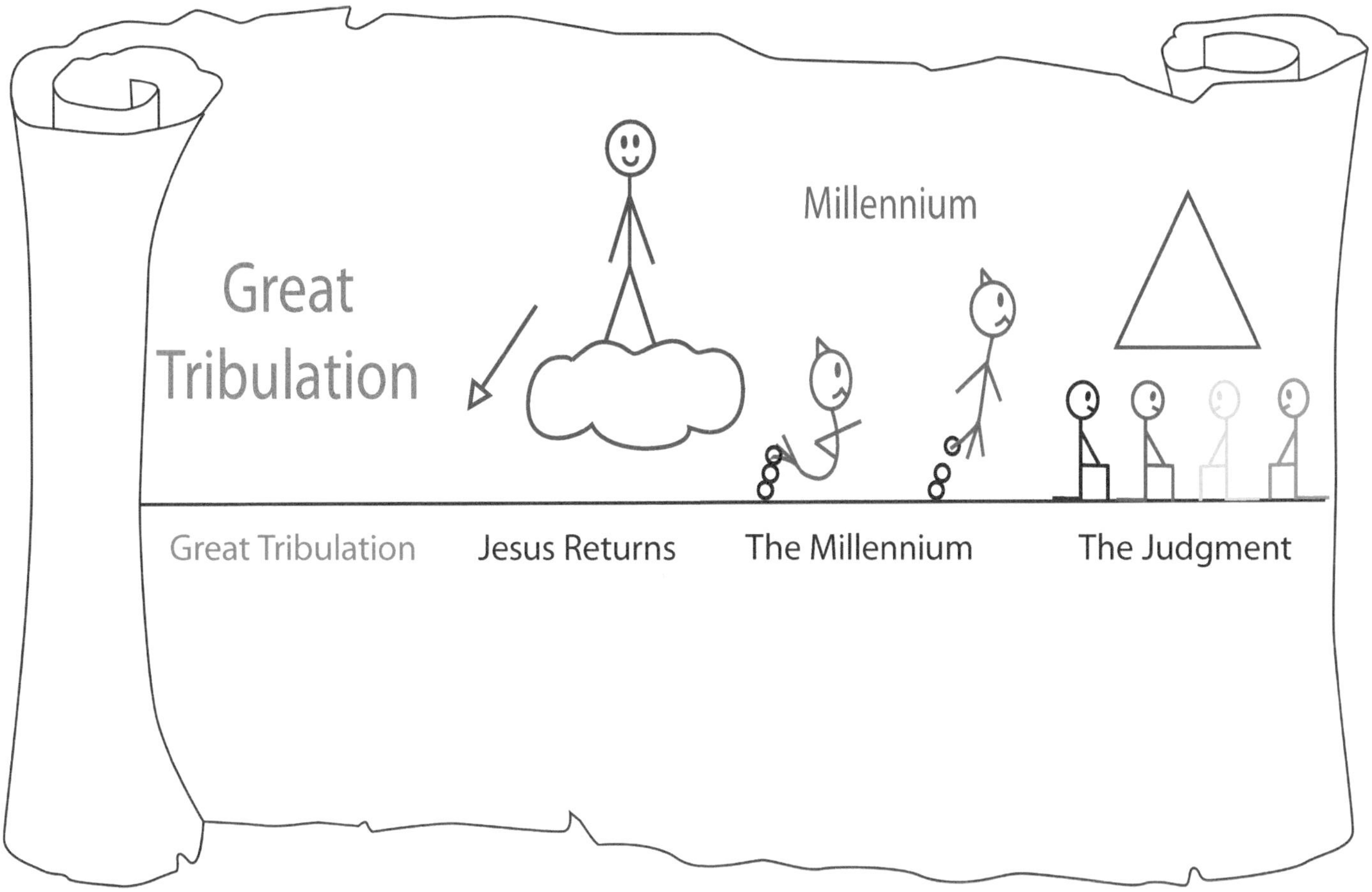

Great Tribulation

Millennium

| Great Tribulation | Jesus Returns | The Millennium | The Judgment |

Memory Verse Review

Revelation 20:15

Revelation 1:7

Revelation 9:20

Revelation 5:9

Memory Work: The Apostles' Creed: Recite the entire Apostles' Creed. See page 350.

Heaven

Memory Verse: Revelation 21:3

God's Patience

Read aloud: II Peter 3:1-9

Discuss God's Patience: Peter here warns believers that in the last days men will scoff at the thought of Jesus coming again. But Peter reminds us that what appears to us to be a delay is really the patience of God and His desire to see no man perish.

Draw and have students draw: A man praying and repenting, turning back to God.

New Heaven and New Earth

Read aloud: II Peter 3:10-13; Revelation 21:1

Discuss New Heaven and New Earth: Although God is patient; the day will come when the heavens and earth will be replaced with a new heaven and new earth where righteousness will reign.

Draw and have students draw: The earth with golden rays going out.

Look up the following words in a Bible Dictionary:

new

holy

tabernacle

blessed

reward

tree of life

God's Dwelling Place

Read aloud: Revelation 21:2-3

Discuss God's Dwelling Place: In this new heaven and new earth, God will once again dwell among His people.

Draw and have students draw: God dwelling among His people.

No tears

No death

No pain

No sorrow

Everyone worships God

Heaven

Read aloud: Revelation 21:4, 5:9, 7:15-17

Discuss Heaven: Where there will be no tears, death will be defeated, pain will not be felt, sorrow will be no more, and everyone will worship God as He dwells among us.

Write and have students write: No tears, no death, no pain, no sorrow, and everyone worships God.

Completed Student Page

Teacher Notes:

The New Jerusalem

Read aloud: Revelation 21:9-26

Discuss The New Jerusalem: This is a beautiful description of the New Jerusalem.

Draw and have students draw: The New Jerusalem.

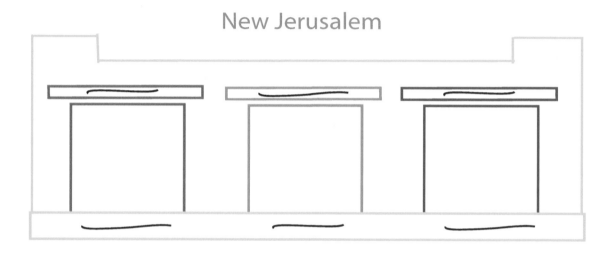

New Jerusalem

Teacher Notes

Completed Student Page

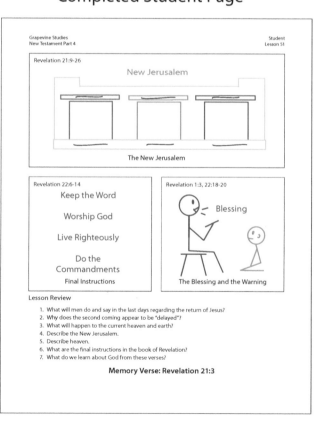

Final Instructions

Worship God

Read aloud: Revelation 22:6-14

Discuss Final Instructions: John records some final instructions to the reader of Revelation, encouraging them to continue in righteousness.

Live
Righteously

Write and have students write: Worship God and Live Righteously.

Blessing

The Blessing and the Warning

Read aloud: Revelation 1:3, 22:18-20

Discuss The Blessing and the Warning: God promises a blessing to those who read and heed the book of Revelation. But God also issues a warning that no words should be added to or taken away from this book.

Draw and have students draw: A man reading, a blessing going forth, and a son hearing what is being read.

Lesson Review:

1. What will men do and say in the last days regarding the return of Jesus? They will scoff and ask "When is He coming?"

2. Why does the second coming appear to be "delayed"? God is giving time for all men to repent.

3. What will happen to the current heaven and earth? They will be destroyed with fire, and there will be a new heaven and new earth.

4. Describe the New Jerusalem. A city built by God for His people.

5. Describe heaven. No tears, no death, no sorrow, no crying, no pain, a place where people of every tribe, nation, and tongue will worship God!

6. What are the final instructions of Revelation? Keep the words of the book, worship God, continue to live a holy and righteous life, and do God's commandments.

7. What do we learn about God from these verses? God will one day dwell among His people in heaven.

Memory Verse: Revelation 21:3

Early Elementary and Elementary

Student Drawing Page

Information for the Heaven card:

- Men will think that Jesus is not coming because God is patient, not wanting men to die without repenting.

- God will destroy the old heaven and earth with fire and bring forth a new heaven and earth.

- Heaven will be a place of:

    1. No tears

    2. No death

    3. No sorrow

    4. No crying

    5. No pain

    6. God dwelling among His people.

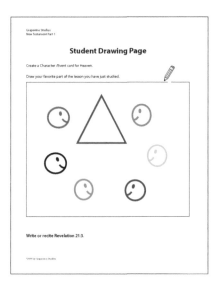

Memory Verse: Revelation 21:3

Final Review

1. What was Paul's mission from God? To preach the Gospel to the Gentiles, to kings, and to the Jews.

2. What other name was Paul known by? Saul.

3. What was the response of the Gentiles when Paul preached? Many received the Word with gladness and glorified the Lord.

4. What was the response of King Agrippa to Paul's preaching? He was almost persuaded.

5. What was the response of the Jews to Paul's preaching? Some opposed but some believed, including the ruler of the synagogue.

6. Name some of the things Paul suffered for the name of Jesus. Stoning, shipwreck, and beatings.

7. What was Paul's view of his death? He looked forward to the crown of righteousness.

8. Recite II Timothy 4:7-8.

9. Why were the letters written to the Churches? To teach, exhort, correct and encourage believers.

10. Name four books written by Paul. See lesson.

11. Who were the three authors of the books to the Church at Thessalonica? Paul, Silvanus, and Timothy.

12. Recite II Timothy 3:16-17.

13. Which New Testament letters were written to Churches? Romans, I & II Corinthians, Galatians, Ephesians, Philippians, Colossians, I & II Thessalonians, Hebrews, I & II Peter, I John, Jude, and Revelation.

14. Which New Testament letters were written to individuals? I & II Timothy, Titus, Philemon, II & III John.

15. Recite Romans 15:4.

16. What was the relationship between God and man at Creation? Perfect and complete.

17. What happened when Adam and Eve sinned? The relationship between God and man was broken.

18.   **What promise did God give Adam and Eve in Genesis 3:15?** That one day a Messiah would be born who would restore the broken relationship between God and man.

19.   **Who was the Messiah, and what did He do?** He was Jesus of Nazareth. He was born, lived a sinless life, was crucified, buried, rose again after three days, and ascended to heaven.

20.   **What did Jesus do to the relationship between God and man?** Through His death and payment for our sins, Jesus provided a way for us to be forgiven and for our relationship with God to be restored.

21.   **What is to come?** One day Jesus will come again, and all men will be judged.

22.   Recite Matthew 24:44.

23.   **Why is obedience to biblical doctrine important?** Obedience shows our love for God.

24.   **How does fellowship help us grow in faith?** Through encouragement, correction, and exhortation.

25.   **What are two ways we can pray?** In private and with others.

26.   **What do we remember when we celebrate communion?** The Lord's death and the New Covenant in His blood.

27.   **Why should I be baptized?** In obedience to the Lord.

28.   **What should I share with others?** The Gospel.

29.   Recite James 1:22.

30.   **Who is worthy to open the seals?** Jesus, The Lamb of God.

31.   **What are the seven seals judgements?** 1) White horse; 2) Red horse; 3) Black horse; 4) Pale Horse; 5) Martyrs crying out; 6) Sun, moon and stars darkened and the earth quakes; 7) Silence in heaven then noise and lightning.

32.   **What are the first four trumpets?** 1) 1/3 of the trees and grass burn; 2) 1/3 of the sea becomes blood, 1/3 of the sea creatures die, and 1/3 of the ships sink. 3) A 1/3 of the waters become bitter; 4) 1/3 of the sun, moon and stars are darkened.

33. Recite Revelation 5:9.

34. What are the last three trumpets? 5) locust from the pit, 6) 1/3 mankind die, 7) lightnings and noise

35. How does mankind respond to the seals, bowls, and trumpets? They blaspheme God and refuse to repent of their sins.

36. What are the seven bowls? 1) boils, 2) all sea creatures die, 3) rivers and springs turn to blood, 4) scorching heat, 5) darkness and pain, 6) gathering of an army, 7) earthquakes and hail.

37. Why would men want to take the mark of the beast? To be able to buy and sell.

38. Recite Revelation 9:20.

39. What is Armageddon? A battlefield located in northern Israel in which the kings of the earth will gather their armies and be defeated at the coming of Jesus Christ.

40. Describe the second coming of Jesus. When Jesus returns every eye will see Him.

41. During the Millennium, who is reigning over the earth? Jesus and the saints.

42. During the Millennium, where is Satan? Chained to the bottomless pit.

43. What happens at the end of the Millennium? Satan is released and deceives man again.

44. What is Satan's end? The lake of fire for eternity.

45. Recite Revelation 1:7.

46. Who will be judged at the White Throne? All mankind.

47. Who will be condemned to hell? Anyone whose name is not found written in the Book of Life.

48. What did the story about Jesus separating the sheep and the goats represent? How God will separate believers from unbelievers at the end of time.

49. What did you learn about Hell from the story of the rich man and Lazarus? All men will be judged after death; judgment is final; there is no crossing over from hell to heaven or back to earth after judgment.

50. What was the original purpose for hell? A place of punishment for Satan and his angels.

51. Describe hell. A place of torment and weeping. Outer darkness, where the fire never ends.

52. Recite Revelation 20:15.

53. What will men do and say in the last days regarding the return of Jesus? They will scoff and ask "When is His coming?"

54. Why does the second coming appear to be "delayed"? God is giving time for all men to repent.

55. What will happen to the current heaven and earth? They will be destroyed with fire, and there will be a new heaven and new earth.

56. Describe the New Jerusalem. A city built by God for His people.

57. Describe heaven. No tears, no death, no sorrow, no crying, no pain, a place where people of every tribe, nation, and tongue will worship God!

58. What are the final instructions of Revelation? Keep the words of the book, worship God, continue to live a holy and righteous life, and do God's commandments.

59. Recite Revelation 21:3.

For Early Elementary and Elementary Levels:

60. How many books are in the Bible? 66.

61. In what language was the New Testament written? Greek.

62. Name the Gospels. Matthew, Mark, Luke, and John.

63. Name the Book of Church History. Acts.

64. Name the Epistles? Romans, I & II Corinthians, Galatians, Ephesians, Philippians, Colossians, I & II Thessalonians, I & II Timothy, Titus, Philemon, Hebrews, James, I & II Peter, I, II, & III John, Jude and Revelation.

65. Name the Twelve Apostles: Andrew, Simon (Peter), Phillip, Matthew (Levi), James, John, Bartholomew, Thomas, James (Son of Alhpaeus), Lebbaueus, Simon (the Canaanite), and Judas Iscariot.

66. Recite the Apostles' Creed. See page 349.

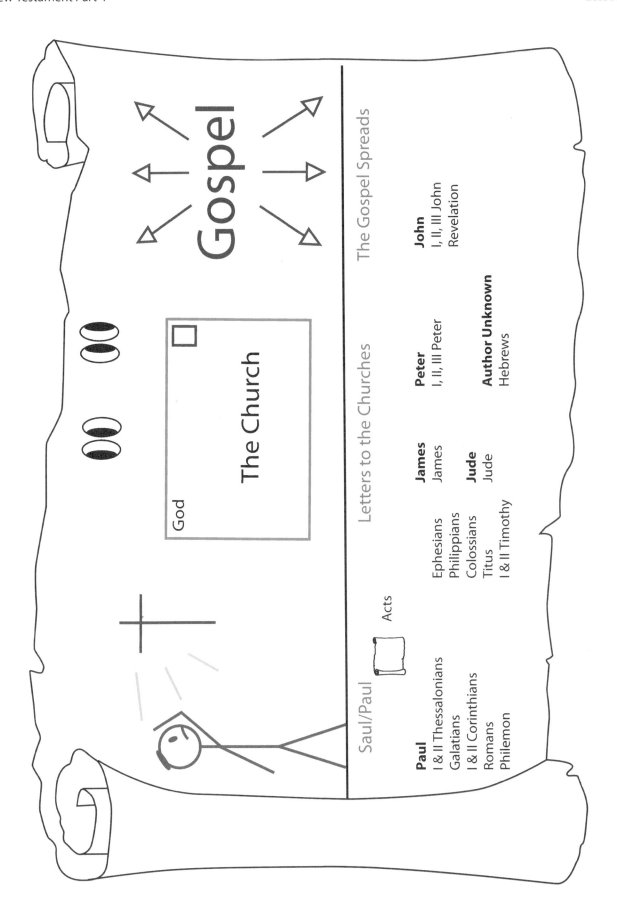

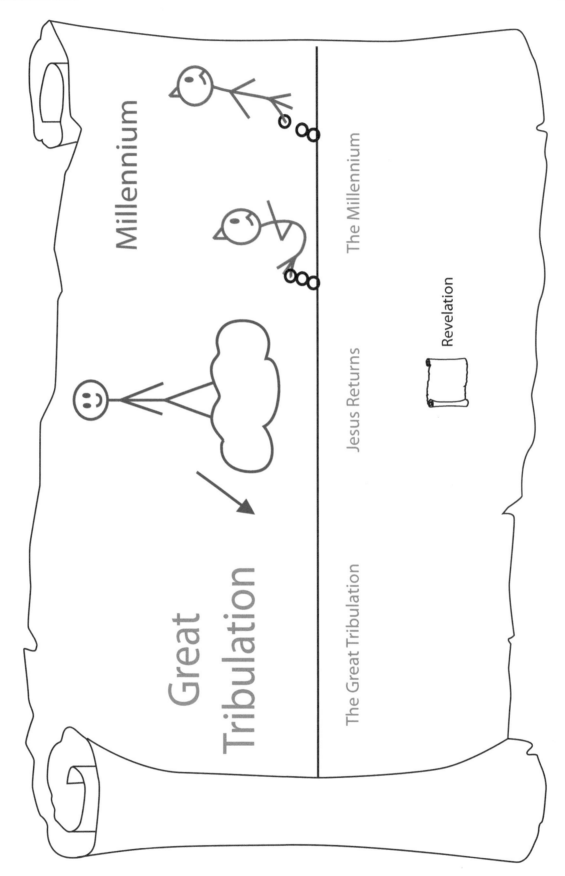

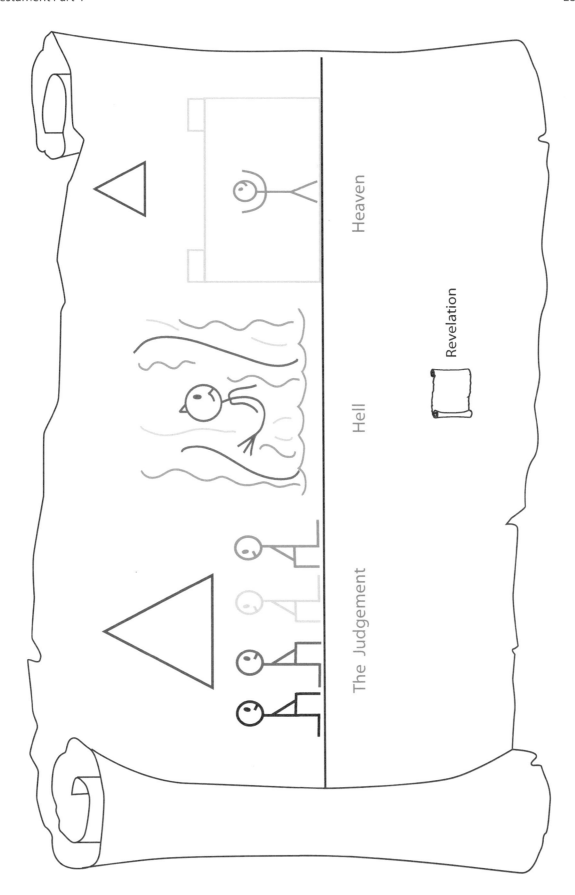

Heaven

Hell

Revelation

The Judgement

The Apostles' Creed

I believe in God, the Father Almighty,

Creator of heaven and earth.

I believe in Jesus Christ, God's only Son, our Lord,

Who was conceived by the Holy Spirit,

Born of the Virgin Mary,

Suffered under Pontius Pilate,

Was crucified, died, was buried;

On the third day He rose again;

He ascended into heaven,

He is seated at the right hand of the Father,

and He will come again to judge the living and the dead.

I believe in the Holy Spirit,

the holy catholic church,

the communion of saints,

the forgiveness of sins,

the resurrection of the body,

and life everlasting.
Amen.

Map

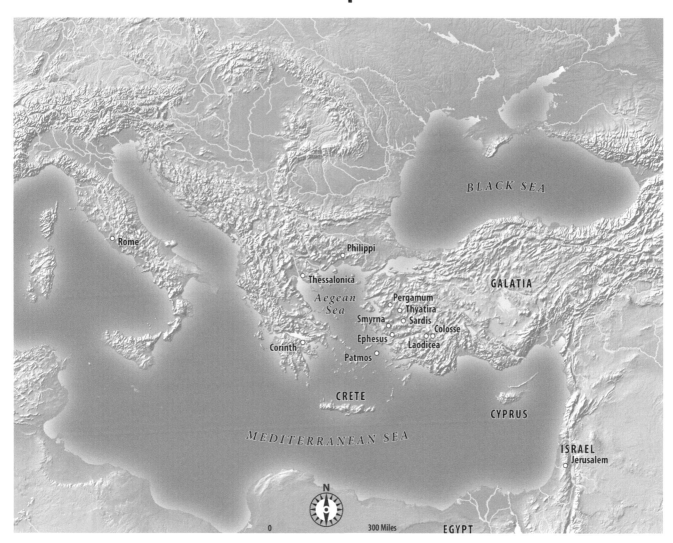

Label:

1. The city of Rome.

2. The city of Corinth.

3. The region of Galatia.

4. The city of Ephesus.

5. The city of Philippi.

6. The city of Colossi.

7. The city of Thessalonica.

Optional: 7 Churches of Revelation

1. City of Ephesus.

2. City of Smyrna.

3. City of Pregamon.

4. City of Thyatira

5. City of Sardis

6. City of Philadelphia

7. City of Laodicea

Page intentionally left blank

New Testament Overview

~

Schedules

Daily Schedule

Day	Date	Lesson Name	Teacher Book Pages	Early Elem. (Traceable) Pages	Elementary Book Pages	Middle School Pages
Day 1		Timeline/Quest Page	2-9, 13	3-6	3-6	3-6, 9
Day 2		Birth of John	14-15	8-9	8	10
Day 3		Birth of John	16-17	10-11	9	11
Day 4		Drawing Review/Quest Page	18	12	10	12
Day 5		Timeline Review	19	13	11	13
Day 6		Birth of Jesus	20-21	14-15	12	14
Day 7		Birth of Jesus	22-23	16-17	13	15
Day 8		Drawing Review/Quest Page	24	18	14	16
Day 9		Timeline Review	25	19	15	17
Day 10		Herod and the Wise Men	26-27	20-21	16	18
Day 11		Herod and the Wise Men	28-29	22-23	17	19
Day 12		Drawing Review/Quest Page	30	24	18	20
Day 13		Timeline Review	31	25	19	21
Day 14		Jesus at the Temple	32-33	26-27	20	22
Day 15		Jesus at the Temple	34-35	28-29	21	23
Day 16		Drawing Review/Quest Page	36	30	22	24
Day 17		Timeline Review	37	31	23	25
Day 18		John Baptized Jesus	38-39	32-33	24	26
Day 19		John Baptized Jesus	40-41	34-35	25	27
Day 20		Drawing Review/Quest Page	42, 50	36	26	36
Day 21		Section Review	43-45	38-40	28-30	30-32
Day 22		Section Review	46-47	41-42	31-32	34-35
Day 23		Timeline Review	51	43	33	37
Day 24		The Temptation of Jesus	52-53	44-45	34	38
Day 25		The Temptation of Jesus	54-55	46-47	35	39

Daily Schedule

Day	Date	Lesson Name	Teacher Book Pages	Early Elem. (Traceable) Pages	Elementary Book Pages	Middle School Pages
Day 26		Drawing Review/Quest Page	56	48	36	40
Day 27		Timeline Review	57	49	37	41
Day 28		Satan	58-59	50-51	38	42
Day 29		Satan	60-61	52-53	39	43
Day 30		Drawing Review/Quest Page	62	54	40	44
Day 31		Timeline Review	63	55	41	45
Day 32		The Twelve Apostles	64-65	56-57	42	46
Day 33		The Twelve Apostles	66-67	58-59	43	47
Day 34		Drawing Review/Quest Page	68	60	44	48
Day 35		Timeline Review	69	61	45	49
Day 36		Jesus Taught	70-71	62-63	46	50
Day 37		Jesus Taught	72-73	64-65	47	51
Day 38		Drawing Review/Quest Page	74	66	48	52
Day 39		Timeline Review	75	67	49	53
Day 40		Jesus Prayed	76-77	68-69	50	54
Day 40		Jesus Prayed	78-79	70-71	51	55
Day 41		Drawing Review/Quest Page	80	72	52	--
Day 42		Final Review	81	74	53	58
Day 43		Final Review	82	75	54	59
Day 44		Final Review	83	76	55	60
Day 45		Final Review	84	77	56	61
Day 46		Final Review	85	78	57	62
Day 47		Timeline Review	86-87	79-80	58-59	63-64
Day 48		Timeline Review	88	81	60	65

Daily Schedule

Day	Date	Lesson Name	Teacher Book Pages	Early Elem. (Traceable) Pages	Elementary Book Pages	Middle School Pages
Day 49		Timeline/Quest Page	94-101	82-84	64-66	68-70, 73
Day 50		Jesus and the Sea	102-103	86-87	68	74
Day 51		Jesus and the Sea	104-105	88-89	69	75
Day 52		Drawing Review/Quest Page	106	90	70	76
Day 53		Timeline Review	107	91	71	77
Day 54		Jesus Fed the Multitudes	108-109	92-93	72	78
Day 55		Jesus Fed the Multitudes	110-111	94-95	73	79
Day 56		Drawing Review/Quest Page	112	96	74	80
Day 57		Timeline Review	113	97	75	81
Day 58		Jesus Healed the Sick	114-115	98-99	76	82
Day 59		Jesus Healed the Sick	116-117	100-101	77	83
Day 60		Drawing Review/Quest Page	118	102	78	84
Day 61		Timeline Review	119	103	79	85
Day 62		Jesus Healed the Demon-Possessed	120-121	104-105	80	86
Day 63		Jesus Healed the Demon-Possessed	122-123	106-107	81	87
Day 64		Drawing Review/Quest Page	124	108	82	88
Day 65		Timeline Review	125	109	83	89
Day 66		Jesus Raised the Dead	126-127	110-111	84	90
Day 67		Jesus Raised the Dead	128-129	112-113	85	91
Day 68		Drawing Review/Quest Page	130, 138	114	86	98
Day 69		Section Review	132-133	116-117	88-89	94-95
Day 70		Section Review	134-135	118-119	90-91	96-97
Day 71		Timeline Review	139	121	93	99
Day 72		Jesus Entered Jerusalem	140-141	122-123	94	100
Day 73		Jesus Entered Jerusalem	142-143	124-125	95	101

Daily Schedule

Day	Date	Lesson Name	Teacher Book Pages	Early Elem. (Traceable) Pages	Elementary Book Pages	Middle School Pages
Day 74		Drawing Review/Quest Page	144	126	96	102
Day 75		Timeline Review	145	127	97	103
Day 76		The Last Supper	146-147	128-129	98	104
Day 77		The Last Supper	148-149	130-131	99	105
Day 78		Drawing Review/Quest Page	150	132	100	106
Day 79		Timeline Review	151	133	101	107
Day 80		The Garden of Gethsemane	152-153	134-135	102	108
Day 81		The Garden of Gethsemane	154-155	136-137	103	109
Day 82		Drawing Review/Quest Page	156	138	104	110
Day 83		Timeline Review	157	139	105	111
Day 84		The Trials of Jesus Pt. 1	158-159	140-141	106	112
Day 85		The Trials of Jesus Pt. 1	160-161	142-143	107	113
Day 86		Drawing Review	162	144	108	114
Day 87		Timeline Review	163	145	109	115
Day 88		The Trials of Jesus Pt. 2	164-165	146-147	110	116
Day 89		The Trails of Jesus Pt. 2	166-167	148-149	111	117
Day 90		Drawing Review	168	150	112	--
Day 91		Final Review	170	151	114	120
Day 92		Final Review	171	152	115	121
Day 93		Final Review	172	153	116	122
Day 94		Final Review	173	154	117	123
Day 95		Timeline Review	174	155	118	124
Day 96		Timeline Review	175	156	119	125
Day 97		Timeline Review	176	157	120	126

Daily Schedule

Day	Date	Lesson Name	Teacher Book Pages	Early Elem. (Traceable) Pages	Elementary Book Pages	Middle School Pages
Day 98		Timeline/Quest Page	180-85, 189	160-162	124-126	130-32, 135
Day 99		The Crucifixion	190-191	164-165	128	136
Day 100		The Crucifixion	192-193	166-167	129	137
Day 101		Drawing Review/Quest Page	194	168	130	138
Day 102		Timeline Review	195	169	131	139
Day 103		The Death of Jesus	196-197	170-171	132	140
Day 104		The Death of Jesus	198-199	172-173	133	141
Day 105		Drawing Review/Quest Page	200	174	134	142
Day 106		Timeline Review	201	175	135	143
Day 107		The Burial and Resurrection	202-203	176-177	136	144
Day 108		The Burial and Resurrection	204-205	178-179	137	145
Day 109		Drawing Review/Quest Page	206	180	138	146
Day 110		Timeline Review	207	181	139	147
Day 111		Jesus Ascended	208-209	182-183	140	148
Day 112		Jesus Ascended	210-211	184-185	141	149
Day 113		Drawing Review/Quest Page	212	186	142	150
Day 114		Timeline Review	213	187	143	151
Day 115		Was Jesus the Messiah Pt. 1	214-215	188-189	144	152
Day 116		Was Jesus the Messiah Pt. 1	216-217	190-191	145	153
Day 117		Drawing Review/Quest Page	218, 226	192	146	160
Day 118		Section Review	220-221	194-195	148-149	156-157
Day 119		Section Review	222-223	196-197	150-151	158-159
Day 120		Timeline Review	227	199	153	161
Day 121		Was Jesus the Messiah Pt. 2	228-229	200-201	154	162
Day 122		Was Jesus the Messiah Pt. 2	230-231	202-203	155	163

Daily Schedule

Day	Date	Lesson Name	Teacher Book Pages	Early Elem. (Traceable) Pages	Elementary Book Pages	Middle School Pages
Day 123		Drawing Review/Quest Page	232	204	156	164
Day 124		Timeline Review	233	205	157	165
Day 125		The Holy Spirit	234-235	206-207	158	166
Day 126		The Holy Spirit	236-237	208-209	159	167
Day 127		Drawing Review/Quest Page	238	210	160	168
Day 128		Timeline Review	239	211	161	169
Day 129		The Early Church	240-241	212-213	162	170
Day 130		The Early Church	242-243	214-215	163	171
Day 131		Drawing Review/Quest Page	244	216	164	172
Day 132		Timeline Review	245	217	165	173
Day 133		The Persecution	246-247	218-219	166	174
Day 134		The Persecution	248-249	220-221	167	175
Day 135		Drawing Review/Quest Page	250	222	168	176
Day 136		Timeline Review	251	223	169	177
Day 137		Saul	252-253	224-225	170	178
Day 138		Saul	254-255	226-227	171	179
Day 139		Drawing Review	256	228	172	--
Day 140		Final Review	257	230	174	182
Day 141		Final Review	258	231	175	183
Day 142		Final Review	259	232	176	184
Day 143		Final Review	260	233	177	185
Day 144		Timeline Review	261	234	178	186
Day 145		Timeline Review	262	235	179	187
Day 146		Timeline Review	263	236	180	188

Daily Schedule

Day	Date	Lesson Name	Teacher Book Pages	Early Elem. (Traceable) Pages	Elementary Book Pages	Middle School Pages
Day 147		Timeline/Quest Page	270-75, 277	238-240	184-186	193-94, 197
Day 148		Paul	278-279	242-243	188	198
Day 149		Paul	280-281	244-245	189	199
Day 150		Drawing Review/Quest Page	282	246	190	200
Day 151		Timeline Review	283	247	191	201
Day 152		Letters to the Churches Pt. 1	284-285	248-249	192	202
Day 153		Letters to the Churches Pt. 1	286-287	250-251	193	203
Day 154		Drawing Review/Quest Page	288	252	194	204
Day 155		Timeline Review	289	253	195	205
Day 156		Letters to the Churches Pt. 2	290-291	254-255	196	206
Day 157		Letters to the Churches Pt. 2	292-293	256-257	197	207
Day 158		Drawing Review/Quest Page	294	258	198	208
Day 159		Timeline Review	295	259	199	209
Day 160		The Gospel in Stick Figures	296-297	260-261	200	210
Day 161		The Gospel in Stick Figures	298-299	262-263	201	211
Day 162		Drawing Review/Quest Page	300	264	202	212
Day 163		Timeline Review	301	265	203	213
Day 164		Sharing the Gospel	302-303	266-267	204	214
Day 165		Sharing the Gospel	304-305	268-269	205	215
Day 166		Drawing Review/Quest Page	306, 312	270	206	222
Day 167		Section Review	307-308	272-273	208-209	218-219
Day 168		Section Review	309	274	210	220
Day 169		Timeline Review	313	275	211	223
Day 170		Revelation Pt. 1	314-315	276-277	212	224
Day 171		Revelation Pt. 1	316-317	278-279	213	225

Daily Schedule

Day	Date	Lesson Name	Teacher Book Pages	Early Elem. (Traceable) Pages	Elementary Book Pages	Middle School Pages
Day 172		Drawing Review/Quest Page	318	280	214	226
Day 173		Timeline Review	319	281	215	227
Day 174		Revelation Pt. 2	320-321	282-283	216	228
Day 175		Revelation Pt. 2	322-323	284-285	217	229
Day 176		Drawing Review/Quest Page	324	286	218	230
Day 177		Timeline Review	325	287	219	231
Day 178		The Second Coming of Jesus	326-327	288-289	220	232
Day 179		The Second Coming of Jesus	328-329	290-291	221	233
Day 180		Drawing Review/Quest Page	330	292	222	234
Day 181		Timeline Review	331	293	223	235
Day 182		Hell	332-333	294-295	224	236
Day 183		Hell	334-335	296-297	225	237
Day 184		Drawing Review/Quest Page	336	298	226	238
Day 185		Timeline Review	337	299	227	239
Day 186		Heaven	338-339	300-301	228	240
Day 187		Heaven	340-341	302-303	229	241
Day 188		Drawing Review	342	304	230	--
Day 189		Final Review	343	306	232	244
Day 190		Final Review	344	307	233	245
Day 191		Final Review	345	308	234	246
Day 192		Final Review	346	309	235	247
Day 193		Timeline Review	347	310	236	248
Day 194		Timeline Review	348	311	237	249
Day 195		Timeline Review	349	312	238	250

Weekly Schedule

Day	Date	Lesson Name	Teacher Book Pages	Early Elem. (Traceable) Pages	Elementary Book Pages	Middle School Pages
Week 1		Timeline	2-9, 13	3-6	3-6	3-6, 9
Week 2		Birth of John	14-18	8-12	8-10	10-12
Week 3		Birth of Jesus	19-24	13-18	11-14	13-16
Week 4		Herod & Wise Men	25-30	19-24	15-18	17-20
Week 5		Jesus at the Temple	31-6	25-30	19-22	21-24
Week 6		John Baptized Jesus	37-42, 50	31-36	23-26	25-27, 36
Week 7		Section Review	43-47	38-42	29-32	30-35
Week 8		Temptation of Jesus	51-56	43-48	33-36	37-40
Week 9		Satan	57-62	49-54	37-40	41-44
Week 10		Twelve Apostles	63-68	55-60	41-44	45-48
Week 11		Jesus Taught	69-74	61-66	45-48	49-52
Week 12		Jesus Prayed	75-80	67-72	49-52	53-55
Week 13		Final Review	81-88	73-80	53-60	58-65

New Testament Overview
Part 2

Weekly Schedule

Day	Date	Lesson Name	Teacher Book Pages	Early Elem. (Traceable) Pages	Elementary Book Pages	Middle School Pages
Week 14		Timeline	94-100	82-84	64-66	68-70, 73
Week 15		Jesus and the Sea	102-106	86-90	68-70	74-76
Week 16		Jesus Fed the Multitudes	107-112	91-96	71-74	77-80
Week 17		Jesus Healed: Sick	113-118	97-102	75-78	81-84
Week 18		Jesus Healed: Demon	119-124	103-108	79-82	85-88
Week 19		Jesus Raised the Dead	125-130, 138	109-114	83-86	89-91, 98
Week 20		Section Review	132-135	116-119	88-91	94-97
Week 21		Jesus Entered Jerusalem	139-144	121-126	93-96	99-102
Week 22		The Last Supper	145-150	127-132	97-100	103-106
Week 23		Garden of Gethsemane	151-156	133-138	101-104	107-110
Week 24		Trials of Jesus Pt 1	157-162	139-144	105-108	111-114
Week 25		Trials of Jesus Pt 2	163-168	145-150	109-112	115-117
Week 26		Final Review	170-176	151-157	114-120	120-126

New Testament Overview
Part 3

Weekly Schedule

Day	Date	Lesson Name	Teacher Book Pages	Early Elem. (Traceable) Pages	Elementary Book Pages	Middle School Pages
Week 27		Timeline	180-85, 189	160-162	124-126	130-32, 135
Week 28		The Crucifixion	190-194	164-168	128-130	136-138
Week 29		Death of Jesus	195-200	169-174	131-134	139-142
Week 30		Burial and Resurrection	201-206	175-180	135-138	143-146
Week 31		Jesus Ascended	207-212	181-186	139-142	147-150
Week 32		Was Jesus Messiah? Pt 1	213-18, 226	187-192	143-146	151-53, 160
Week 33		Section Review	220-223	194-197	148-151	156-159
Week 34		Was Jesus Messiah? Pt 2	227-232	199-204	153-156	161-164
Week 35		The Holy Spirit	233-238	205-210	157-160	165-168
Week 36		The Early Church	239-244	211-216	161-164	169-172
Week 37		The Persecution	245-250	217-222	165-168	173-176
Week 38		Saul	251-256	223-228	169-172	177-179
Week 39		Final Review	257-263	230-236	174-180	182-188

Weekly Schedule

Day	Date	Lesson Name	Teacher Book Pages	Early Elem. (Traceable) Pages	Elementary Book Pages	Middle School Pages
Week 40		Timeline	270-75, 277	238-240	184-186	193-94, 197
Week 41		Paul	278-282	242-246	188-190	198-200
Week 42		Letters to the Church Pt 1	283-288	247-252	191-194	201-204
Week 43		Letters to the Church Pt 2	289-294	253-258	195-198	205-208
Week 44		The Gospel	295-300	259-264	199-202	209-212
Week 45		Sharing the Gospel	301-306, 312	265-270	203-206	213-15, 222
Week 46		Section Review	307-309	272-274	208-210	218-220
Week 47		Revelation Pt 1	313-318	275-280	211-214	223-226
Week 48		Revelation Pt 2	319-324	281-286	215-218	227-230
Week 49		The Second Coming	325-330	287-292	219-222	231-234
Week 50		Hell	331-336	293-298	223-226	235-238
Week 51		Heaven	337-342	299-304	227-230	239-241
Week 52		Final Review	343-349	306-312	232-238	244-250

Continue your *Stick Figure* Journey through the *Bible*

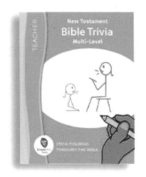

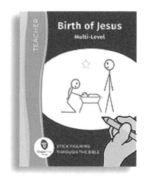
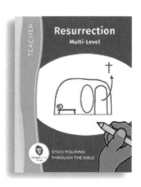

GrapeVine
Bible Studies

www.GrapevineStudies.com